# Sydney School: Formative Moments in Architecture, Design and Planning at the University of Sydney

**Edited by Andrew Leach and Lee Stickells**

# Acknowledgments

We are grateful for the School's support in bringing this book to completion, particularly the faith kept by Jonathan Hulme, Dean John Redmond and Professor Robyn Dowling, even when it seemed production challenges would get the better of the project. The work of the book's authors was given tremendous support by colleagues who assisted with background research, including: Zoe Skinner, Rebecca Hawcroft, Mark Dunn, Joni Taylor, Maren Koehler, Amelia Kelly and Iakov Amperides. Further assistance was ably provided by the School's library liaison JohnPaul Cenzato, Julie Price at University Library's Rare Books and Special Collections, and Nyree Morrison and Karin Brennan from the University of Sydney Archives.

We thank the organisers and participants in the University of Auckland's symposium "Educating Architects and Planners, 1917-2017" for the chance to test some of the ideas and material contained in the book; especially Julia Gatley, Lucy Treep, Linda Tyler, Philip Goad, Robert Freestone, and Kirsty Volz. We appreciate the patience of students in the 2017 and 2018 iterations of the unit DAAE2001 Australian Architecture, who encountered aspects of the book very much in progress.

Work on all chapters was greatly assisted by individuals and organisations who offered insights, anecdotes, images and feedback that furthered the stories being told. On behalf of the authors we would like to recognise the cooperation of: Tim Gooding, Tone Wheeler, Michael Muir, Sue Clarke, Karine Shellshear, Jane Dillon, Mark Arbuz, Regina Haertsch, Stephen Stokes and family, Sandra Meihubers, Lasse Kaukomaa, Katie Molnar, National Gallery of Australia, RMIT Design Archives, Richard de Dear, Michaela Dunworth, Adrian Snodgrass, Art Gallery of New South Wales, the State Library of New South Wales, Alan Rees, The Estate of Lloyd Rees, Toowoomba Regional Gallery, Huw Ap Rees, the ACT chapter of the Australian Institute of Architects, Jiat-Hwee Chang, Dick Holroyde, Huw Ap Rees, Laura Jolley, Warren Julian, Peter Smith

The timelines imposed on the authors were, at times, remarkably short. We are grateful to each writer for their efforts to ensure that this volume would be ready to mark the school's centenary.

And, of course, the team at Uro—Maitiú Ward, Andrew McKenzie and Amelia Willis—who worked quickly and diligently to get this book to press.

At the time of his sudden death in 2015, Trevor Howells had begun working on a book marking the centenary of Wilkinson's appointment. While we wouldn't claim this volume offers anything like Trevor's mischievous wit, we hope it goes some way to fulfilling the aspirations he had for recognising the School's century of achievements. ≡

# Contents

**Foreword** — John Redmond — 5

**Introduction** — Andrew Leach and Lee Stickells — 7

**Chapter 1:**
"...thoroughly equipped in all respects..." — 9
— Andrew Leach

**Drawing in the Wilkinson Decades** — 27
(With an introduction by Andrew Leach)

**Chapter 2:**
Town and Country Planning to 1949 — 35
— Paul Jones

**Chapter 3:**
The Arts of Architecture — 57
— Simon Weir

**Chapter 4:**
Architects in White Coats — 71
— Daniel J Ryan

**The Inaugural Wilkinson Lecture** — 91
An Urban Nation – Gough Whitlam
(With an introduction by Peter Phibbs)

**Chapter 5:**
The Sydney School — 103
— Catherine Lassen and Julie Willis

**Chapter 6:**
Pig Education — 121
— Lee Stickells

**The Expanded Field** — 143
(With an introduction by Lee Stickells)

**Chapter 7:**
The Seventies Science Wars — 151
— Glen Hill

**Chapter 8:**
A Theory Moment — 165
— Duanfang Lu and Peter Webber

**Postscripts** — 177
What Universities Are For — Andrew Leach
Prospects — Martin Tomitsch

# Foreword
— John Redmond

It's fitting that Australia's first university also produced the country's first university faculty of architecture—100 years ago. It is a foundation preceded by over 30 years of preparation, during which architecture was offered in other faculties of the university.

Its history has been characterised by a strong desire to be at the cutting edge of the evolving built environment and to advance initiatives to achieve it, resulting in the appointment of strong high-principled leaders, who undertook the long periods of development necessary to establish their discipline or foci firmly in the faculty.

The pre-faculty work prior to 1918 resulted in Leslie Wilkinson's appointment as Chair in Architecture. He dominated the development of the faculty and the development of the university's campus until his retirement 30 years later. Similarly, with the development of the other disciplines, the internal and external debates and agendas resulted in the university appointing outstanding leaders who stayed the distance: Henry "Jack" Cowan with architectural science, Denis Winston with urban planning, John Gero with design. Its remit was further expanded by Lloyd Rees with art and architecture, Col James with social activism, and Trevor Howells with heritage conservation. Certainly, the faculty has been blessed with outstanding leaders to develop each new discipline it has added.

They, and the faculty they attracted to work with them, were characterised by high aspirations for their discipline, outstanding intellects, deep commitment to advancing their professions, and government, social and community engagement. It is, therefore, perhaps not surprising that these qualities have come to define the faculty's graduates and have marked them out as "Sydney" architects, planners and designers.

The most recent period of its history has been characterised by linking and weaving together the constituent disciplines and developing a common focus for the diversity it spawned in its middle period. The current vision is of "one-school" in which everyone in it is deeply committed to developing and improving the built environment for people. To meet this commitment, some of the faculty use the methodologies of science, some architecture, some social science, some the humanities and some design. But whatever the methodology, the objective is the same—improving the human condition. It's a high aspiration that fuels high ambition, and while it's the current mantra, the reality is that such high principles and aspirations combined with high intellect and art have characterised the faculty throughout its first 100 years.

The success of its approach is acknowledged with its ranking by *Quacquarelli Symonds* (QS) at number one in Australia for architecture/built environment, and its inclusion in the very top group of the global rankings.

The "one-school" philosophy and its aspirations puts it in a good position to help shape and create humanity's environment during the next 100 years, which will see developments beyond our current imagination and even comprehension, and the challenge of global urbanisation and the conflicting challenge of global sustainability.

This will require the faculty (now known as the Sydney School of Architecture, Design and Planning) and all its members to assert the methods, values and philosophies that make up our culture, and to provide people-focused environments that serve to enable, enhance and celebrate human life.

# Introduction
— Andrew Leach and Lee Stickells

The occasion of a centenary presents an obvious opportunity for commemoration, but also prospect; that is, the chance to look backwards and forwards at once. One hundred years is, by any count, a substantial amount of time, and its passage suggests a degree of endurance that we could reasonably expect to continue into the foreseeable future. Neat though it is, a centenary is also somewhat arbitrary. As with the chance, taken here, to commemorate the appointment and arrival of Leslie Wilkinson in 1918, one hundred years marks a moment in time. But, while the emphasis on the moment can sharply illuminate, it can also reduce veracity. A little more difficult to bend into the units of an institution's history are the steps leading toward a moment and away from it: the creation of the chair Wilkinson came to occupy, the university's first tentative moves in teaching architecture, town and country planning, architectural science, design computing and so forth.

This book therefore takes Wilkinson's arrival at the University of Sydney, not as its subject, but as an occasion to reflect on a number of formative moments and figures, who have shaped the profile of what was, for most of the 20th century, the Faculty of Architecture. Accordingly, each of those moments provides an entry point into the discussion of important, overlapping phases in its history. The university has trained thousands of architects, designers and planners; sometimes directly for their professions and sometimes for a world beyond the most obvious uses to which their degree might have been put. These thousands of alumni have likewise been taught by hundreds of lecturers and tutors, each of whom advanced, challenged or otherwise extended what has since 2017 been called the Sydney School of Architecture, Design and Planning. As a consequence, this is not a chronicle of all that has happened in this century-long project, or in the 135 years during which architecture and its cognate disciplines have been taught at Sydney. Anyone anxious to find their name in these pages is likely to be disappointed. Instead of a complete chronology of the school's life, we have sought to reflect on those moments that have shaped its profile since the 1880s, contextualising the formation of Australia's first Chair in Architecture into what was, by the end of World War One, already more than a quarter-century-long experience of teaching courses in construction and architectural history. This book looks into that moment, and into what came after, to understand the ambitions that were expressed by the establishment not only of this first chair, but also of those that followed.

The chapters of *Sydney School* therefore look into a series of episodes in which the school (or the university, or their professional constituents, or a broader public) took stock of the education being offered at the University of Sydney, and of the activities of its faculty and students, and responded with change. Such changes have, of course, driven internal transformations in the personalities, organisation and activities of what has variously been a department, faculty or school. However, the chapters also acknowledge that these changes have been performed against a more or less noisy backdrop of developments in professional education and practice, university-based research and broader societal and cultural shifts. The formative moments through which the book is configured are inevitably spread out in an uneven way. Some individuals loom large over the story, while deserving others, influential teachers or significant graduates, are overlooked as we pursue a story about how the university has positioned itself for architecture, town planning and the disciplines that grew up around these two disciplinary chairs. As a result, the chapters reflect on the stakes of teaching architectural design in the university, as well as on teaching town and country planning and on the new necessities of what the university called architectural science. They consider how it responded to changes in historiography in the 1960s and 70s and its contribution to the project to lend legitimacy to the notion of a distinctively Australian architecture. They position the university's embrace of the so-called soft sciences and its embrace of (architectural) theory. We have isolated these moments as crucial to the trajectory of the university's education in architecture, design and planning over the past century. Crucial, too, is that which is specific to the University of Sydney's architecture school insofar as it is a product of its history.

We have conceived of this book as something that can sit comfortably within the growing library of centenary or anniversary histories of architecture schools that have, like us, welcomed the opportunity to think about the pasts of their various institutions so as to understand the positions and structures that are built into their school's very fabric. The story of *Sydney School* is, in one sense, a story of innovation, but, in another, of persistent conservatism and, hence, of a tension between addressing, on one hand, the needs and provisions agreed between the university and the profession and, on the other, the inherent restlessness of students, who sense the fragility of these institution-to-institution agreements and seek out other ways to use their education; that is, for ends other than those anticipated by professional bodies or school boards. In this sense, like our neighbours on the bookshelf, we have found a new way into the history of architectural culture through the institutions that educate architects and advance a corporate idea of architecture itself, which is to be advanced and tested in the studio and lecture theatre. This tension plays out, too, in the reciprocity of continuities and breaks that has given the Sydney School of Architecture, Design and Planning a consistency across decades.

As Martin Tomitsch recalls in his concluding account of the state of the school's present, the scale and organisation of its architectural education cannot be compared across one end of the century to the other. While the first cohorts of students could be counted on two hands, for each of these students the school now teaches close to 100 more in a wide range of degrees. While each chair led a department—first, a single chair within the Faculty of Architecture, then two, then chairs of the Departments of Architecture, Town Planning, and Architectural Science—the University of Sydney now has nearly a dozen full professors leading aspects of a school that prides itself on a productive interdisciplinarity. Once a department in the Faculty of Science, then a Faculty of Architecture in its own right and then renamed to reflect the expansive range of fields offered within the walls of the Wilkinson Building, it has now been recalibrated as a university school. One could have the sense of an initial clarity being undermined, while it instead changes, as all things should, in response to a fluid world beyond the edges of the school.

The authors of the chapters that follow take a variety of approaches to the task of recalling the moments in which these tensions proved productive. Some essays are, therefore, more personal, bound up in their authors' experience of the school, while others are aiming for the kind of historical and critical distance for which the passage of time and a degree of neutrality are vital. Between the scholarly, reflective and polemical, then, this book advances a history of a problem. How should we train design professionals in the university? How should we weigh the many qualities considered vital to the formation of a well-disposed young practitioner and university graduate? Within this reckoning, how should we accommodate the jostling expectations for an education in architecture, design or planning as held by the professions, the university, its stakeholders or the students themselves? In the absence of the kind of dogmatic positions that would make one answer or another seem natural, the history of this institution is one of balancing the merits of the pragmatic and the esoteric, the professional and the scholarly. As such, it reflects the tensions within the subjects taught within the school, with their origins in the humanistic disciplines, the fine and applied arts, construction and the trades, the social sciences, engineering, hygiene and psychology. There is no monolithic position against which to test the history of the Sydney School, beyond an enduring sense of the importance it placed on weighing things up. This process sometimes resulted in accord, sometimes in partisan bickering. The particular moments in the school's history taken up by each author illuminate distinctive facets of the problem of thinking about the conceptualisation, construction and delivery of courses, diplomas, professional degrees and research degrees as a question of education beyond training.

A history of the school emerges that is both complex and orderly. It unfolds as a story about how the school and the figures who have populated it have positioned and re-positioned themselves with respect to the task of educating architects, designers and planners. By following the chronological arc of the chapters, readers will acquire an impression of the evolution of the school; a development contained, in one sense, by the walls of the Main Quadrangle or the Wilkinson Building, as well as an evolution installed in a relationship with the larger ideas and events that are addressed in the design of degrees, the appointment of teachers and the polemics of our most vocal precursors. The pivotal role and development of studio teaching (across multiple disciplines), the increasingly prominent position of the "laboratory" in the formation of disciplinary knowledge and the social responsibilities attendant to it feature in a number of chapters. This reflects a sustained introspection around design pedagogy and the new challenges reaching the university from the world beyond. Taken together, the chapters that follow reveal the ways in which some of the expectations for the university-based training of design professionals, including a preoccupation with relevance, have been drivers of sometimes sudden instances of change and transformation in the institution and its activities, while also enduring as subjects of perennial deliberation.

*Sydney School* has set out to mark a moment in the institutional life of our school, but to do so by reflecting on the implications of the first move: to bring architecture into the modern university. The University of Sydney was not the first to make this accommodation, but it watched those earlier examples (London, Liverpool, Pennsylvania) with great interest, hoping to replicate their importance, not only as an antipodean counterweight, but also on the same terms, ignoring the challenge of distance. In the decades following the appointment of Sydney's first Chair in Architecture, universities across Australia (indeed the world) embraced architecture as a discipline with its own departments and faculties, just as institutions of technical education in Australia and elsewhere, where architecture had been taught decades before it was offered as a university degree, were recalibrated as universities. At the University of Sydney, the Chair in Architecture would be joined subsequently by chairs in Town and Country Planning and in Architectural Science, within a faculty of increasing scale and multidisciplinarity.

But what are the stakes of a university education in architecture? Or in town planning? Or for interaction design? These questions return us to the existential conundrum of today's universities. They suggest something about the environment and ambitions of the University of Sydney as an institution that, at a crucial moment in which interests from all directions aligned, opened up to the design disciplines, laying the foundations for this school.

To provide training in the standards meant university education. A university education required an assured reward, which led back to registration. And the mark of full acceptance into a university was the establishment of a Chair in the discipline.

— JM Freeland, *The Making of a Profession* (1971)

**Figure 1** — University of Sydney, view of grounds and the front of the main building, 1887, photographer unknown. University of Sydney Archives.

# Chapter 1: "... thoroughly equipped in all respects ..."
— Andrew Leach

From the very beginning, the history of architectural education at the University of Sydney has been inflected by the question of usefulness: of the graduate to his or her profession; of the university to society; and of the quality of the work undertaken by students and graduates to Sydney itself. These questions have surfaced with each major reconfiguration of the syllabus, with each new degree added to the university's stable, and with each new discipline or specialisation given a home in what was long called the Faculty of Architecture. What subjects are proper to a professional course of study in architecture? What should distinguish those architecture graduates with a *university* education? And an education from the University of Sydney in particular? Questions of these sort might now tend to hover somewhere between curriculum planning and marketing. However, in anticipation of the first class of enrolments in the Bachelor of Architecture (BArch) in 1918, the appointment of the university's inaugural Chair in Architecture later that year, and the foundation of the Department and then Faculty of Architecture in 1918 and 1920, these were existential questions that involved not only the university community, both within and well beyond those teaching courses in architecture, but also the leadership of the Institute of Architects of New South Wales (IANSW) and those whose voices gave shape to cultural commentary in Sydney. [^1]

Although all Australia's graduate architects now hold university degrees, the idea that the university was the natural place to secure a professional formation in architecture was far from obvious a century ago. The question of which institution was best equipped to examine the skills and knowledge of prospective architects—the institutes of architecture, technical colleges or, looking to British, French, and American models, the academy or the university—was likewise a subject of deep contention. Architects could become so by learning from other architects on the job, either entirely or, as the 19th century wore on, as architects-in-training whose daytime, on-the-job experience was supplemented by evening classes in colleges of technical education. [^2] Those behind the decision to establish Australia's first university Chair in Architecture grappled with the implications of the university's expanding involvement in the profession. As did the inaugural chair. This issue shaped the tone and actions of those advancing architectural education at the University of Sydney for its first decades, indeed from the very first moments in which the university began contributing to the education of architects in Sydney and New South Wales. The history of architectural education at the University of Sydney is, therefore, also a history of the stakes of a university education in architecture and of the debate around what the university has to offer the profession.

[^1]: Predicating further discussion on internal discussions within the university, see C Turney, U Bygott and P Chippendale, *Australia's First: A History of the University of Sydney*, vol. 1, 1850-1939 (Sydney: Hale and Iremonger, 1991), 386–96; J Horne and G Sherington, *Sydney: The Making of a Public University* (Melbourne: Melbourne University Publishing, 2012), 386–95. On professional debate, see JM Freeland, *The Making of a Profession: A History of the Growth and Work of the Architectural Institutes of Australia* (Sydney: Angus & Robertson, 1971), 218–21.

[^2]: For further reading on the ways in which the Australian debate on architectural registration and education mirrored that of British architecture, see M Crinson and J Lubbock, *Architecture – Art or Profession? Three Hundred Years of Architectural Education in Britain* (Manchester: Manchester University Press, 1994); D van der Plaat, "Architectural Ignorance and Public Indifference: Harold Desbrowe-Annear's Lecture on 'Some Methods of Architectural Criticism' (1893)," *Fabrications: The Journal of the Society of Architectural Historians, Australia and New Zealand* 19, no. 1 (2009): 163–75.

Leslie Wilkinson's appointment as the Chair in Architecture was a significant moment in this story, but it occurred at the culmination of more than three decades of experimentation and debate. Most of all, his appointment followed more than three decades of contributions by others to the education of Sydney's architects, dating back to the 1880s, which were to be largely overshadowed by Wilkinson's profile in the university's history.

## First Moves

In 1882, the University of Sydney added to its statutes a Certificate in Engineering, in which a concentration in civil engineering and architecture was taught alongside other concentrations in mechanical engineering and mining engineering. [^3] Initially conceived as an extension of the discipline of engineering that might lead to an autonomous course of study, architecture was, at this moment, taught as a technical subject offered in the polytechnic mode, with courses in architecture and building, and architectural history, and was offered through electives to third-year students who would, by and large, become engineers. (In this, it shares a disciplinary heritage with architecture at the University of London. [^4]) These subjects, therefore, sat alongside others, including materials science, geometrical drawing, surveying, building physics, geology, and studies in harbours and sewerage works. The certificate was built on a foundation of studies in the arts so that graduates would understand their force moments and their Latin declensions, as would have seemed proper to students at Australia's earliest university, with its Oxbridge pretensions.

The third-year courses in architecture were offered to both matriculated students and to those who had not entered the university as such. Lectures were, furthermore, offered in the evenings, with interlopers paying their lecturer directly. These provisions allowed for what became a sustained practice of courses in the history of architecture and in those dimensions of planning and construction that owed much to the kind of knowledge fostered in the Department of Engineering. They were taken by young members of both engineering and architecture professions and by students otherwise engaged in technical training in architecture at the Sydney Technical College—one of the foundation institutions of the University of New South Wales—which had inherited a technical training mission established by the Sydney Mechanics' School of Art in 1865. [^5]

The architecture courses at Sydney were first offered in 1884 (a course of 30 lectures) and taught by Cyril Blacket, who was son of the former University Architect and Colonial Architect Edmund Blacket, and who had previously taught at what was then the Sydney Technical College and had only recently been appointed head of the Department of Architecture. [^6] After three years, Cyril Blacket left his post due to ill health, ultimately returning to education at the Sydney Technical College in the 1890s. Specific training in design was noticeably absent, with the courses taught by Blacket intended to supplement the design training of the office and of the technical college. The university

[^3]: *University Calendar* (University of Sydney, 1882), 49. All subsequent references to the *University Calendar* refer to this serial source. On the comparable path of architectural education at the University of Melbourne, see M Lewis, "The Development of Architectural Teaching in the University of Melbourne," in *Report to the Committee to Consider all Aspects of the Teaching of Architecture and Building in the University* (University of Melbourne, 1970).
[^4]: Bartlett School of Architecture, *Bartlett: 175 Years of Architectural Education at UCL* (London: Bartlett School of Architecture, 2016).
[^5]: N Neill, *Technically & Further: Sydney Technical College, 1891-1991* (Sydney: Hale & Ironmonger, 1991).
[^6]: Turney, Bygott and Chippendale, *Australia's First*, 386, suggest that, in this, the university's formal education in architecture preceded the foundations of the New South Wales Institute of Architecture. As Freeland notes, however, the institute had been founded much earlier, although it experienced something of a hiatus in these years. Freeland, *The Making of a Profession*, 210, records that early architectural education in Sydney was aimed primarily at aspiring engineers and was directed by Normal Selfe, who taught mechanical drawing, and William Cruickshank, Chief Surveyor to the Marine Board. A more substantial program of study was established in 1878 and led by the City Architect, William Sapsford, and his assistant, Alexander Elphinstone. Turney, Bygott and Chippendale also recall that Sydney was preceded in its efforts to establish a course in architecture by the University of Melbourne, which had tabled a parallel initiative several years earlier, likewise failing for various reasons to put the course in place (386). Describing Blacket's conditions, they note that he "received an honorarium of £100 and all the students' fees" (387).

**Figure 2** — Winsome A Hall, tapestries of the transition period with borders from the illuminated manuscripts of the 9th to 14th centuries, student drawing, 1927. McConnel Drawings Collection, University of Sydney Library, Rare Books and Special Collections.

made a claim, at first, upon those kinds of subjects that naturally extended from its existing offerings in engineering and the humanities.

Replacing Blacket, the British architect John Sulman was appointed as a lecturer in architecture on a year-to-year contract in 1887, teaching the courses Blacket had established: Architecture and Building (effectively construction) and History of Architecture (20 lectures in each subject). These early developments were supported to no little extent by the Chair of Engineering, William H Warren, who had advocated for the place of engineering in the university since his own appointment in 1882 and understood the stakes for architecture as a traditionally technical domain making its way into the cloisters. The IANSW likewise lobbied from outside the university, even securing a place for its president, Thomas Rowe, on the University Senate from 1885, in an attempt to assert the profession's interests in any governing body that might have a role in architectural education. [^7] In 1888, Warren oversaw an amplified offering comprised of a two-year, 60-lecture program on an expanded curriculum intended to complement the offerings of the Sydney Technical College, thereby luring its students down from Harris Street. [^8] The fact that no courses in architectural design had so far been included in the university's course catalogue was seen by Warren, Sulman and others as a major impediment to granting certificates to students who had followed the architecture courses at Sydney. [^9] Further efforts to table a "complete" course in architecture as a major within the established Bachelor of Science were considered by the University Senate in a number of meetings between 1889 and 1892. During this time, the architecture schedule was adopted in principle by the University Senate, pending funding. The course considered by the senate in July 1890 was structured around a wide variety of subjects, ranging from the humanities to the sciences, from fine arts to engineering, as follows:

> In the first year it was recommended that students pursue existing courses in chemistry, physics, mathematics and geometrical drawing, together with a special course on building construction (with practical exemplification) at the junior level, and a course on drawing. In second year existing courses in geology, surveying and applied mathematics were to be taken, to which were to be added special studies in building construction (senior level), [the] history of architecture and of

[^7]: Freeland, *The Making of a Profession*, 62. Freeland also notes IANSW representation on the Board of Technical Education and the Australasian Association for the Advancement of Science.
[^8]: Turney, Bygott and Chippendale, *Australia's First*, 388. "During their initial year students would pursue studies in maths, physics, chemistry and natural history as in first-year Arts, and would also complete courses in building construction (20 lectures) and the history of architecture (20 lectures). In second year students would attend courses on designing and planning buildings (20 hours) and materials and structures (30 lectures). On the successful completion of examinations on the courses, certificates would be issued."
[^9]: Turney, Bygott and Chippendale, *Australia's First*, 387.

design (at the junior level), and drawing. In the final year, the only existing courses to be taken were materials and structures and sanitary engineering. Major emphasis was to be on special courses in the history of architecture and of design (both at the senior level), together with courses on specification, ornament, and drawing. [^10]

A long delay had been introduced by measures that had been tabled with the intention of rendering the course more robust, requiring students entering the degree to first undertake two years' practical experience in the profession. The Institute of Architects had once more found its feet during the 1880s and had a view on this matter (and, indeed, on the entire course), but it was Sulman's lobbying that swung the senate away from this practical requirement, as he argued that the requirement would simply deter students from entering the university. A back and forth, which would seem familiar to anyone now involved in architectural education, ensued over enrolment levels, staffing and other resources needed to effectively offer the courses outlined in the proposal before the senate. In 1892 and early 1893, Sulman undertook a study tour in the United States. [^11] However, it seems that no sooner were these matters resolved than the financial crash of 1893 forced these plans on to ice, where they remained until Sulman began agitating for their resuscitation over the course of the following two decades. In this interregnum, the Institute of Architects also suffered poor fortunes and itself confronted the possibility of winding up its activities in 1897, thereby undermining an important source of advocacy in the senate's considerations. [^12] It is no exaggeration to describe the early history of architectural education at the University of Sydney as a history of initiatives thwarted by circumstance.

## Solid Footings

In 1896, a gift to the university of £50,000, made by the iron-founder Peter Russell, allowed the establishment of a number of endowed lectureships in the Department of Engineering, among which was the PN Russell Lectureship in Architecture. Having taken up the architecture courses established by Blacket, Sulman was appointed as the first Russell Lecturer in Architecture and remained in this role until his tentative retirement from the university in 1912, at which point the lectureship was taken up by John F "Jack" Hennessy. Although he taught in the evenings, maintaining a thriving practice, Sulman's role in the formative years of the university's architectural education cannot be overstated. [^13] Leaving London in 1885 for

[^13]: On Sulman's involvement with the university, see Edwards, *A Life of Purpose*, 132–34.

**Figure 3** — Marjorie SD Hudson (later Holroyde), *Design for a Country School to Accommodate 100 Boys*, student drawing, 1924. McConnel Drawings Collection, University of Sydney Library, Rare Books and Special Collections.

[^10]: Turney, Bygott and Chippendale, *Australia's First*, 388–89.
[^11]: Z Edwards, *A Life of Purpose: A Biography of John Sulman* (Haberfield, NSW: Longueville Media, 2017), 133–34.
[^12]: Freeland, *The Making of a Profession*, 75.

the sake of his wife's health (ultimately losing her in 1888), he had left the opportunity to direct the Architectural Association, of which he had been elected President. In Sydney, he lost little time in becoming involved in both professional life and professional education, establishing the Palladian Club as a venue for architectural criticism and discussion around new books, an alternative to the IANSW that had been resuscitated from a period of inaction only five years earlier. [^14] Sulman taught the two engineering courses in architecture for a period of 25 years, all while assuming an increasingly secure voice in the professional world on issues of town planning and urban sanitation (as Paul Jones further explores later in this volume). Sulman's involvement in architecture was fundamental to its early expansion into town and country planning, just as his practice and advocacy alongside a quarter-century's involvement at the university shaped his incredibly productive career in retirement. (Not least among his achievements was chairing the Federal Capital Advisory Committee in its efforts to implement the ex novo national capital, Canberra.)

The scope and ambitions of Sulman's course in the history of architecture (as indicated by its exam) appeared to change little over that quarter-century, considering, as the *University Calendar* notes, "the historical evolution of design in buildings from the earliest times to the present day, embracing Egyptian, Assyrian, Grecian, Roman, Romanesque, Byzantine, Saracenic, Gothic, Renaissance and modern Work." [^15] That his textbooks were the four-volume *History of Architecture* by James Fergusson and Banister Fletcher's own volume of the same title is hardly remarkable in light of the course description, except to say that it indicates a serious curriculum directed to the training of architects that was commensurate with the historical education being received by students in London, Liverpool and elsewhere in the United Kingdom. The number of architects who took Sulman's courses thoroughly outweighs the number of students who sought degrees from the University of Sydney at this time. His courses extended those students who were not content with the technical training offered in Harris Street or the professional experience of the office. Indeed, Hennessy's own son was among those technically trained architects who sought out a rounder education with Sulman. [^16]

As an indication of the modest scale of this endeavour, only four names are given as students in these courses in 1912: BC Duckworth, RH Goddard, E (Eric) Heath and RC Hill. Heath, for one, had been primarily a student of the Sydney Technical College, as others may also have been, and it is notable that two of these names appear as "also-rans" in a competition to design an ideal home in 1926, indicating at the very least a long-term commitment to architecture as a profession. [^17]

Sulman's ambitions were broader, of course, and he continued to push for the adoption of the full course in architecture that had been approved but not funded in 1892. Turney, Bygott and Chippendale describe him as "frustrated but optimistic," which he certainly must have been to sustain the serial delays, first in considering the matter at the senate and then in putting the plan into action. [^18] All the while, pressure increased on all fronts for the university to take up what had been increasingly regarded within professional circles as its responsibility to educate architects. As the authors of *Australia's First* put it, while courses continued to be taught at the technical college and as Sulman continued to offer his own evening classes in history and construction,

---

[^14]: Freeland, *The Making of a Profession*, 63. Freeland offers an amusing account of its trajectory: "Sulman formed the Palladian Club as part of his plan to bring respectability to the architecture profession. The club met one a month for the purpose of showing and criticizing the work of its members. Some of them proved to be sensitive to the frank opinions of their colleagues and a reluctance to producing work for criticism developed. On Sulman's suggestion they decided to become a book club, importing books from Batsford's in London, reading them, discussing them and finally recouping most of their money by putting them up for auction."

[^15]: *University Calendar* (1907), 177.

[^16]: Freeland, *The Making of a Profession*, 218. Freeland names a number of figures who passed through Sydney in this way while following the technical training path, including Herbert E Ross, Henry Budden, Carlyle Greenwall, John Clamp (who employed the future Florence Taylor), Esplin, Hubert Corlette, Thomas Cosh, Joseph A Kethel and George Taylor (the other half of the formidable Taylor partnership).

[^17]: "The Ideal Home Competition Promoted in Sydney: A Review of the Designs Submitted," *Building* 38, no. 225 (1926): 50–64.

[^18]: Turney, Bygott and Chippendale, *Australia's First*, 390.

"the Institute of Architects maintained its efforts to raise the education and professional qualifications of architects and became adamant ... that a Chair of Architecture should be established at the University." [^19] This was in 1906 and, notwithstanding efforts both within and beyond the university discussions, the debate tipped into 1907. The necessary funding was not forthcoming from the State Government, so the delay extended to the end of the decade, when the profession's own capacity to advocate for the establishment lost momentum.

## Advancements Towards a Chair

Freeland recounts the argument that had underscored debates around education and registration since the 1880s. [^20] At base was a question of how to "control ... the standards of those practicing architecture," which had to be raised consistently to elevate the social status of the architect. As Freeland writes, "Education was one essential, but long-term way of doing it. Registration, by making it possible to cut out the worst wood immediately, was the necessary short-term complement to education." [^21] While the young architect could be educated in all manner of situations, the standing of the three universities that had been founded by the 1880s (those of Sydney, Melbourne and Adelaide in 1850, 1853 and 1874, respectively) mapped neatly against the aspirations of the profession itself. [^22] The investment in university study, as Freeland put it, would be secured by the professional process of registration, controlling the size and quality of the profession's membership. [^23] "And so the case closed back in on itself. Higher standards of architecture meant legally enforceable qualifications for architects—registration. To provide training in the standards meant university education. A university education required an assured reward, which led back to registration. And the mark of full acceptance into a university was the establishment of a chair in the discipline." [^24]

Appointed to succeed Sulman in 1912, Hennessy was a highly vocal advocate for the establishment of the chair. [^25] Just four years younger than Sulman, Hennessy deployed his seniority to pursue the profession's advancement through a campaign waged on several fronts. He had been instrumental in bringing together the Palladian Society and the IANSW, following a period in the 1880s and 1890s during which the stand-off between John Sulman and John Horbury Hunt had coloured both institutions. Hennessy resolved, through this action, an image of the profession as driven by both technical expertise and the applied arts. He understood the deep connection that necessarily held the university to the profession and, in 1908, had led the committee that prepared the Registration Bill on behalf of the IANSW, even though it would not reach the floor of the State legislature for more than a decade. [^26] Delivering the 1910 inaugural address to the IANSW as its Acting President, he asserted: "It may well be asked why the architect should escape examination, and why such a noble profession—on which depends, to a greater extent than any other, the health and well-being of the citizens—should be a happy

[^19]: Turney, Bygott and Chippendale, *Australia's First*, 390. Freeland traces a tumultuous decade from the end of the 1880s to the end of the 1890s, during which internal disputes and administrative difficulties that were well-aired in the press can only have served to undermine the Institute of Architects' capacity to forcibly advance its position. Likewise, the publicly recognised animosity between John Horbury Hunt, who long held the presidency of the IANSW, and Sulman himself, as the profession's most prominent representative in the university. After matters came to a head in 1891, Freeland writes, "Sulman had nothing to do with the Institute for twenty years." Freeland, *The Making of a Profession*, 64–73, especially pages 70 and 72–73, with particular quotations from page 73.
[^20]: Freeland, *The Making of a Profession*, 211–13.
[^21]: Freeland, *The Making of a Profession*, 211–13. Developments in the 1880s and 1890s were limited to Sydney and Melbourne, with widespread engagement in architectural education across the Australian colonies in colleges of technical education before Federation.
[^22]: Freeland, *The Making of a Profession*, 211–13.
[^23]: Freeland, *The Making of a Profession*, 203.
[^24]: Freeland, *The Making of a Profession*, 203. While Warren's efforts at Sydney to secure a path to the appointment of a Chair in Architecture were underpinned by the recent experience of securing a Chair in Engineering, the precedence of engineering's success in this matter spurred on the architecture profession to gain equivalent recognition as a university-trained profession. It is significant, in light of Freeland's observations, that Wilkinson was the first to register on the Roll of the Board of Architects in 1923 and later served two terms as president of the IANSW in the 1930s. For further reading, see D Wilkinson, "Epilogue," in *Leslie Wilkinson: A Practical Idealist*, ed. S Falkiner (Woollahra, NSW: Valadon 1982), 112.
[^25]: Freeland, *The Making of a Profession*, 210.
[^26]: Freeland, *The Making of a Profession*, 236.

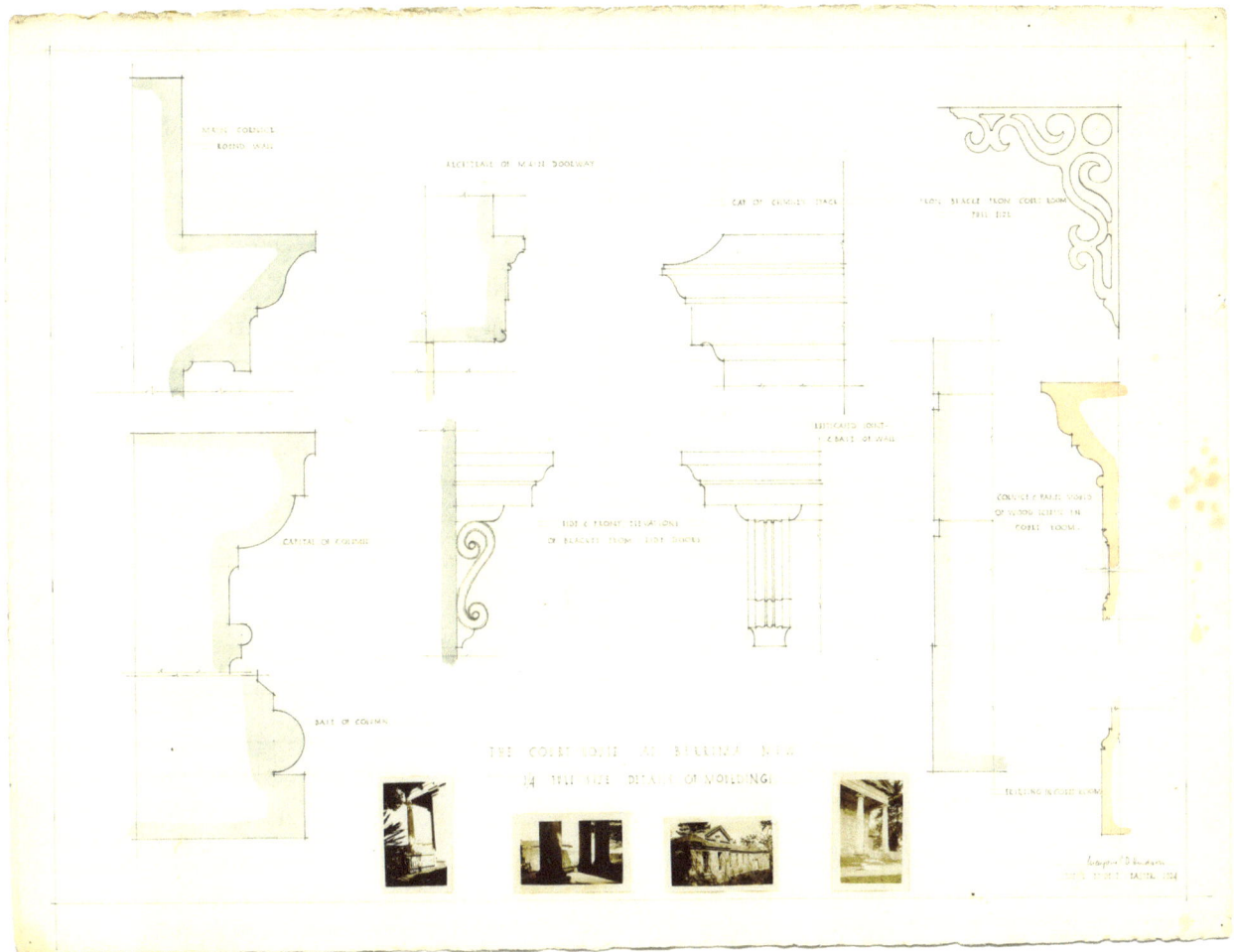

**Figure 4** — Marjorie SD Hudson, *Courthouse at Berrima, NSW*, 1/4 Full Size Details of Mouldings, student drawing, 1924. McConnel Drawings Collection, University of Sydney Library, Rare Books and Special Collections.

hunting ground for the charlatan? … The higher standard must be taken up by the future architects, and as each must live his own life, and no other man can live it for us, so it behoves us to ascertain what the true value of it is." [^27]

Having himself studied in London at the Royal Academy of Art, Hennessy was convinced that the "establishment of a Chair of Architecture at the Sydney University" would advance these aims, enabling Australia to join the ranks already filled by the chairs at Liverpool, London (at the University and the Architectural Association) and Pennsylvania. [^28] He returned to this matter in opening an exhibition of architects' drawings at the Royal Arts Society's Rooms in 1912, now as President of the Institute (since 1911) and soon to become Sulman's successor to the Russell Lectureship. On that occasion he observed:

… we have no Architecture School connected with this Institute, and I feel that until we establish such classes, we shall not attract students in large numbers. It is true that some of the subjects are taught by excellent masters at the Technical College, but the atmosphere of an Architecture School is wanting—that indefinable influence of school or college life which penetrates every young man's being and character and impels him to study. That influence I say is wanting at present, and we can expect larger and better things from our students only when we, as an Institute, have established classes, or better still, when a complete Architecture School is started at Sydney University. [^29]

[^27]: Turney, Bygott and Chippendale, *Australia's First*, 390–91.
[^28]: Turney, Bygott and Chippendale, *Australia's First*, 391.
[^29]: Turney, Bygott and Chippendale, *Australia's First*, 391–92.

**Figure 5** — Frank W Turner, *A Study of the Ionic Order*, student drawing, watercolour elevation, 1927. McConnel Drawings Collection, University of Sydney Library, Rare Books and Special Collections.

Noting that, in the absence of these initiatives, Australia would lose its talented students to overseas schools, he continues: "This is not as it should be; a young country such as ours should attract and endeavour to retain the best brains in architecture as in all other lines of work." [^30] He vigorously pursued the two levers of professional standardisation, registration and education, and agitated consistently from within the university to see an inaugural Chair in Architecture appointed.

Efforts continued over the years to put the right combination of people into the rooms where discussion over the funding and scope of the chair might advance. It was hoped that these discussions would prompt others about a coherent and full curriculum for a university degree in architecture, promoted by Sulman and Hennessy alike as the gold standard of entry to the profession by examination. Meanwhile, the university continued to offer courses in building construction and in architectural history to both matriculated and external students. The pieces came together in 1915 and 1916, resulting in an amendment to the University Act that provided the funds needed to establish a Chair in Architecture. In the middle of the First World War, the university was sceptical at its prospects of attracting a suitable candidate, especially a suitable candidate from Britain (the source of choice).

The senate resolved to test the market, however, after a series of providential meetings in February 1917 saw tabled a government commitment to fund a statutory endowment for the Chair in Architecture at Sydney and an expansion of the university's facilities to support a larger student cohort engaged in a wider range of subjects. [^31] Three representatives of the Institute (Pritchard, Kent and Sydney Jones) advised the senate to establish a committee of selection in London, ostensibly to avoid any delay should circumstances become more favourable, and to advance planning at home around a degree that would equip students for professional registration. In both respects, the proposed actions were somewhat speculative, supported by neither a firm decision to proceed with the search nor any legislative tool to support professional registration. Nonetheless, Hennessy oversaw the development of a curriculum for a four-year BArch, available to students who met the entry requirements of the science degree. Its first-year subjects would be architecture (including building construction), descriptive geometry ("with practical work"), architectural drawing and design, mathematics, physics or chemistry, and subjects from the Bachelor of Arts (BA) schedule. [^32] The full curriculum for subsequent years of study would be determined at a later point in time, drawing on the ideas and expertise of the chair. Thus, from the appearance of the means in February, the profession's expectations were laid out in March; Hennessy had concocted

[^30]: Turney, Bygott and Chippendale, *Australia's First*, 391–92.

[^31]: Freeland, *The Making of a Profession*, 219. Freeland recounts the progress made in each meeting from July 1916 to February 1917. The university made a formal request for funds for the chair in October 1916, with the University (Amendment) Bill passing in December 1917.

[^32]: Turney, Bygott and Chippendale, *Australia's First*, 393.

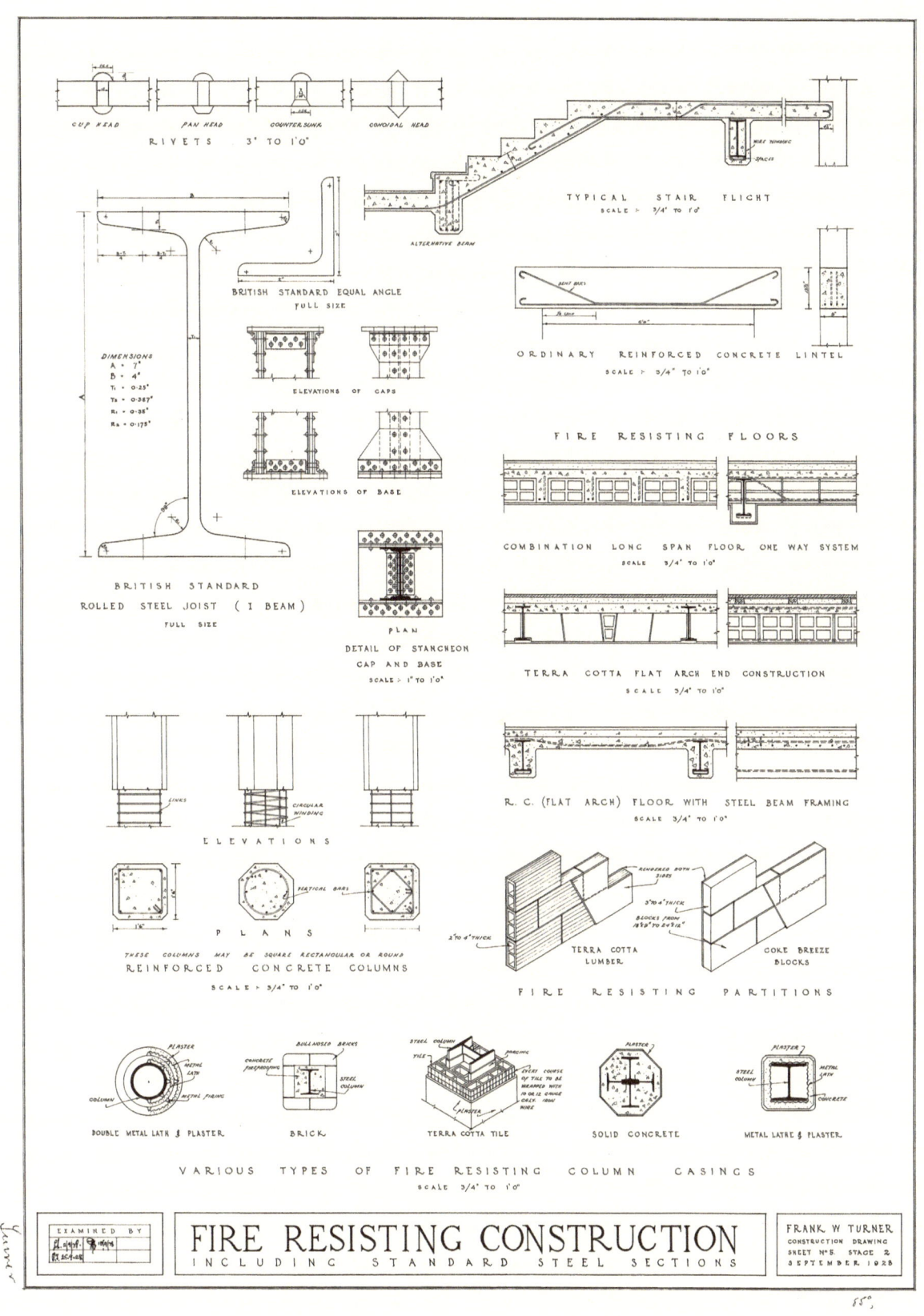

**Figure 6** — Frank W Turner, *Fire Resisting Construction, including Standard Steel Sections*, student drawing, 1928. McConnel Drawings Collection, University of Sydney Library, Rare Books and Special Collections.

Figure 7 — David W King, *Gothic Woodwork, Churches*, student drawing, 1929. McConnel Drawings Collection, University of Sydney Library, Rare Books and Special Collections.

the start of the degree by April, receiving senate approval in May 1917. [^33] In the second reading of the University (Amendment) Bill, in December 1916, it was noted that the State's endowment of the chair and its expanded support of additional "exhibitions" fulfilled "a promise which was given some time ago" and already captured in the University Amendment Act of 1912. [^34] The first nine students enrolled at the start of 1918 included four women and five men.

Anticipating government support, although still in the midst of war-time, the senate had established a committee to mount a global search for a chair in 1916. [^35]

The position was open, but the senate expressed its collective hope that the appointee would be British. This reflected Australia's enduring relationship with the imperial centre, as well as a keen awareness of the model being pursued at Sydney, which followed the precedents set by such institutions as University College London and the University of Liverpool. All deliberations were, therefore, held in London by a committee appointed by the senate and chaired by Aston Webb, Reginald Blomfield, and Charles Nicholson—all knights of the realm—as well as FM Simpson, then professor at University College London and former chair at Liverpool, and the scientist Archibald Liversidge, a professor emeritus of Sydney who had retired to London and presided over the meeting that approved the BSc in Architecture in 1890. [^36] The Agent General of New South Wales sat on the committee as well, sending and

[^33]: Turney, Bygott and Chippendale, *Australia's First*, 393.
[^34]: NSW, Parliamentary Debates, Legislative Council, 14 December 1916, 3745–46.
[^35]: Turney, Bygott and Chippendale, *Australia's First*, 392. The university's official history notes that the senate had originally anticipated making a temporary appointment that would last until after the end of the war, reflecting difficulty in securing candidates both for the chair and for the search committee itself. Provisions made in the State legislature, however, gave impetus to proceed with a "full" search for a permanent appointment.

[^36]: Turney, Bygott and Chippendale, *Australia's First*, 388.

receiving cables to keep the University Senate informed. This was not necessarily an unusual process, as can be gauged by the concurrent search for a Chair in Zoology, which was likewise being conducted by a London-based committee and likewise mediated through the Agent General. The committee shortened a list of 16 candidates to three names, records of which have since been expunged from the senate papers, ultimately recommending Leslie Wilkinson, who was then teaching alongside Simpson at the Bartlett. Curiously, as the university's official history reports, Hennessy himself was considered for the chair, enjoying the support of Warren and Catherine Dwyer, a fellow of the senate. A motion to this effect was put to the senate by Warren, only to be amended to reflect the recommendation made through the Agent General. [^37] The senate ultimately voted to accept the recommendation of the London-based committee. For all those local interests who had shaped the opportunity to appoint a Chair in Architecture, Wilkinson was announced as a *fait accompli*.

## A Turning Point

Wilkinson had studied figure drawing at the Hornsey School of Art and undertaken technical training at London's Northern Polytechnic (one of the antecedent institutions of London Metropolitan University) before enrolling in 1902 at the Royal Academy, where he won numerous honours. Upon graduation, he travelled extensively around Britain, France, Spain and Italy, studying architecture and the "allied arts" while passing the examinations of the Royal Institute of British Architects. He was appointed an assistant to Simpson at University College in 1908, winning a post as assistant professor two years later. There he taught building construction, design principles, perspective drawing, sciography, and site sketching and directed the Evening School of Design. He lectured widely in Britain, and his drawings were published in both professional journals and in major monographs of the moment. [^38] His early practical experience was in the studio of Charles E Kempe (renowned for his stained glass and altar-pieces) and in the office of James Gibson and Samuel Russell, where he worked on competitions and commissions for public libraries in Hull and Walsall, the Queen Victoria Memorial at Hull, the Walsall Town Hall, and a school at Eastbourne, as well as a number of churches, office blocks, and houses. His private practice, corresponding in duration with his time at University College, resulted in a number of houses and flats, a gymnasium and laboratory at Guisborough Grammar School in Yorkshire, and a chapel and surgery at the Wellcome Institute in Millwall. This was alongside a thriving consultancy that contributed drawings and models to the work of "well-known Architects" unnamed in his résumé (on projects likewise unnamed) and that submitted numerous competition entries, some of which earned commendations and placings. His own drawings had been exhibited at the Royal Academy on four separate occasions before the outbreak of war. His military service was spent in the University of London Officers' Training Corps, commanding an infantry company and lecturing full-time in topography and field engineering. Among the 11 names given to speak on his behalf, no fewer than three were on the selection committee: Blomfield, Simpson and Webb. In a written reference, James Gibson endorsed Wilkinson's candidacy with the observation that: "He would vitalise the study of Architecture and impress Students with the fact that it is a living Art." [^39]

[^37]: This was a turn of events also recorded in P Johnson, "Leslie Wilkinson at Sydney University," in *Leslie Wilkinson*, 53–86; and Turney, Bygott and Chippendale, *Australia's First*, 393.

[^38]: His resume specifies the following journals: F Simpson, *A History of Architectural Development*, vols 1–3 (New York: Longman Green, 1905-1911); WJ Anderson, *Architecture of the Renaissance in Italy* (London: Batsford, 1909); AE Richardson, *Monumental Classic Architecture in Great Britain and Ireland during the Eighteenth & Nineteenth Centuries* (London: Batsford, 1914). All of these editions are, naturally, in the Sydney library collection.

[^39]: All details in this paragraph have been synthesised from "Application for the Post of Professor of Architecture from Leslie Wilkinson, ARIBA," in the *Wilkinson Papers* (University of Sydney, October 1917). Quotations are drawn specifically from correspondence to the Agent-General for New South Wales from James S. Gibson on 6 September 1917. Portions of this document are narrativized at greater length and are illustrated with drawings by Wilkinson, in "Early Days," *Leslie Wilkinson*, 11–29.

While Wilkinson prepared his application to the chair, Hennessy developed an initial curriculum into which the first students of the BArch entered in 1918. The first full curriculum of architecture had been tabled by Hennessy in 1917 within the Faculty of Science and included as first year subjects architecture (including building construction), descriptive geometry (including practical work), architectural drawing and design, mathematics, physics or chemistry, and a subject from the BA schedule. "The curriculum will probably cover a period of four years," noted the *University Calendar*, accommodating the distinct possibility that the new chair would seek to make immediate changes to the program as initially conceived. The Senate Report observed that the State legislature had provided, not only for the chair (in 1916), but also for an expanded cohort of students. The second, third and fourth years of the degree would maintain courses in design, drawing and history and technical subjects shifting in scale from buildings to towns and cities.

Having been offered the post, Wilkinson went about resigning his commission and extracting himself from his responsibilities at both University College (where he taught architectural design, drawing and construction) and the Officers Training Corps. His arrival in August 1918 was the culmination of decades of manoeuvring and foiled plans. [^40] Speaking to the Institute of Architects a mere fortnight after Wilkinson took up his post, the Institute's president, Arthur Pritchard, expressed hope that this moment might position Sydney "as the Art centre and Paris of the southern hemisphere" and that the university might help Australia to "evolve a national architecture, the most glorious and imperishable record of a Nation's greatness." [^41] High hopes, indeed.

Wilkinson taught his first class on 16 September and quickly appointed his first lecturers. The artist Norman Carter, who taught freehand drawing, had held the fort along with Jack Hennessy in temporary positions while the chair search was underway in 1918; while Hennessy's time at Sydney concluded at the end of 1918, Carter was kept on. (A review of those student drawings that survive from the early Wilkinson years indicate the importance of studies in visual composition and, in particular, the composition of stained glass panels. Carter taught students drawing even as he continued to compose important glass panels.) [^42]

Wilkinson gave his inaugural address more than a year after his arrival, having settled in and assessed the institutional landscape and the professional prospects it had to offer. Titled "Australia and Architecture," the event on 3 September was reported by Florence Taylor in her journal *Building*, for some time the go-to place for unauthorised yet comprehensive accounts of Wilkinson's lectures. [^43] It would now seem ill-considered to begin as Wilkinson did when he said: "Australia is remarkable in the nations of the world in not possessing any indigenous architecture, and [more defensibly] the University of Sydney, in establishing the

[^40]: G Sydney Jones, personal correspondence to L Wilkinson, 4 March 1918. His formal welcome was held at Admiralty House on 29 August 1919, but an institute event one week later offers the sharpest assessment of the importance of his appointment. Jones had written to Wilkinson to enquire after his plans so that the institute could offer "a hearty welcome to Australia." The event was attended by "the Premier, Mr W Holman, the Lord Mayor of Sydney, J Joynton-Smith, the Speaker of the Legislative Assembly, representatives of the judiciary, the Mitchell Library, the Art Gallery, the Chamber of Commerce, newspaper editors, well known architects of the day and many other worthy citizens and their wives." His first significant professional contact appears to have been William Hardy Wilson, with whom he spent much time during his first week in Sydney. See Wilkinson, "Early Days," 21, 56; Johnson, "Leslie Wilkinson at Sydney University," 56. Furthermore, according to Freeland, *The Making of a Profession*, 219, Jones had been advocating for the Chair in Architecture since the 1890s, so the arrival of Wilkinson must have been particularly rewarding.

[^41]: Johnson, "Leslie Wilkinson at Sydney University," 56.
[^42]: On Carter, see Simon Weir's essay later in this volume.
[^43]: [F Taylor], "Architecture and Australia: The Inaugural Address of Professor Wilkinson, of the Chair of Architecture, University of Sydney," *Building* 24, no. 145 (September 1919): 55–56. In the very next article, Florence Taylor, "'The New Broom': Sydney's New Architectural Critic," *Building* 24, no. 145 (September 1919): 57–64, she offers a rebuke to Wilkinson's apparent neglect, in his lecture, to the issue of housing. See also and Freeland, *The Making of a Profession*, 221. On Taylor herself, and, by extension, Sydney's architectural culture around the time of this event, refer to B Hanna and R Freestone, *Florence Taylor's Hats: Designing, Building and Editing Sydney* (Ultimo, NSW: Halstead Press, 2007). It is noteworthy that Taylor had, as Florence Parsons, studied both at the Sydney Technical College and at the Sydney University, gaining an education in architecture, surveying, and engineering before embarking upon the career for which she is famous.

new School of Architecture, was the first in Australia in following the example of Europe and America [and hence the tradition initiated by the Parisian *École des Beaux-Arts*] in placing architecture in its proper place, that its importance called for in the great Arts." [^44] The future development of the Australian profession, he argued, would quickly become contingent on the academic work of the schools. It was not sufficient to stick rigidly to a view of architecture as either a fine art or a form of engineering, nor to attempt a half-hearted reconciliation of the two views. He advocated for "a thorough grounding in scientific principles and the details of modern work," while encouraging and developing the "artistic sense." [^45] "We must build up the deficiency," he continued, "and aim at turning out students thoroughly equipped in all respects, possessed of fine taste, good sense, broad sympathies, full of imagination and ideas, supported by the practical common sense of the skilled constructor, organiser, and supervisor." [^46] By flourishing in the university, architecture would likewise flourish in the community beyond, with the university leading society beyond its 19th-century errors in building and city planning, embracing "something better and more expressive of our life and ideals." [^47]

Figure 8 — 1918 Freehand Drawing class, comprised of John Fairlie-Cunninghame, William (Bill) Laurie, Leonore (Lorna) Lukin, Beryl McLauchlan, Ellice Nosworthy, Gregory Roarty, Mary Alice Sheffer and Stanley Vickers. Photographer unknown, 1918. University of Sydney Archives. Several of these students were among the first graduating BArch cohort: Cunninghame, Laurie, Vickers, Lukin, McLaughlan and Nosworthy (receiving their degrees alongside Charles Hollinshed and Frederick Lucas). Thanks to Kirsty Volz for clarification of the identities and datation of this photograph.

Wilkinson quickly moved to re-work Hennessy's BArch. In particular, he laid out a professional curriculum for the balance of years that was overtly oriented to professional needs, including significant commitments to the design studio and to those practical subjects that would equip students to enter the professional world upon graduation. Students in their second and third years would take courses in "design, drawing, history of architecture and construction," as well as courses in materials and structures for second-year students, surveying and hygiene for third-year students. [^48] The fourth and final year comprised further studies in design and drawing, history of art, professional practice, and town planning. Engineering staff taught courses in hygiene and surveying and contributed to the teaching of construction and structures. The balance of teaching was undertaken by the School of Architecture, with Wilkinson at the helm. Hennessy returned to the permanent staff to meet these needs, and he was joined by new colleagues Alfred Coffey and AW Gerard; these three taught construction, freehand drawing, and design, respectively. [^49]

The importance of the new school for the closely related professional ambition to register architects was hardly lost on Wilkinson: where the university's examinations would assess the knowledge acquired by the prospective architect, the registration process would

[^44]: [Taylor], "Architecture and Australia," 55.
[^45]: [Taylor], "Architecture and Australia," 55.
[^46]: [Taylor], "Architecture and Australia," 55.
[^47]: Wilkinson, quoted in "Architecture and Australia," 55–56.
[^48]: Turney, Bygott and Chippendale, *Australia's First*, 394
[^49]: Turney, Bygott and Chippendale, *Australia's First*, 394. This paragraph follows the official account very closely.

confirm the aspirant's application of that knowledge to specific commissions. Wilkinson spoke two years before the Architect's Act was passed in New South Wales but already foresaw a moment when the "amateur opinion" would be eclipsed by the new expertise to be fostered in the university, and when "the amateur and unqualified architect [would] be grouped with the lay lawyer and the quack." [^50] It was part of the university's purview, then, and hence part of the mission of the Department of Architecture, to equip graduates, not only with the means to design well, but also to serve as good cultural citizens. [^51] His hopes to position architecture at the centre of the university's development is captured by his success in having the Faculty of Architecture named among the expanded range of 10 faculties despite nobody having yet been awarded the BArch. (The first eight graduates received their degrees in 1922.) Wilkinson was appointed as dean, remaining in that position until his retirement in 1947 and directing more than a quarter of the faculty's nearly century-long history.

Wilkinson's contributions to the university were hardly limited to his tenure as dean. Over the course of 1919, Wilkinson secured a place on the University Building and Grounds Committee before manoeuvring, by the year's end, to set aside the historical arrangement under which the Colonial or Government Architect was also the University Architect, instead establishing himself as University Architect. In this role, he contributed a significant number of new buildings and helped the university to plan for future expansion. [^52] The pairing of the Chair in Architecture with the role of University Architect was neither predicated in the university's search for a chair, nor especially well regarded when it did come to the attention of the senate. An early and anonymous query, posed through the Agent-General, as to whether the conditions of the appointment might allow a parallel professional practice prompted the senate to bluntly reiterate its original conditions of appointment, which allowed no more than a consulting practice alongside university duties. This response went unchallenged at the time. However, a unanimous recommendation by the search committee that the new chair be allowed to run a practice for the good of the students followed Wilkinson's senate-confirmed appointment, which not only suggests the origin of the query, but also the views of the committee on the value of keeping a hand in, as it were.

The prominence of institutional buildings in Wilkinson's portfolio makes perfect sense, given his location within the university itself, and predicates, for instance, the involvement of Dean Peter Johnson's practice in the expansion of the Wilkinson Building in the 1970s (as Lee Stickells describes in a later chapter). It noticeably builds on the experience gained by Wilkinson in assisting Simpson in the design of the new building for the School of Architecture at University College London, on which he had worked from 1911 to its completion in 1915 and which was the first purpose-built facility for architecture education realised in Great Britain. [^53] As early as 1920, Wilkinson recommended eight new projects, including the completion of Blacket's quadrangle and its cloisters, buildings for the Departments of Physics and Chemistry, and works for the School of Public Health and Tropical Medicine. The volume of work precluded a single hand, and Wilkinson used the opportunity to foster relationships with a number of the city's architects. [^54] He tabled a masterplan for the university in 1920, rationalising the

[^50]: Johnson, "Leslie Wilkinson at Sydney University," 56.
[^51]: Johnson, "Leslie Wilkinson at Sydney University," 56.
[^52]: Falkiner, ed., *Leslie Wilkinson*, 60.
[^53]: "Application for the Post of Professor of Architecture from Leslie Wilkinson, ARIBA," October 1917. Wilkinson specifically notes: "In that capacity [as Simpson's assistant] I was intimately connected with the building and especially with its furnishings and the equipment of its Library and Collections of Models and Casts."
[^54]: For a full account of Wilkinson's tenure as University Architect, see Johnson, "Leslie Wilkinson at Sydney University," 53–86, especially page 68, and 117–23. See also T Howells, *University of Sydney Architecture* (Sydney: Watermark Press, 2007). It is notable that, in an earlier era, Sulman too had built for the university, as in Edwards, *A Life of Purpose*, 189–96.

relationships between buildings both extant and possible across the campus, describing tree-lined lanes, indicating where animals should be prevented from grazing, and articulating sight-lines across the campus. He did not enjoy the free-rein in implementation for which he had hoped, but such projects as the Quadrangle and the Physics Building are enduring testimonials to his vision. [^55]

If Wilkinson's buildings offer a complement to his work as an educator, an architectural allegory offers insights into another element of the academic culture he advanced. It is a quirk of history that the statutes first admitting courses in architecture into the university (1882) were passed in the same year in which women were likewise first allowed through its doors to take a limited range of subjects. This latter change to the university's legislation prompted an unrelated but nonetheless architectural problem: the need for "a suitable retiring room and other necessary conveniences set apart exclusively for female students." [^56] This was the "small cottage ... erected at the rear of the University buildings" according to the design of Colonial Architect James Barnet, who had been Clerk of Works at the time when Edmund Blacket had designed the University's Great Hall. [^57] The Women's Common Room, as it was called, was later torn down to allow for further development of the complex suite of buildings articulated around the main quadrangle, a mark of normalisation as much as anything. These events both suggest, in their own ways, an early willingness on the university's part to modernise a mere three decades after its foundation and hence to move deftly beyond the image fostered by the four founding faculties: arts, science, medicine and law. [^58]

# Interior Tensions

Despite the efforts of the university, it is telling that the courses offered to engineering students were largely taken up by non-degree students (those students enrolled in the Sydney Technical College) under the University Extension program. It is telling, too, that while the BArch established by Hennessy and refined by Wilkinson offered a path for women to enter the profession, the distance maintained between town and gown fostered a professional distrust in the capacities of those early graduates, and of the women especially, who had received no additional exposure to the architect's office during their studies. [^59]

There has surely never been a more rollicking tale told of the history of architecture's professional regularisation than that of Max Freeland's *The Making of a Profession*, the research and insights of which have had no small role in recalling the first decades of Sydney's experiences in educating students in architecture, as recounted above. The parallel histories of architectural education and professional registration inform a narrative about defensible standards that the establishment of the Chair in Architecture at Sydney was intended to advance, as was the development of a full university degree in architecture that would test skills through examination. [^60] Freeland writes:

> ... the course that Wilkinson instituted was a far cry from any that had been seen in Australia to that time. ... If all the previous courses in Australia had been too practically and scientifically based, which they were, Wilkinson's course went to the other extreme and

[^55]: On the 1920 University Plan in particular, see Johnson, "Leslie Wilkinson at Sydney University," 66–67; Howells, *University of Sydney Architecture*, 61, 222–25.
[^56]: *University Calendar* (1882), 149.
[^57]: *University Calendar* (1882), 149.
[^58]: Compare with M Wigley, "Prosthetic Theory: The Disciplining of Architecture," *Assemblage* 15 (1991): 6–29. Wigley's essay concerns the tentative early accommodation, and accommodations, of architecture at the Massachusetts Institute of Technology, which has enough differences from the Sydney case not to sustain closer comparison.

[^59]: This subject was thoroughly explored in K Volz, "Early Woman Architects at the University of Sydney: An Examination of Nell McCredie's Student Portfolios, 1918-1923," in *Educating Architects and Planners, 1917-2017* (Auckland: University of Auckland, 8 September 2017) and in B Hanna, "Australia's Early Women Architects: Milestones and Achievements," *Fabrications* 12, no. 1 (2002): 26–57, which builds on her doctoral dissertation, "Absence and Presence: A Historiography of Early Woman Architects in New South Wales" (PhD diss., University of New South Wales, 1999).
[^60]: For more information on the path to registration in New South Wales, see Freeland, *The Making of a Profession*, 236–38.

emphasised philosophy, theory and practice of design, aesthetics and attractive rendering. In each of its four years the main subjects covered, under various names, the different aspects of design, freehand drawing, watercolour drawing and the history of architecture. Construction and the sciences became a secondary appendage tacked, like an unwanted tail, on to the end. [^61]

Freeland's diagnosis is that the tendencies concretised at Sydney under Wilkinson were the culmination of three decades of tensions between the most pragmatic expectations around architectural education, which fed the position of those "registrationist" members of the profession, and the memorialist's identification of architecture with arts both liberal and applied.

Was architecture an art or a profession? Were its qualities to be defended by institutional structures or the honesty of the "craft"? Something of Wilkinson's early introspection is exposed by the return of John Sulman to the university in 1919 to deliver the Vernon Memorial Lectures in Town Planning (taken up by Paul Jones in the next chapter). Sulman had never been so busy, or so significant, as he was in his retirement years and in lecturing on town planning, he lectured too on a view of architecture that did not retreat from the world or imagine new worlds so much as it went into battle with the conditions of the city. Nevertheless, between the water-coloured perspective and the technical operations of the city remain several scales of knowledge that were regarded by some circles as problematically absent from the training of the University of Sydney's architecture graduates. [^62] Indeed, the question of relevance that the profession itself addressed through later appointments in construction and architectural science would continue to agitate at the edges of Wilkinson's faculty, eventually spilling over in the student protests of the 1960s and 1970s.

[^61]: Freeland, *The Making of a Profession*, 219–20.

[^62]: That said, when Australia returned to war in 1939, Wilkinson joined a group of artists, scientists and designers who were concerned with the contribution their work could make to the war effort, specifically in the realm of camouflage design. On this episode, see A Elias, *Camouflage Australia: Art, Nature, Science and War* (Sydney: Sydney University Press, 2015).

# Drawing in the Wilkinson Decades

**Introduction —** From his arrival in 1918, Wilkinson emphasised drawing as the architect's favoured medium. Together with drawing instructor Norman Carter and later John D Moore he shaped the culture of the University of Sydney's architecture studios around compositional exercises, hypothetical design problems within building and planning types that enjoyed the master's sympathies, and studies of fine buildings drawn from across the historical canon. These 10 drawings offer a cross-section of the visual culture of the Wilkinson years, including fine student works by figures who went on to become giants in their respective domains: Frank Turner at the helm of the NSW Small Homes Service; Peter Priestley in his celebrated modernist practice and Urmila Eulie Chowdhury (née Saksena) alongside Pierre Jeanneret in Chandigarh. Their work here represents the first generation of students who were taught according to consistent principles that privileged fine skills in communication, a keen sense of compositional balance, and a balanced appreciation of the great repository of precedents to be found in history (both immediate and distant). As the office building study by Judith Macintosh (née Moreau) suggests, and as drawings into the 1950s and 1960s would further attest (once Lloyd Rees entered the fray), these skills and values mediated the arrival of modernism to the architecture studios of the University of Sydney.

    These drawings are reproduced from the McConnel Drawings Collection, a gift of alumni of what was, at the time, the Faculty of Architecture, to further the place of hand drawings in the studio culture of the Sydney School.

— Andrew Leach

**Figure 1** — Marjorie SD Hudson (later Holroyde),
*A College Chapel, to Seat 500 Students*,
watercolour plan, section and elevations, 1925.
McConnel Drawings Collection, University of Sydney
Library, Rare Books and Special Collections.

**Figure 2** — E Annette (Nancy) Hazelton (later Davey), *Ornament of the Spanish Renaissance* (watercolour study of the stone door to the sacristy of the Cathedral of Sigüenza), 1928. McConnel Drawings Collection, University of Sydney Library, Rare Books and Special Collections.

BANK
ELEVATION
PLAN THROUGH COLUMNS
PLAN OF TRACHYTE BASE
SIDE ELEVATION
SECTION A A
SECTION B B
SANDSTONE
TRACHYTE
CONCRETE
BRICKWORK
WOODWORK
THREE EIGHTHS OF AN INCH TO ONE FOOT DETAIL OF FRONT ELEVATION OF A SUBURBAN BANK.
MASONRY AND BRICKWORK
CHECKED BY
FRANK W. TURNER
CONSTRUCTION DRAWING
STAGE II JUNE 1928

ENMORE ROAD
AUSTRALIA STREET
WILSON STREET
PRINCE'S HIGHWAY
ERSKINEVILLE ROAD
UNION STREET
CIVIC DESIGN
AERIAL VIEW

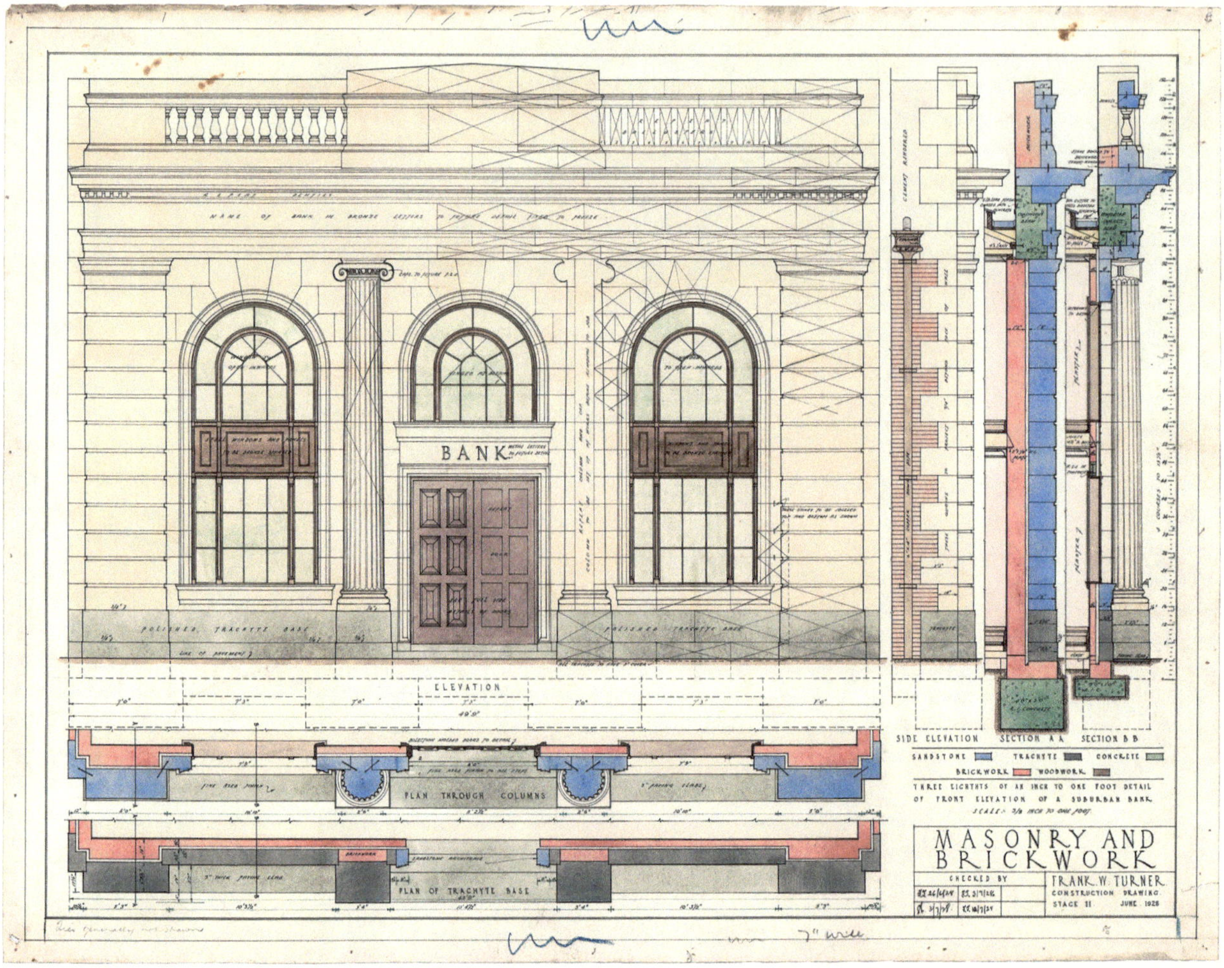

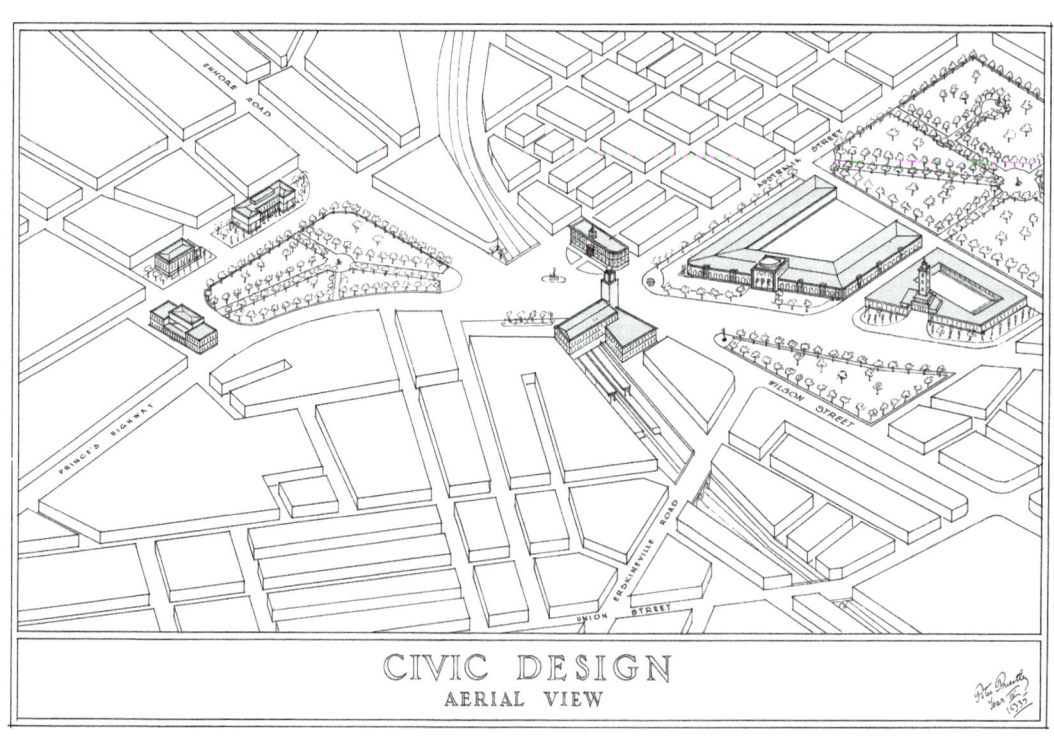

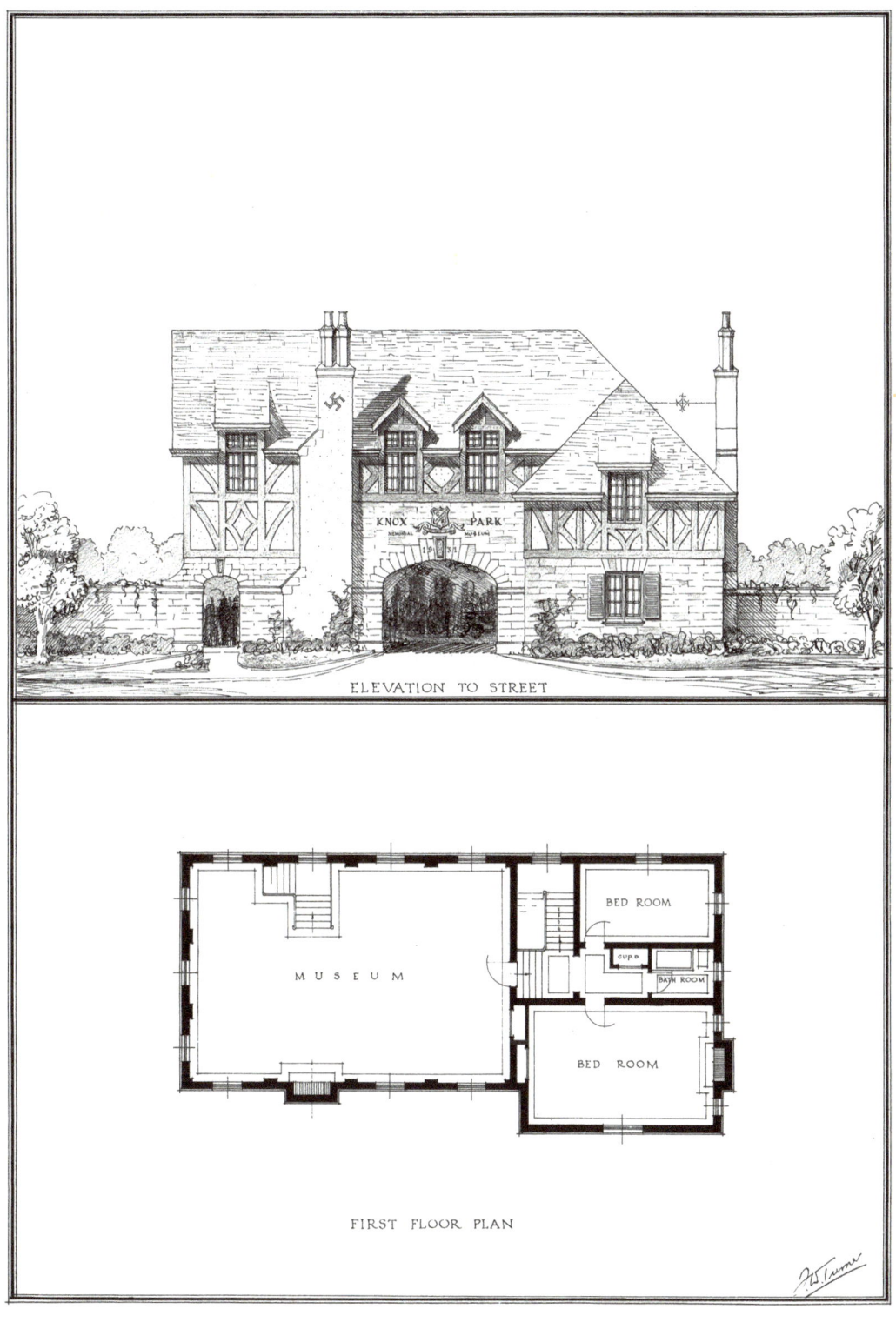

**Figure 3** (opposite top) — Frank W Turner, *Masonry and Brickwork*, watercolour plan, sections and elevation of masonry detail, 1927. **Figure 4** (opposite below) — Peter Priestley, *Civic Design* (aerial perspective), 1935. **Figure 5** (above) — Frank W Turner, *A Memorial Entrance to a Suburban Park with a Museum and Caretaker's Lodge*, one page of a four-page portfolio of plans and pencil-rendered elevations and perspectives, 1931.

All figures this page McConnel Drawings Collection, University of Sydney Library, Rare Books and Special Collections.

**Figure 6** — Peter Priestley, *Decorations and Ornament from the English Gothic Church*, showing examples taken from various sources and of various periods, watercolour drawing, 1936. McConnel Drawings Collection, University of Sydney Library, Rare Books and Special Collections.

**Figure 7** (below) — Eulie Saksena (later Chowdhury), *Medieval Ornament, The Annunciation, St Ouen, Rouen* (14th century), watercolour study of stained glass, 1946. McConnel Drawings Collection, University of Sydney Library, Rare Books and Special Collections.

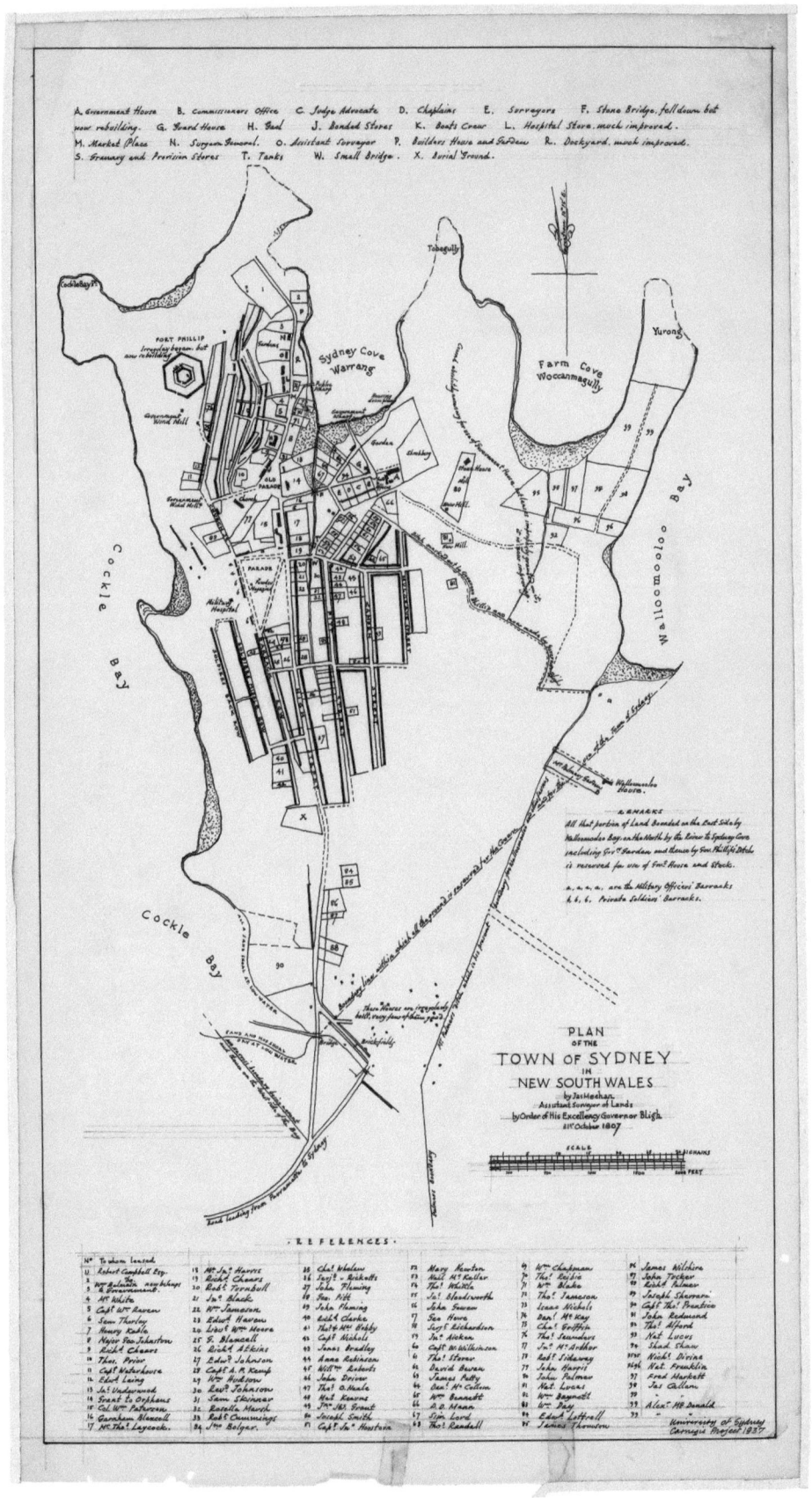

**Figure 8** — Unknown author, copy of a *Plan of the Town of Sydney in New South Wales*, by Jas Mechan, Assistant Surveyor of Lands by Order of His Excellency Governor Bligh, 31 October 1807, 1937. McConnel Drawings Collection, University of Sydney Library, Rare Books and Special Collections.

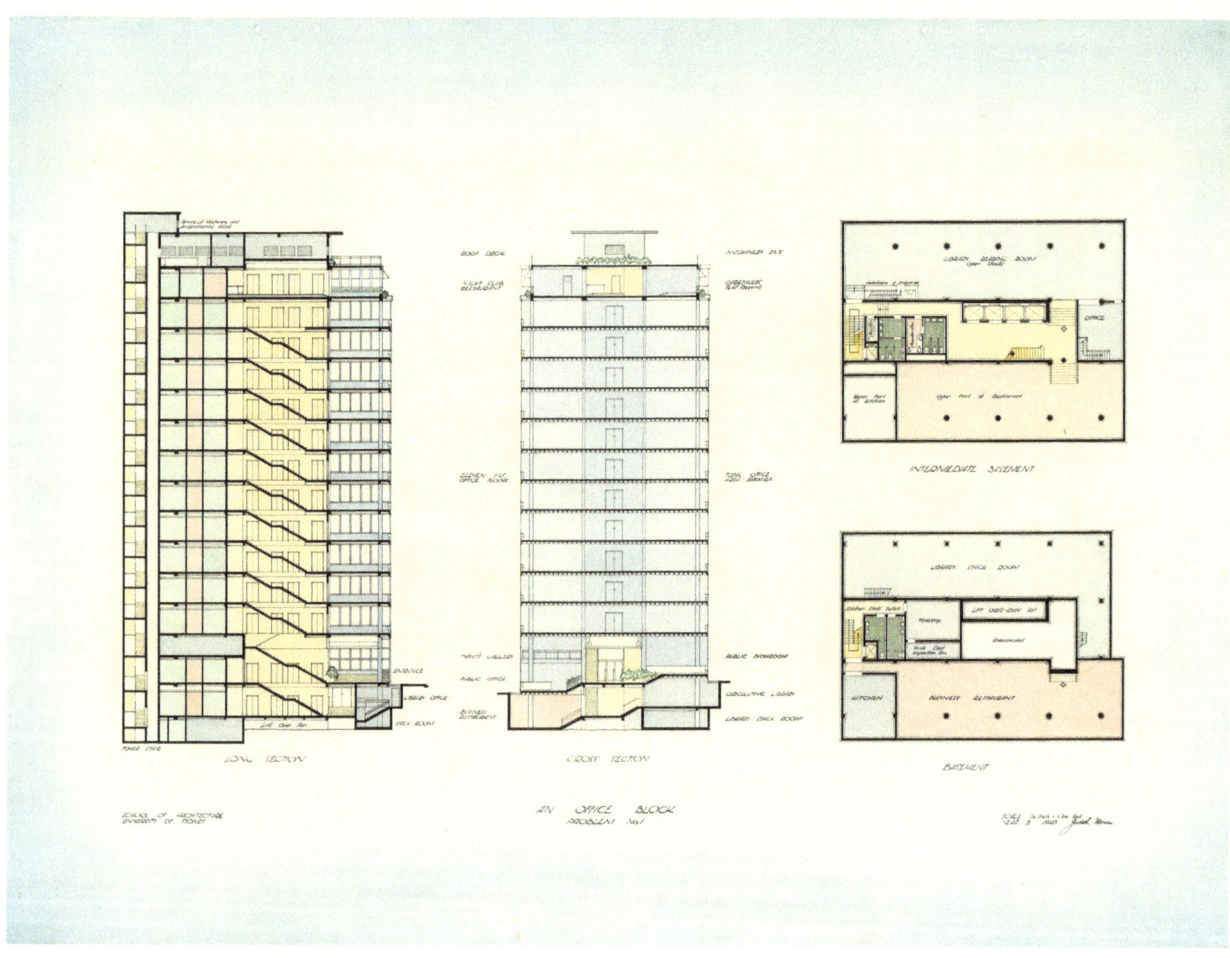

**Figure 9 —**
Judith Moreau (later Macintosh), *An Office Block*
(Problem No. 1), watercolour plans and sections, 1943.
McConnel Drawings Collection, University of Sydney
Library, Rare Books and Special Collections.

… this meeting of subscribers to the Vernon Memorial Fund offers the sum of 810 pounds, six shillings and sixpence to the Senate of the University for the purposes of founding a course of twenty lectures on 'Town Planning' …

— University of Sydney Senate (1915)

**Figure 1** — Portrait of Sir John Sulman (1849–1934), by John Longstaff, 1931. This portrait of John Sulman, who was to have an enduring impact on town planning at the University of Sydney and Australia-wide, won the Archibald Prize in 1931. Art Gallery of New South Wales.

# Chapter 2: Town and Country Planning to 1949
— Paul Jones

This chapter is a contribution to a deeper understanding of the evolution of town planning education within the University of Sydney and, more broadly, to the development of the town planning movement within Australia. The latter topics have been documented from varying perspectives through the prolific and insightful writings of Robert Freestone and others. [^1] These pages aim to identify the origins of town planning education at the University of Sydney, primarily in the first half of the 20th century to 1949. The chapter explores the circumstances of the establishment of the town planning discipline at the University of Sydney up to the appointment of the Chair of Town and Country Planning in 1948 and the commencement of the Diploma in Town and Country Planning in 1949. It outlines the upward trajectory to this point, including the role of the Vernon Memorial Lectures in Town Planning, the influence of key individuals and lobby groups, the growth of the town planning profession generally, and how the Faculty of Architecture, the University of Sydney, and the New South Wales (NSW) State Government responded and reacted to the growing demands for professional town planning education.

It is a narrative that reflects the development of town planning education as concurrent with the emergence of town planning as a fledgling profession, its own discipline, and a major public interest. The chapter is constructed from a combination of sources, both primary and secondary, with a strong emphasis on primary material accessed from the University of Sydney Archives.

Within this context, there are three main themes that can be identified in shaping the development of town planning education at the University of Sydney. The first two run concurrently from 1919 to 1939, and the third evolves from the merging of the latter themes in 1947. Firstly, there is the pivotal role of the Sydney University Extension Board (SUEB), which was responsible for providing community education lectures in Sydney, wider NSW, and other states. After four years of preparatory discussions, in 1919, SUEB commenced the Vernon Memorial Lectures in Town Planning, which were the first organised delivery of publicly accessible, non-faculty based planning education in Sydney and Australia. John Sulman gave the first four lecture series, between 1919 and 1926.

Secondly, there was the establishment of the Department of Architecture in 1918 and the embedding of town planning as a fourth-year subject within the academic curriculum of the Bachelor of Architecture (BArch). The reputation and stature of both the Faculty of Architecture (from 1920) and town planning movement grew in the 1920s and 1930s, and the faculty had developed a clear position on town planning education by the end of 1938; namely, that professional educational courses on town planning should be under their control and management and that the concurrent SUEB biennial town planning offerings via the Vernon Memorial Lectures be stopped.

[^1]: In addition to the publications cited elsewhere in this chapter, see also R Freestone, "The Evolution of Australian Urban and Regional Planning: A Textual Analysis," in *The Routledge Handbook of Australian Urban and Regional Planning*, ed. N Snipe and K Vella (London: Taylor and Francis, 2017), 73–85; R Freestone and N Pullan, "From Wilkinson to Winston: Towards a Planning Degree at the University of Sydney, 1919–1949," *Proceedings of the Society of Architectural Historians, Australia and New Zealand* 32, *Architecture, Institutions and Change*, ed. P Hogben and J O'Callaghan (Sydney: SAHANZ, 2015), 57–169; R Freestone, "Royal Commissions, Planning Reform and Sydney Improvement 1908–1909," *Planning Perspectives* 21 (2006): 213–31; R Freestone, "The Vernon Lectures: Beginnings of Planning Education in NSW," *New Planner* (August 1992): 16–17. The author would like to thank librarian John Paul Cenzato for sourcing secondary material, and archivists Nyree Morrison and Karin Brennan from the University of Sydney Archives, who facilitated access to a range of documents for this chapter.

Thirdly, in an era of expansion by the university, as well as major planning initiatives for Sydney's metropolitan growth and a rise in professional interest in formal town planning education, a Department of Town and Country Planning was established in 1947 in the Faculty of Architecture. By the end of 1948, the Foundation Professor and Chair of Town and Country Planning, Denis Winston, had been appointed and, in early 1949, a postgraduate Diploma in Town and Country Planning commenced. With Winston's appointment, the University of Sydney and the Faculty of Architecture monopolised university educated town planners in Sydney and wider NSW until 1966.

Responding to New Circumstances SUEB was the main conduit for the delivery of public lectures on "new" knowledge and public interest matters in the early years of the university and into the 20th century. Set against criticism of the university for being too exclusive and following its restrained influence in the public arena in the late 1800s, in 1880 the University Senate began debate on the need to widen university education so it was available to the broader public, including working men and women. Major social, economic and industrial change forced the university to review its educational approaches and impact on the community, including providing accessible education to the public well distant from universities.

The extension lectures were based on a wider breadth of topics and were modelled, like many other earlier university initiatives, on the university extension movement in England, which organised public lectures on literary, historical and other related topics. [^2] In 1886, university by-laws and regulations were drafted to govern the extension lectures, which were to be open to the public, subject to a course fee to fund the administration of lectures. [^3] Inaugurated at the end of 1886 with three courses, the SUEB programs were to comprise a minimum of 10 lectures, although many series allowed for a shorter number. At the end of each lecture, questions were to be answered and submitted before leaving class. There was a formal optional examination at the end of the lecture series, after which students received a certificate on passing. Significantly, one of the first SUEB lecture series in 1887 was on architecture and was offered to non-degree students by John Sulman (1849–1934) [Figure 1], who had arrived in Australia in 1885 and was appointed lecturer in architecture that same year. [^4] In 1890, Sulman, who was to go on to become one of the leading advocates of the town planning movement of his generation, showed his early commitment to the study of town planning by presenting his paper, "The Laying Out of Towns," to the engineering and architecture section of the Australian Association for the Advancement of Science in Melbourne. [^5] This seminal paper stood the test of time and was to be part of Sulman's textbook, used for his teaching of town planning under the sponsorship of SUEB at the university from 1921–26.

The SUEB lectures were advertised in the local press, including the *Sydney Morning Herald*, to draw public attention and were offered at the university lecture halls, downtown and metropolitan Sydney, and country centres across NSW. Despite issues in supplying lecturers in distant NSW towns such as Bourke, Hay, Albury, Gunnedah, and Murwillumbah, SUEB targeted the full spectrum of society, including sheep shearers and shed hands isolated from the larger metropolitan centres. [^6] In the early 20th century, lectures were extended to Queensland and Western Australia, with diverse lecture topics representing the growth in global, as well as national knowledge. The 1929 SUEB *Volume of Printed Syllabuses Index* shows that

---

[^2]: D Dymock, "'A Reservoir of Learning': The Beginnings of Continuing Education at the University of Sydney," *Australian Journal of Adult Learning* 49, no. 2 (2009): 248–49.

[^3]: C Turney, U Bygott and P Chippendale, *Australia's First: A History of the University of Sydney*, vol. 1, 1850–1939 (Sydney: Hale and Iremonger, 1991), 194.

[^4]: See Andrew Leach's discussion of John Sulman's arrival in the previous chapter.

[^5]: J Sulman, "The Laying Out of Towns," in *An Introduction to the Study of Town Planning in Australia* (Sydney: Government Printer of New South Wales, 1921), appendix A, 214–16. This paper was originally read before Section J of the Australasian Association for the Advancement of Science at Melbourne University in January 1890.

[^6]: *Sydney University Extension Board Annual Report*, 1909–1910 (University of Sydney, 1910), 8. All subsequent references to the *Sydney University Extension Board Annual Report* refer to this serial source.

the depth and breadth of topics offered in previous years included "The Philosophy of Proverbs," "Historic Italy," "Economic Position of Women," "Rain and Rain Making," "The Constitution of the Universe," "Primitive Man," "The Beginnings of Life," and "Psychology of Salesmanship." [^7] Typical courses delivered in the early 20th century were on literacy, history, biology and geographical subjects, with courses in 1912 provided on "new" subjects such as the "Northern Territory and its Aborigines." [^8]

## A Growing Town Planning Movement

SUEB lectures related to town planning and architecture gained momentum, albeit slowly, alongside an increasing profile of city, state and national town planning issues and international events that were generating a wave of professional, community and government interest and opinion on the public agenda. Much of the initial focus at the beginning of the 20th century was on the urban growth challenges of Australia's largest city, Sydney, where deficiencies in town planning and public health were strongly exposed by the bubonic plague at the end of the 1800s. This event contributed to the NSW Government's decision to undertake the Royal Commission on the Improvement of the City of Sydney and its Suburbs in 1908 and 1909. [^9] Arguably Australia's first town planning review addressing city and suburban expansion, the Royal Commission made a range of recommendations addressing suburb expansion, suburb design, housing reform, public health, and civic design. One result of the Royal Commission was that, in 1912, the NSW Housing Board was established and set about major housing reform, including the development of Sydney's first garden suburb, Daceyville. Also known as Dacey Garden Suburb, the plan was initially designed by the Department of Public Works. It was then modified by leading town planning advocates John Sulman, John Hennessy, and NSW Housing Board chairman John Fitzgerald in 1912, followed by a third reiteration by William Foggitt in 1917. [^10]

In 1910, there was the much publicised, First International Town Planning Conference in London, which was attended by over 1400 architects and town planners looking at the best exemplars in town planning. This included the new English town of Letchworth and model factory villages such as Bournville and Port Sunlight. [^11] Sulman addressed the conference on the proposed new national capital of Australia, Canberra, subsequently won by Walter Burley Griffin in May 1911. Sulman acknowledged that this national initiative was playing an important role in increasing public attention in town planning and adding impetus to the establishment of town planning associations in the respective states. [^12] In 1913, the Greater Sydney Royal Commission was established by the NSW Government to review better arrangements for town planning coordination in Sydney. In the same year, the Town Planning Association of NSW (TPA of NSW) was formed with Sulman as the inaugural president, a position he held until 1925. [^13] At the same time, many high-profile reports were being prepared on town planning and housing for the NSW Government following international study tours. This included a report on housing by Professor Robert Irvine, Chair of Economics at the University of Sydney. [^14]

[^7]: Sydney University Extension Board, *Volume of Printed Syllabuses* (University of Sydney, February 1929), Index.
[^8]: *Sydney University Extension Board Annual Report* (1912–13).
[^9]: *Report of the Royal Commission for the Improvement of the City of Sydney and Its Suburbs* (Sydney: WA Gullick, Government Printer, 1909).
[^10]: S Jackson-Stepowski, *Dacey Garden Suburb: A Report for the Daceyville Heritage Conservation Area within its Historical Context* (Sydney, 2002), 11–12.
[^11]: W Whyte, "The 1910 Royal Institute of British Architects' Conference: A Focus for International Town Planning?" *Urban History* 39, no. 1 (2012): 149–65
[^12]: Sulman, *An Introduction to the Study of Town Planning in Australia*, xvi.
[^13]: R Apperly and P Reynolds, "Sulman, Sir John (1848–1934)," in *Australian Dictionary of Biography*, vol 12 (Melbourne: Melbourne University Press, 1990), http://adb.anu.edu.au/biography/sulman-sir-john-8714/text15255, accessed 29 August 2018.
[^14]: "Australian Town Planning Conference and Exhibition, 1918," in *Official Volume of Proceedings of the First Australian Town Planning and Housing Conference and Exhibition*, 17–24 October 1917 (Adelaide: Vardon and Sons Ltd. Printers, 1918), 7.

As professional, government and community interest in town planning gathered momentum, the inaugural Australian Town Planning and Housing Conference and Exhibition was held in Adelaide from 17 to 24 October 1917. Papers were given by a range of respected professionals, including Griffin himself, then Federal Capital Director of Design and Construction, and John Bradfield, Chief Engineer of the Metropolitan Railway Construction for Sydney, who spoke on the "Transit Problems of Greater Sydney." Sulman was involved in the organisation of the conference through his role as Vice-President of the NSW Conference Executive. In the foreword to the *Proceedings*, conference director Charles Reade acknowledged that, while the momentum in town planning in Australia and New Zealand had been "seemingly tardy in growth" in recent times, it had now gathered sufficient momentum to be a major "national problem." [^15]

Building on the success of this exhibition, the second Australian Town Planning and Housing Conference and Exhibition was held in Brisbane from 30 July to 6 August 1918. Key post-war town planning topics such as the "soldier settlements" scheme for returned soldiers were addressed by a range of speakers such as Senator Millen, Minister for Repatriation, while the detail of the town plans outlined in Millen's paper were presented by Sulman. [^16] Other papers presented included the "Proposed Industrial Garden City at Darra, Queensland" by Thos Price, Mayor of Toowoomba; and the "Districting or Zoning of Cities and Towns" by well-known Sydney and NSW property developer and town planning advocate, Henry Halloran. At this time, Sulman and Bradfield were President and Vice-President, respectively, of the growing Town Planning Association of NSW; Henry Halloran was also a member.

At a university level, SUEB made several attempts to deliver town planning lectures in this period. For example, in 1912, SUEB, in

**Figure 2** — Unknown artist, Walter Liberty Vernon, NSW Government Architect (1890–1911). Vernon was the genesis of the Vernon Memorial lecture series set up by the Town Planning Association (TPA) of NSW and managed by the SUEB. University of Sydney Archives.

conjunction with the University of Melbourne, gave its backing to a 1913 lecture tour by Thomas Mawson, well-known British architect and lecturer in town planning at the University of Liverpool. The series was postponed on several occasions by Mawson and eventually lapsed in 1914 when Mawson took up an offer of high profile work for the Greek Government in Athens. [^17] Another lecture series was proposed to be undertaken by Charles Reade and William Davidge from the British Garden Cities and Town Planning Association. SUEB agreed to part-fund the proposed lecture series, subject to contribution by the NSW State Government. However, State funding was not forthcoming, and the proposed lecture series did not come to fruition. [^18] In October and November 1919, the newly appointed Dean of Architecture, Leslie Wilkinson, gave lectures under the SUEB banner on "The Appreciation of Architecture." [^19] This four-lecture series included one lecture with material on town planning. This material included references

---

[^15]: "Australian Town Planning Conference and Exhibition, 1918," 5.
[^16]: AJ Comming, "Australian Town Planning Conference and Exhibition, 1918," *Volume of Proceedings of the Second Australian Town Planning Conference and Exhibition*, Brisbane, 30 July–6 August 1918 (Brisbane: Government Printer, 1919), 46–51.
[^17]: *Sydney University Extension Board Annual Report* (1913–14), 4. All SUEB documents are sourced from the University of Sydney Archives.
[^18]: Freestone, "The Vernon Lectures," 16.
[^19]: *Sydney University Extension Board Annual Report* (1919–20), 11.

to planning, town planning, and the siting of buildings. [^20] Wilkinson later gave another lecture for SUEB on architecture, in which he addressed the town plan and housing. [^21] At the same time, SUEB introduced a major town planning lecture series under the banner of the Vernon Memorial Lectureship.

This time marked an important shift in the growing town planning movement from ad hoc success via new lobby groups, conferences, model suburbs, land subdivisions, and the like to a formalised lecture series organised by Australia's premier university. Despite the interruption of the First World War, this was an important time in the evolution of town planning education, with events and activities headlined by individuals such as Sulman slowly building momentum for a new era of professionalisation and responses in town planning.

## The Vernon Memorial Lectures and John Sulman 1919–26

The role of the University of Sydney in the move towards providing town planning education gained major traction in 1915, when the University Senate approved the introduction of the Vernon Memorial Lectures in Town Planning, organised and managed under the auspices of SUEB. The lecture series was established in honour of Walter Liberty Vernon, who served as the Colonial and then Government Architect for NSW for over twenty years before his death in 1914 [Figure 2]. As Government and University Architect, he was responsible for designing many university buildings, including the original Fisher Library. Vernon was also active in promoting town planning, including suburb design in Sydney, as well as advocating for the new national capital, Canberra. Vernon served alongside Sulman as an inaugural committee member of the TPA of NSW. His death provided a timely opportunity for the recently established association to put forward a proposal for an ongoing lecture series on town planning, architecture, or related subject as a memorial of Vernon's life. It was to be underwritten by a gift of 810 pounds, six shillings and sixpence from subscribers. Their resolution was approved in full by the University Senate on 5 July 1915 based on a resolution emanating from the Faculty of Science.

> **That this meeting of subscribers to the Vernon Memorial Fund offers the sum of 810 pound 6s 6d to the Senate of the University for the purposes of founding a course of twenty lectures on "Town Planning," to be delivered biennially and to be known as the Vernon Memorial Lectureship, the Senate having the power to reconsider the disposal of the income at ten-year intervals, provided always that the object to which it is applied shall be within the limits of Architecture, Town Planning, or some allied subjects.** [^22]

With the fund administered by the senate, SUEB was requested to organise and manage the biennial lectureship foundation, with the first series due to commence in 1917. However, the advent of the First World War halted commencement until 1919. The SUEB Annual Reports from 1919 to 1937, corresponding with the beginning and end of the Vernon Memorial Lecture series under the original format prescribed by the senate, indicate that they were presented a total of nine times by three eminent architects and town planners of the day. Sulman, who was by this time highly respected as a public commentator, lobbyist, adviser and teacher on town planning, architecture, and art, was given the honour of delivering the inaugural lecture in 1919 and then biennially in 1921, 1923 and 1926. The latter lectures were delayed a year due to Sulman's ill health. David Davidson gave the series in 1928, while Alfred Brown gave the final four lecture series in 1931, 1933, 1935 and 1937.

---

[^20]: *Volume of Printed Syllabuses* (1919), Index, 857.
[^21]: *Volume of Printed Syllabuses* (1919), Index, 859.
[^22]: *University Calendar*, vol. 1 (University of Sydney, 1973), 292. All subsequent references to the University Calendar refer to this serial source; *Sydney University Extension Board Minutes* (University of Sydney, 1915).

The first Vernon Memorial Lecture series by Sulman commenced on Wednesday 23 July 1919 in the Geological Theatre at the University of Sydney and spanned 20 weeks, with the course fee of 10 shillings paid in advance. At the completion of the course, an exam was held, and certificates given to those who successfully passed. Tickets were available for single lectures, with all lectures illustrated with lantern slides. [^23] The number of students enrolled for the initial series was over 150, the largest in the total series, with the SUEB Annual Report of 1918-19 noting, "a large class of earnest students were drawn chiefly from Architects, Surveyors, Engineers, and Municipal Officers of Sydney and its neighbourhood." [^24]

The names of the 20 lectures provide insight into the extent of knowledge and expertise Sulman had acquired, with strong emphases on town planning as an art and on the key role of civic design, architecture, and beauty as pivotal in the layout and arrangement of towns and cities. The themes of the lectures were:

1. The Towns of the Past
2. The Towns of the Present and the Future
3. The Health of Towns
4. The Transportation of People and Commodities
5. The Road System of Towns
6. Civic Centres
7. Other Centres, Squares and Open Spaces
8. Traffic Centres, Road Junctions, Intersections, Street Spacing and Size of Allotments
9. Suburbs and Subdivisions
10. Suburbs and Subdivisions (cont.)
11. Parks and Parkways
12. Playgrounds, Gardens and Tree Planting
13. Civic Aesthetics
14. Civic Aesthetics (cont.)
15. Building Regulations
16. Drainage, Road Construction, Lights and Power and other Services
17. The Improvement of Existing Cities and Towns
18. Re Housing
19. Financing Town Planning
20. Town-Planning and Municipal Government [^25]

By the end of the lecture series in early December 1919, SUEB expressed strong gratitude for the outcome of the first Vernon Memorial Lectures on town planning, stating they were "clear proof both of the interest in the subject and of Mr. Sulman's reputation as an authority on Town Planning." [^26] Some 70 students had managed to complete the course, with 42 sitting the examination and 37 passing. [^27] Students had to answer six out of the 11 exam questions; the depth and breadth of town planning knowledge; and the skills tested by the exam were extensive. This included a strong emphasis on the ability to draw and illustrate by sketching. A copy of what is believed to be the first examination paper in town planning as given on 10 December 1919 under the Vernon Memorial Lectureship and the auspices of SUEB is shown in [Figure 3].

Sulman gave subsequent editions of the Vernon Memorial Lectures in Town Planning in 1921 and again in June 1923 and April 1926. In the 1920-21 SUEB annual report, it was noted that 80 students enrolled in the course in 1921, with the average attendance being 63 and some 42 students sitting the exam at the end of the lecture series. The lectures were well received, with the board proceeding to "congratulate Mr. Sulman heartily on this repetition of his earlier success," following the successful delivery of the previous series in 1919 and now 1921. [^28]

Sulman maintained the 20-lecture program he devised for his 1919 lectures in subsequent series. His lectures were offered in the evening to allow practitioners

[^23]: *Volume of Printed Syllabuses* (1919), 729-31.
[^24]: *Sydney University Extension Board Annual Report* (1918-19), 6.
[^25]: *University Calendar* (1919), 280-81.
[^26]: *Sydney University Extension Board Annual Report* (1918-19), 7.
[^27]: *University Calendar* (1920), 692.
[^28]: *Sydney University Extension Board Annual Report* (1920-21), 9.

> **UNIVERSITY OF SYDNEY**
> **TOWN PLANNING**
>
> Wednesday, 10 December, 1919
> 6.30 p.m. TO 9.30 p.m.
>
> Answer six questions only.
>
> 1. What is a civic survey? Describe the information it should supply and how it may be obtained.
>
> 2. Describe the districting of towns, the objects aimed at, and the advantages anticipated.
>
> 3. What are the essentials of the quick and cheap transportation of goods and persons? Give examples of the improvements already made or proposed in different cities.
>
> 4. Describe and illustrate by rough sketches the different methods of planning the road system of towns, and the advantages and defects of each; also state the desirable widths and grades of main avenues, secondary roads, and short dead-end residential roads.
>
> 5. Describe the various kinds of open spaces required or desirable in connection with the road system of towns, and illustrate them by rough sketches.
>
> 6. In planning suburbs and subdivisions, what are the common defects to be avoided and the improvements that may be introduced? Illustrate by rough sketches.
>
> 7. Describe shortly the types of parks required in city, suburbs and country; also parkways, playgrounds, and other open spaces required for recreation, &c., and their size, lay-out, and distances apart.
>
> 8. How may towns be made more pleasing to the eye by
>    (a) Elimination of ugliness.
>    (b) Artistic treatment?
>
> 9. Describe the various means of securing better health for town dwellers which are afforded by more town planning regulations.
>
> 10. How may the deficits of existing Towns be remedied? Give your views as to the best way of financing the same.
>
> 11. Describe the present system of local government in Australia; give your views as to how it may be improved, and as to the main principles required in a Town Planning Act.

**Figure 3** — First Town Planning Exam at Sydney University under the auspices of the Vernon Memorial Lectures. University of Sydney Archives.

in the workplace to attend, a tradition that continues to strongly permeate the urban programs offered today. With Sulman's lectures gaining popularity for their breadth of coverage of planning issues, he saw an opportunity to compile the 20 lectures from his 1919 lectures into a comprehensive 256-page book called *An Introduction to the Study of Town Planning in Australia*. This work was to be published in 1921 by the Government Printer of NSW, with the book's front page proudly acknowledging Sulman as a "Member of the Town Planning Institute" and as the "Vernon Lecturer on Town Planning in the University of Sydney," among other notable citations. The chapter structure of the book replicates the same sequence as the Vernon Memorial Lectures given by Sulman, with students encouraged to consult the book before attending each individual lecture to ensure they were aware of the subject matter to be delivered. [^29] Importantly, in the Preface, Sulman acknowledges the lectures on town planning at the University of Sydney as the "first of their kind in Australia," with the book resulting from student requests to have the lecture information publicly available. [^30] Attached to the main text are appendices that include Sulman's 1890 paper, "The Laying Out of Towns," as well as two articles written by Sulman: "On Improvements to Sydney" from 1907; and "The Federal Capital" from 1909.

This comprehensive book by Sulman provides deep insights into the content of the lecture material delivered between 1919 and 1926 and subsequently borrowed and adapted by Davidson and Brown when presenting their own Vernon Memorial Lectures following

[^29]: *Volume of Printed Syllabuses*, Index, 733–39.
[^30]: Sulman, *An Introduction to the Study of Town Planning in Australia*, xv.

Sulman's final series in 1926. Importantly, the book reflects the concerns and preoccupation of planning for towns and cities as learned from his professional experience and international travel. Sulman outlines that his interest in town planning emanated from a visit to Paris in 1873, when he compared the tree-lined boulevards and avenues of Paris with the narrow streets of London and contrasted the ease of traffic movement between the cities. These issues, plus Sulman's subsequent work on London slums in 1876, collectively drove his desire for the need for town planning and "re-housing" to be a discipline with special focus. Sulman states that his main criticism of Australian planning on his arrival in the mid-1880s was that, while slums were limited in number, there was a "haphazard" placement of many public buildings and a "commonplace chessboard system of planning being almost universal." [^31] The "chessboard system" refers to Sulman's critique of repetitive rectangular layouts, which, in his view, were the bane of traffic congestion and visual monotony. Sulman argued that existing cities should be remodelled and new towns and suburbia designed along garden city and garden suburb values. [^32]

There are several cross-cutting themes that recur throughout Sulman's book and that were central in the delivery of the Vernon Memorial Lectures on Town Planning. Distilled from the 20 lecture themes and his subsequent book, these are the key concerns: the paramount role of public health considerations, including fresh air and sunlight as drivers of planning standards; land use zoning, termed "The Districting of Towns" by Sulman, reflecting popular American town planning jargon of the time. Also of importance was the "dignified" civic centres, parks, playgrounds, gardens and tree planting; the promotion of the "spiderweb" city layout based on radial avenues from the city centre and joined by ring road connections, as first raised by Sulman in his 1890 paper and reflected in practice in the layout of Canberra; replanning of existing suburbs and the need for new garden suburbs; limits to population growth; public transport connectivity; the pivotal role of civic design, proper placing of public buildings and parks, and "high quality" civic aesthetics; the importance of planning and building regulations; and, finally, the key role of local government in achieving town planning goals. In many ways, these central themes reflected core elements of the prevailing British and American planning movements at the time, which Sulman acknowledged were inspired from a combination of Garden City and City Beautiful approaches to town planning.

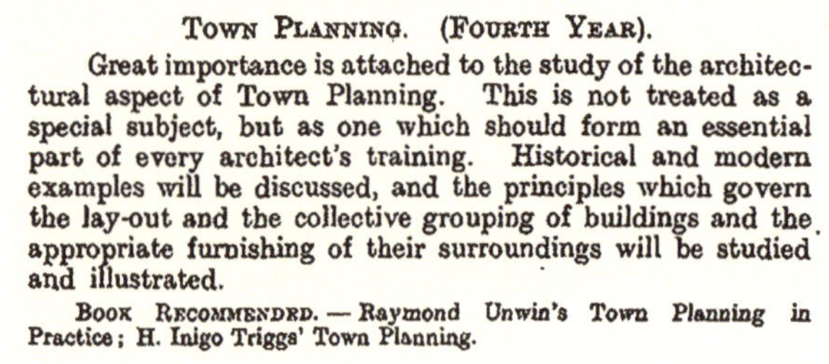

TOWN PLANNING. (FOURTH YEAR).

Great importance is attached to the study of the architectural aspect of Town Planning. This is not treated as a special subject, but as one which should form an essential part of every architect's training. Historical and modern examples will be discussed, and the principles which govern the lay-out and the collective grouping of buildings and the appropriate furnishing of their surroundings will be studied and illustrated.

BOOK RECOMMENDED. — Raymond Unwin's Town Planning in Practice; H. Inigo Triggs' Town Planning.

**Figure 4** — Description of the fourth-year town planning unit in the Bachelor of Architecture, 1920. *University Calendar* (1920). University of Sydney Archives.

Sulman's depth of scholarly reading and his citation of leading British and American texts for students to further pursue was exemplary. Key texts cited included Raymond Unwin's *Town Planning in Practice* (1909), Nelson Lewis's *The Planning of the Modern City* (1916), and Charles Purdom's *The Garden City* (1913), as well as references to various volumes of the English *Town Planning Review* and *The Builder*.

While issues like heritage conservation, community participation, and the natural environment dominate contemporary planning debate, Sulman's curriculum reflected a comprehensive view of top down modern town planning, which characterised that period. The town planning narrative advocated by Sulman strongly emphasised both strategic and detailed town planning in its wider context, linked by the pivotal role of civic design, public buildings and spaces, and planned suburban expansion. In new subdivisions, for examplc, Sulman

[^31]: Sulman, *An Introduction to the Study of Town Planning in Australia*, xv.

[^32]: Sulman, *An Introduction to the Study of Town Planning in Australia*, 106.

recommended one tenth of every new block be collectively given over to community facilities in the form of public gardens, playgrounds, and parks to contribute to achieving garden city and garden suburb ideals. In Sulman's view, a variety of design was allowed if it was in context with the surrounds and if places and spaces did not suffer from excessive contrast in architectural design.

Given Sulman's obsession with a city's appearance and civic ideals, including notions of beautification and aesthetics as central to the skills of a town planner, it was only natural that he was an advocate of a design review model emerging in Europe at that time, which he termed a "Council of Taste," to adjudicate building design. [^33] This would be an advisory review of building design elements, such as height, but eventually would become a mandatory regime. [^34] Such foresight would eventually come to fruition in Sydney in the 1970s with the advent of urban design advisory committees, now a commonplace and accepted planning assessment tool. In the context of the times, Sulman was a visionary, strongly informed by national and international practice, who advocated a holistic view of town planning principles in his high profile public lectures delivered at the University of Sydney.

## The Evolving Position of Town Planning in the Faculty of Architecture, 1919–26

Alongside the commencement of the Vernon Memorial Lectures in 1919, interest by governments and the emerging profession meant matters associated with town planning were gradually increasing on the university's agenda. Town planning was not only included as a subject in the BArch, but also emerged within subject material taught in other faculties. It also figured in high level discussion within the university at this time. In 1917, for example, Sulman attended the inaugural Australian Town Planning Conference and Exhibition, held in Adelaide, alongside James Nangle (Fellow of the Royal Astronomical Society and Superintendent of Sydney Technical College) and John Bradfield, as representatives of the University Senate. [^35] Town planning was taught in the Bachelor of Arts in 1920 alongside topics such as city government, housing, and municipal finance in a unit called "Municipal Administration." [^36] A town planning subject was also offered by the Faculty of Engineering, with student Romeo completing his Master of Engineering degree in 1921 on the topic of "The Survey, Design, and Lay Out of a Model Suburb on Modern Town Planning Lines." [^37]

With the appointment of Leslie Wilkinson as the Chair of Architecture in 1918 and the commencement of the Vernon Memorial Lectures in 1919, town planning education made major gains when it was embedded in the architecture curriculum as a specific subject. In 1919, the university by-laws specified town planning as a fourth-year subject as part of the curriculum for the new four-year BArch. [^38] A short description of the town planning lecture subject, including reference to two seminal books on town planning and city design by Raymond Unwin (1909) and Inigo Triggs (1909), was provided in the 1919 University Calendar [Figure 4]. [^39]

The subject description is subsequently repeated word for word in calendars until the late 1940s, providing insight into the relationship between architecture and town planning, which was perceived to be important at that time. There is clear emphasis on the need to understand the impact of architecture on its wider spatial setting and the principles that govern such arrangements individually, collectively and aesthetically. It is only in the university calendars after 1939 that the town planning unit description offered by the Faculty of Architecture contains an

---

[^33]: Sulman, *An Introduction to the Study of Town Planning in Australia*, 173.
[^34]: Sulman, *An Introduction to the Study of Town Planning in Australia*, 173.

[^35]: *University Calendar* (1918), 610.
[^36]: *University Calendar* (1920), 193.
[^37]: *University Calendar* (1921), 512.
[^38]: *University Calendar* (1919), 93.
[^39]: *University Calendar* (1919), 280.

addendum indicating that the town planning lectures now offered in that period included material attributed to funding from the Vernon Memorial lectureship fund.

Town planning was one of six final-year subjects in the BArch. In 1922, it was taught as a one-hour lecture on a Monday each semester. [^40] By 1923, it was available as an alternate to "The History of Sculpture and Painting." The subjects were to be taken in either third or fourth year, with the town planning unit taught by lecturer Keith Harris. [^41] After a year's practical experience was introduced into the BArch in the late 1920s, the curriculum was changed in 1930 to allow the unit to be taken by students as an alternate subject in the fourth or fifth years. [^42] In 1948, the faculty agreed to dispense with the alternate arrangement, and the town planning unit had to be taken in the fourth year. [^43] This became a fifth-year requirement in 1949. [^44]

With the first cohort of BArch students graduating in 1922, the first examination in the town planning subject for fourth-year students was offered in 1921. The examination shown in [Figure 5] was the first town planning examination in the BArch at the University of Sydney. In the examination, there was strong emphasis on understanding existing town layouts in Europe and America; types of public spaces; the principles to underpin new town layouts, including industrial suburbs; and an understanding of the Garden City movement that was emerging at that time.

As the Faculty of Architecture flourished in the early 1920s, interest in town planning education permeated discussions at varying levels. Wider interest in town planning gathered momentum at this time due to lobbying by key individuals and emerging educational activities of professional interest groups. The TPA of NSW, for example, was running its own lecture series in 1925 on

[^40]: *University Calendar* (1922), 164.
[^41]: *University Calendar* (1923), 328.
[^42]: Minutes of the Meeting of the Faculty of Architecture (1930), 69. All minutes are held in the University of Sydney Archives.
[^43]: Minutes of the Meeting of the Faculty of Architecture (1948), 130.
[^44]: Minutes of the Meeting of the Faculty of Architecture (1949), 154.

### TOWN PLANNING

Five questions only to be attempted, but all must attempt Nos. 3 and 4.

1. (a) To what circumstances do we owe the origins of towns?

    (b) What were the main characteristics of definitely planned towns in ancient and medieval times? Quote examples.

    (c) Of preconceived plans, what are the main types? Contrast the more usual layout of European with American cities.

2. What information would you consider essential and what desirable in setting out to plan –

    (a) an entirely new town;
    (b) an industrial suburb to an existing town?

3. Having obtained the necessary data, what do you consider the most important factors in deciding the general layout of a town?
    Give in order of importance.

4. (a) What are the main factors to take into consideration in the plotting and designing of streets?

    (b) Give the relative advantages of straight and curved streets, and quote successful examples of both.

5. (a) What are the main causes of traffic congestion? Suggest remedies or palliatives for each.

    (b) Contrast German and French theories in regard to crossings or street junctions.

6. (a) Give a short description of classic and medieval " places ";

    (b) What are the main types of " places "? State the functions of each, and quote examples.

7. (a) What are the principles and objects of the "The Garden City Movement"?

    (b) Differentiate between
    (i) garden cities;
    (ii) garden villages;
    (iii) garden suburbs.

Quote examples.

**Figure 5** — First town planning examination in the Bachelor of Architecture, 1921. "Examination Papers of the University of Sydney," (1921–22). University of Sydney Archives.

aspects of town planning. [^45] At the same time, the TPA argued for the establishment of an "independent faculty" for town planning to leverage on the "good work" in town planning done by the university. [^46] Sulman also advised the university in 1925 that, in his view, the Vernon Memorial Lectures were "basic" and only a "permanent introduction" and that additional courses in town planning needed to be introduced. [^47]

George Taylor, another town planning advocate and Sulman's former student, was strongly involved in the TPA and conveyed his views to the university at the same time. Taylor, along with his wife Florence Taylor, who was a keen advocate for town planning and women in architecture, was well credentialed and committed to progressing the town planning movement [Figure 6]. In 1914, Taylor authored the book *Town Planning in Australia* (which contains an introduction by Sulman), and was the first editor of the magazines *Building and Town Planning and Housing*. [^48] Not surprisingly, Taylor stressed to the university the important contribution of the Vernon Memorial Lectures and the role of town planning in "human development," as well as the need for an independent faculty on town planning within the university. [^49]

## The Merging of the Vernon Memorial Lectures into the Faculty of Architecture, 1925–38

With the continued growth of the Faculty of Architecture and growing interest in town planning matters, on 16 April 1925, the University Senate requested a report from SUEB on issues arising in the delivery of the Vernon Memorial Lectures. Arguably reflecting the successful impact of Sulman's work, SUEB responded that "nothing should be done at present regarding the lectures and subjects of the memorial lectures in future years." [^50] At the same meeting, SUEB also agreed to endorse Sulman for the 1925 lectures in view of his forthcoming visit to Europe and America to study town planning. [^51] In June 1925, Sulman, then aged 76, cancelled his lecture series due to ill health, citing possible impacts on his well-being from evening teaching during the cold winter months. SUEB agreed to postpone the series to 1926. However, this would be Sulman's last lecture series at the Colonial Institute Hall in downtown Sydney. [^52]

Sulman was knighted in 1925 and gradually stepped back from his professional life. In 1926, SUEB noted that the "Senate had accepted a gift from Sir John Sulman to the sum of 2500 pounds for the encouragement of the teaching of Town Planning in perpetuity." [^53] SUEB endorsed the proposal to be funded by Sulman's gift, with such lectures to be given biannually in the years there were no scheduled Vernon Memorial Lectures. [^54] However, in June 1926, Sulman stipulated that funding would only be subject to the Vernon Memorial Lectures being ongoing and based in Sydney. SUEB resolved that this could only be dealt with by the senate and was not a matter for SUEB. Sulman's frustration with the slowness of formal town planning education coming to fruition was evident in his subsequent request to SUEB in 1926 that "architecture or other similar object" be deleted from the terms of the Vernon Memorial Fund and that a separate "advisory committee" on town planning be established. SUEB again advised Sulman it was not possible to alter the terms of the fund and that this would be at the discretion of the senate. [^55] As a result, the question of the Sulman-funded lecture series lapsed. [^56]

---

[^45]: R Freestone and M Park, "Spreading the good news about town planning in Sydney 1913–34," in *Cities, Citizens and Environmental Reform: Histories of Australian Town Planning Associations* (Sydney: Sydney University Press, 2009), 27–63.
[^46]: Corr. George Taylor to the Registrar, 22 June 1925, Minutes of the Vernon Memorial Lectureship (University of Sydney Archives).
[^47]: Corr. John Sulman to the Registrar, 27 April 1925, Minutes of the Vernon Memorial Lectureship.
[^48]: G Taylor, *Town Planning for Australia* (Sydney: Building Limited, 1914).
[^49]: Corr. George Taylor to the Registrar, 22 April 1925.

[^50]: Minutes of the Sydney University Extension Board, 1923–44, 31.
[^51]: Corr. John Sulman to the Registrar, 12 May 1925, Minutes of the Vernon Memorial Lectureship.
[^52]: *University Calendar* (1927), 840.
[^53]: Minutes of the SUEB (1923–44), 53.
[^54]: Minutes of the SUEB (1923–44), 54.
[^55]: Minutes of the SUEB (1923–44), 53–54.
[^56]: Minutes of the SUEB (1923–44), 57.

Wilkinson viewed the teaching of town planning within the university as increasingly within the domain of the Faculty of Architecture. This was reflected in the town planning unit being contained within the BArch curriculum and in his wish to be involved in the selection of lecturers for the ongoing Vernon Memorial Lecture series. Within this context, on 30 April 1929, Wilkinson and the faculty executive agreed to "enter a protest against the appointment by the senate of a lecturer in a subject covered by the curriculum of a university faculty without reference to that faculty." [^57] The latter was arguably a complaint about the process of appointing Alfred Brown as the Vernon Memorial Lecturer in 1931. Wilkinson led the discussion and strongly expressed his displeasure that the faculty had not been consulted. [^58]

[^57]: Minutes of the Meeting of the Faculty of Architecture (1929), 58.
[^58]: Minutes of the Meeting of the Faculty of Architecture (1931), 59.

**Figure 6** — A testimonial certificate given to Florence Taylor by the TPA of NSW dated 12 December 1928, following the sudden death of George Taylor early in 1928. The memento contains the signatures of many well-known luminaries and supporters of town planning of the time, including Vernon Memorial lecturers John Sulman and David Davidson, AE Sulman (John Sulman's wife), John Bradfield, Henry Halloran and Aubrey Halloran. Original held by Paul Jones, Sydney School of Architecture, Design and Planning, University of Sydney.

Despite this, the Vernon Memorial Lectures in Town Planning continued independently of the Faculty of Architecture. In 1928, David Davidson, a sanitary engineer and strong advocate of town planning legislation, commenced his single lecture series on 13 June 1928, with the latter half of the lecture series rearranged due to his appointment as Town Planning Commissioner of Western Australia. An Alderman of Willoughby Council, John Bates, gave the final lecture on municipal government on Davidson's behalf. Student interest was still healthy, with 50 students enrolled in 1928 and an average attendance of 43 students. Davidson's lectures had strong structural similarities to the themes presented earlier in the series by Sulman. However, new material was introduced, reflecting the evolution of planning theory and practice at that time. The most noticeable additions by Davidson were the inclusion of "Philosophy and Ethics of Town Planning" in week one, "Town Planning Reports and Civic Surveys" in week 14, and "Regional and National Surveys" in week 15. [^59]

With Davidson's departure, a special SUEB committee agreed that the Vernon Memorial Lectures in Town Planning be given in 1931 by Brown, who was also to give the lectures in 1933, 1935 and 1937. Brown was a British trained architect and well known as a leading advocate for town planning. He had strong practical experience in architecture and planning in England, New Zealand and Australia, including more than two years' experience in the planning of Welwyn Garden City, a new town in England. The 20 lectures were attended by a "keen and enthusiastic body of students," some 63 in total. The State Government Architect Edwin Smith contributed to the course material, as did Sulman, the latter offering the use of his lecture notes, including his "lantern slides." [^60] Leslie Wilkinson attended the first lecture on 10 June and was "well satisfied with the result." [^61]

[^59]: Sydney University Extension Board Annual Report (1928–29), 3.
[^60]: Sydney University Extension Board Annual Report (1930–31), 2–3.
[^61]: Minutes of the Sydney University Extension Board (1923–44), 197.

The lectures presented by Brown followed the general pattern of the earlier lecture themes presented by Sulman and Davidson. However, Brown introduced his own knowledge and approach, most noticeably bringing new lecture material to "Introduction: Definition of Town Planning" in week one; his planning experiences as learned from "Welwyn Garden City: The First of London's Satellite Towns" in week eight; "Residential Estate Development" in week nine; and an appreciation of the technical aspects of planning including engineering in week 19. Like Sulman, Brown emphasised the importance of architecture and design in attaining good town planning outcomes, strongly promoting "Aesthetic Considerations in Town Planning" in weeks 15 and 16. [^62] Like Sulman, Brown's material for all four series was practically identical for each year given. The impact of Sulman's textbook was enduring, with SUEB noting in its 1933 assessment of Brown's lecture delivery that Sulman's *Town Planning in Australia* still formed the key reading material for the series. [^63]

For reasons that are unclear, only 14 lectures were given by Brown in the 1935 series. Student numbers were low, with around 20 to 25 in attendance. [^64] The 1935 lectures were well publicised, with the advertisement by SUEB in the *Sydney Morning Herald* on Saturday, 8 June 1935 advising that "while the course is primarily intended for students of architecture, surveying, and engineering, they will be much of interest to students of public health and civic improvement." [^65] Likewise, in 1937, the Vernon Memorial Lectures were targeted, not only at architecture, surveying and engineering students, but also at "students of Local Government, and of Public Health, Social Economists, Welfare Workers, and those generally interested in Civic Improvement." [^66]

On 14 April 1937, the meeting of the faculty executive endorsed Brown as the Vernon Memorial Lecturer in Town Planning for 1937. However, at the same meeting, the faculty agreed to review how the objectives of the Vernon Memorial trust could be best achieved before the next scheduled lecture series in 1939. [^67] This recommendation was endorsed by the University Professional Board, and, in 1938, the future of the Vernon Memorial Lectureship was seriously in doubt when the University Senate asked for a review of how the income from the foundation could be dispersed. This assessment led to the Faculty of Architecture and the University Professional Board recommending to the senate that the biennial Vernon Memorial Lectureship be discontinued in its current format. [^68] This major shift in the delivery of town planning education was helped by the fact that the lectures given by Brown in 1937 were noted as "incomplete," with only 17 lectures given and 35 students enrolled. [^69]

The minutes of the faculty executive on 21 July 1938 provide insight into the logic of discontinuing the Vernon Memorial Lectures under the stewardship of SUEB and transitioning to a singular town planning curriculum under the control of the faculty. The faculty was of the view that interest in town planning had increased, and it noted that town planning legislation was already being passed by other state governments. The advent of such legislation in NSW, which stipulated planning activities and processes to be undertaken, would generate a demand for qualified town planners, and it seemed sensible from the faculty's perspective that the funds supporting the Vernon Memorial Lectures be redirected to underpin a professional course in town planning based in the faculty. [^70] On 14 October 1938, the Faculty of Architecture noted that the University Senate and Professional Board had endorsed their

[^62]: *Sydney University Extension Board Annual Report* (1930–31), 2–3.
[^63]: *Sydney University Extension Board Annual Report* (1932–33), 5.
[^64]: *Sydney University Extension Board Annual Report* (1934–35), 8.
[^65]: "Lectures in Town Planning," *Sydney Morning Herald*, 8 June 1935, 19.
[^66]: Flyer promoting the Vernon Memorial Lectures in Town Planning to potential participants (University of Sydney Archives); Minutes of the Vernon Memorial Lectureship, 1937 (University of Sydney Archives).

[^67]: Minutes of the Meeting of the Faculty of Architecture (1937), 91.
[^68]: Minutes of the Vernon Memorial Lectureship (1937); *University Calendar* (1973), 292–93.
[^69]: *Sydney University Extension Board Annual Report* (1936–37), 14.
[^70]: Minutes of the Meeting of the Faculty of Architecture (1938), 96.

recommendation to dis-continue the Vernon Memorial Lectures in their current form and transition towards a "professional course." [^71]

The faculty executive agreed that Wilkinson and town planning lecturer Keith Harris would finalise the proposal for new professional arrangements. [^72] The proposal, which must have been in an advanced stage of development, was presented to the faculty executive a few days later on 18 October 1938, when it was agreed to advise the Professional Board that "in place of the two distinct and unrelated courses in Town Planning" a single course of 18 lectures be offered to architectural students and other "qualified persons" under the auspices of the faculty and supported by the Vernon Memorial Fund. [^73] In this setting, Wilkinson and the faculty were marking out territorial boundaries as to who was responsible for education in town planning within the university and the evolving profession, with the current format of the Vernon Memorial Lectures clearly in their sights.

Brown was not happy with the decision to pull back the public lecture series. In 1938, he expressed his displeasure at not being formally invited to give his views on the future series to the senate and the Faculty of Architecture. Among other matters, Brown cited that the proposed number of lectures to be given on town planning (16 rather than 20) was insufficient to do the required content justice. Brown was also concerned that the public would be excluded as lectures would be controlled by the Faculty of Architecture. Importantly, Brown was apprehensive that the "memorial" nature of the lectures dedicated specifically to honour Vernon's legacy would be eroded over time. [^74] Notwithstanding such efforts, the public biennial lecture series on town planning, under the esteemed Vernon Memorial Trust, as originally agreed by the university, would now cease to exist. In 1938, the senate agreed on a downgraded Vernon Memorial Lectures in Town Planning to situate them within the Faculty of Architecture. The latter would comprise lectures not accessible to the general public but which would be available to fifth-year architectural students within the faculty and at the Sydney Technical College, as well as to other "qualified"' professionals [Figure 7]. [^75]

> The lectures will be devoted to Town Planning, including History, Theory, Practice, Law, Procedure, Finance, Engineering in its relation to Town Planning, and Surveying in its relation to Town Planning; they will be given in the evening during Lent and Trinity Terms. The lectures will be open to fifth-year students in the School of Architecture, fifth-year Architectural Diploma students at the Sydney Technical College, holders of the Local Government Engineers' Certificate, qualified architects, engineers, or surveyors, and persons with such other qualifications as the Faculty of Architecture may approve.

**Figure 7** — The "new" format for the Vernon Memorial Lectures, 1938. *University Calendar*, University of Sydney Archives.

The implication of the above was that the Vernon Memorial Lectures in Town Planning would be absorbed by the BArch after 1939. The lectures were undergoing a major transition from being publicly accessible on a biennial basis to being part of specialist "professional" educational curriculum within the Faculty of Architecture, though still resourced by the Vernon Memorial Lectures fund. [^76] Tampering with the format of the original biennial Vernon Memorial Lectures meant the role of SUEB in coordinating publicly available town planning lectures would no longer continue. Harris oversaw the rebadged Vernon Memorial Lectures in the faculty in 1939 and 1940, noting that only eight and subsequently 40 participants enrolled over and above the basic architectural student cohort in these respective years. [^77] Although the Vernon Memorial Lectures were no longer publicly available, educational offerings to the public on town planning continued to be made available via SUEB in the war years. For example, on 26 August 1943, the faculty's town planning

[^71]: Minutes of the Meeting of the Faculty of Architecture (1938), 98.
[^72]: Minutes of the Meeting of the Faculty of Architecture (1938), 98.
[^73]: Minutes of the Meeting of the Faculty of Architecture, (1938), 100–01.
[^74]: Corr. Alfred Brown to Registrar, 15 November 1938, Minutes of the Vernon Memorial Lectureship.

[^75]: *University Calendar* (1939), 297.
[^76]: *University Calendar* (1941), 545.
[^77]: Minutes of the Meeting of the Faculty of Architecture (1940), 106.

**Sulman argued that existing cities should be remodelled and new towns and suburbia designed along garden city and garden suburb values.**

— Paul Jones, "Town and Country Planning to 1949"

lecturer, Harris, gave a lecture on behalf of SUEB at Cessnock, NSW, on "Towns and Their Purpose." [^78] The advent of the Second World War, however, was to put a temporary hold on plans for new ways of integrating town planning education within the faculty, including revisiting the "basic" arrangement agreed by the senate for the faculty in 1938.

## The Department and Chair of Town and Country Planning

The early to mid-1940s saw a major interest in city expansion, followed by national post-war reconstruction, including regional development. In 1943, the Ministry for Post-War Reconstruction was established and, in 1944, a major report on the role of the Commonwealth Housing Commission was released. It advocated major changes in social housing provision and in the role of town planning in community development across the varying states. Not surprisingly, the term "town planning" and the scope of what it could deliver was broadening in usage into terms such as "town and country planning" and "urban and regional planning." [^79] At the same time, the university not only embarked on the introduction of new teaching courses as originally proposed in the late 1930s, but also established a whole range of new departments, with six new chairs established within five years after the end of the Second World War. There was a strong push by the university in the immediate post-war era to ensure it kept abreast of and responded to the educational needs of a "new" set of social and economic drivers underpinning a boom in population and urban and regional development. [^80]

While the university's Professional Board acknowledged the growth of town planning courses introduced in British universities, the move to embed new localised institutional structures and curricula was strongly aligned with rising interest in planning for the growth of Sydney. This included long awaited new legislation in town planning. Also gaining major public attention in Sydney was the first serious attempt at metropolitan planning. This was proclaimed via the establishment of the Cumberland County District on 27 July 1945 and provided for the creation of the Cumberland County Council. In 1945, the NSW Government amended the Local Government Act of 1919, significantly influencing the evolving education arrangements in town planning at the University of Sydney to meet the demand for qualified town planners. In the section on town planning, a new part titled "Town and Country Planning Schemes" was introduced, which not only facilitated the establishment of the Cumberland Council, but also provided provisions that required (i) councils to employ staff with prescribed town or country planning qualifications so as to prepare their planning schemes and (ii) that conditions be set as to which qualifications in town and country planning would be acceptable for those applying for a recognised qualification. [^81] The push for increased professionalism to meet a demand for well-credentialed practitioners with acceptable educational training was gaining ascendancy.

A major implication following this was that the NSW Local Government Town and Country Planning Advisory Committee (LGTCPAC), as now established under the amended Local Government Act of 1919, was to be the arbitrator of appointing staff in local government as town planners. As a rule, such appointments were given to chief engineers, whose staff and departments in local councils would also undertake town planning activities. In this context, both practical experience and the completion of the committee's external annual examination was required to gain a local government qualification as a town planner. On completing the exams, with no local council planning or related experience, a

[^78]: *Sydney University Extension Board Annual Report* (1942–45).
[^79]: Commonwealth Housing Commission Final Report (25 August 1944), Ministry of Post-War Reconstruction.
[^80]: W Connell, G Sherrington, B Fletcher, C Turney and U Bygott, *Australia's First: A History of the University of Sydney*, vol. 2, 1940–1999 (Sydney: Hale and Iremonger, 1995), 46.

[^81]: J Toon and J Falk, eds, *Sydney – Planning or Politics: Town Planning for the Sydney Region since 1945* (Sydney: Planning Research Centre, University of Sydney, 2003), 213.

Provisional Certificate of Qualification as a Town and Country Planner was awarded to applicants after a minimum of two years' work experience on the provision that they were over 23 years of age. On 24 September 1947, architect Peter Harrison was the first person to successfully complete the examination and be awarded the full certificate, and went on to be appointed one of the first lecturers in the new Department of Town and Country Planning in the Faculty of Architecture. [^82]

Concurrent with these legislative changes in 1945 were discussions between the LGTCPAC and key educational institutions, including the University of Sydney, on the urgent need for courses through which existing and aspiring town planners could gain qualification. In 1945, for example, LGTCPAC approached SUEB to arrange a course in town planning, to be held in early 1946. The Faculty of Architecture supported this initiative, but Wilkinson, who was to retire at the end of 1947, was unhappy that SUEB was involved in organising the course without the initial involvement of the faculty. [^83] The result of these ongoing deliberations and training initiatives was that, in July 1947, the University Senate endorsed the establishment of a Chair of Town and Country Planning within the Faculty of Architecture for a five-year term, subject to funding provided by the NSW Department of Local Government. [^84]

The formation of a department and the agreement to appoint a Chair of Town and Country Planning was a strong institutional outcome for the education of town planners and the town planning profession generally. Following this decision, the town planning lectures were rebadged under a downgraded Vernon Memorial Lectures program. The result was that the town planning movement, in combination with the offerings in the Faculty of Architecture, was on a strong upward path, including professional recognition. In October 1947, the Town and Country Planning Institute of NSW, with the endorsement of the faculty and senate, offered a prize to the "best paper submitted in the final examination in Town Planning for Architectural students." [^85] By 1948, the Faculty of Architecture was among the highest ranked faculties in the university for undergraduate enrolments. [^86]

**Figure 8** — Denis Winston was appointed the first Professor of Town and Country Planning at the University of Sydney (1948-73). University of Sydney Archives.

In May 1948, Denis Winston, Borough Architect at Southampton Council, England, was appointed the Foundation Professor and Chair of Town and Country Planning [Figure 8]. [^87] A graduate of the University of Liverpool (1929-33), holding a Bachelor of Architecture with first class honours, Winston's work at Southampton had focused on the development of the central business district and the implementation of that council's major housing schemes. [^88]

The first professorial town planning appointment in Australia, Winston arrived at the end of 1948 and readily set about designing and launching a course targeting "men and women" who were qualified graduates in full-time employment and with minimum knowledge and experience in town

[^82]: Toon and Falk, eds, *Sydney – Planning or Politics*, 213.
[^83]: Minutes of the Meeting of the Faculty of Architecture (1946), 116.
[^84]: Turney, Bygott and Chippendale, *Australia's First*, vol. 1, 277.
[^85]: Minutes of the Meeting of the Faculty of Architecture (1947), 123.
[^86]: Turney, Bygott and Chippendale, *Australia's First*, vol. 1, 45.
[^87]: R Freestone, "The First Professor: Denis Winston Comes to Sydney, 1949," *Australian Planner* 46, no. 1 (2009): 36–37.
[^88]: S Miers, *The Work and Time of Denis Winston*, video, 2015, https://youtu.be/EuLPnMjoi_0, accessed 16 May 2018.

planning. [^89] By March 1949, the Faculty of Architecture commenced a postgraduate Diploma in Town and Country Planning that spanned two years. Based on attendance at evening lectures, the Diploma in Town and Country Planning was "designed to assist architects, engineers, surveyors and certain other qualified persons to supplement their more specialised professional training by a study of the general principles of town and country planning" and be "recognised for the purpose of admission by the Town and Country Planning Institute of Australia, Sydney, and the Planning Institute of Australia, Melbourne." [^90]

Under the stewardship of Winston and Harrison, the diploma comprised 10 units, five in each year, with each unit comprising 24 lectures [Figure 9]. A strong emphasis was placed on "Theory and Practice of Town and Country Planning," with the unit occurring in both years, each instance covering different topics. [^91] Winston covered the development of the diploma and eventually the master's degree and reflected the community outreach objectives of SUEB, as well as meeting the need to build capacity in town planning, especially for staff in the NSW Government. Winston was required to establish courses to meet the needs of the community while also acting as an adviser to the NSW Department of Local Government. This included a major review of Sydney's Cumberland County Plan in the late 1950s. [^92]

DEPARTMENT OF TOWN AND COUNTRY PLANNING.

TIME TABLE OF LECTURES.

| SUBJECT. | Mon. | Tues. | Wed. | Thurs. | Fri. |
|---|---|---|---|---|---|
| **First Year.** | | | | | |
| Theory and Practice of Town and Country Planning ... ... | ... | 6–7 | ... | ... | ... |
| Architecture as related to Planning | ... | ... | 6–7 | ... | ... |
| Geography and Geology as related to Planning ... ... ... | ... | ... | 7–8 | ... | ... |
| History of Town and Country Planning ... ... ... | ... | ... | ... | 6–7 | ... |
| Social and Economic Organisation | ... | ... | ... | 7–8 | ... |
| **Second Year.** | | | | | |
| Civil Engineering as related to Planning ... ... ... | ... | 6–7 | ... | ... | ... |
| Theory and Practice of Town and Country Planning ... ... | ... | ... | 6–7 | ... | ... |
| Public Administration and Town Planning Law ... ... ... | ... | ... | 7–8 | ... | ... |
| Surveying and Valuation as related to Planning ... ... ... | ... | ... | ... | 6–7 | ... |
| Landscape Architecture and Horticulture ... ... ... | ... | ... | ... | 7–8 | ... |

**Figure 9** — Units and lecture times for the new Diploma in Town and Country Planning. *University Calendar* (1951 supplement). University of Sydney Archives.

Winston was passionate about the role of town and country planning, especially the challenges of expanding cities and the quality of rapidly changing urban lifestyles. He was a strong advocate for the need to establish a national association of town planners and went onto become the first president of the Australian Planning Institute. [^93]

With the formal establishment of the Department of Town and Country Planning in the Faculty of Architecture, the influence of the Vernon Memorial Lectures in Town Planning and its relationship to architecture and the new Diploma in Town and Country Planning remained the subject of discussion. Under Winston's guidance, in 1949, the faculty was of the view that specific Vernon Memorial Lectures were no longer needed within the BArch, given this fell within the appointment terms of the new Professor in Town and Country Planning. The faculty thought that the Vernon Memorial Lectures did not need to be given as an extramural course when the Diploma in Town and Country Planning now existed and catered for applicants with an interest in town planning, notwithstanding that they had to have minimum qualifications to gain entry. The faculty recommended that money from the Vernon Memorial Fund should support a series of lectures within a single unit within the diploma. [^94] The public town planning lectures offered during the 1920s and 1930s that were central to the ethos of the Vernon Memorial Lectures and its structure were now off the educational agenda.

[^89]: Minutes of the Meeting of the Faculty of Architecture (1948), 134.
[^90]: *University Calendar* (1951 supplement), 494.
[^91]: Minutes of the Meeting of the Faculty of Architecture (1949), 135, 139–40.
[^92]: Miers, *The Work and Time of Denis Winston.*
[^93]: Turney, Bygott and Chippendale, *Australia's First*, vol. 1, 277.
[^94]: Minutes of the Meeting of the Faculty of Architecture (1949), 148.

In this context, in 1949, the senate revisited its resolution of 1938 regarding the future of the Vernon Memorial Lectures and agreed "that the income from the Vernon Memorial Fund be applied to the maintenance of the course of lectures with the Town and Country Planning post-graduate diploma course called 'Architecture as related to Town and Country Planning,' or to such other lectures within the Town and Country Planning diploma as the Faculty of Architecture may from time to time decide." [^95] In 1949, Winston agreed that a unit in the diploma called "Architecture in Relation to Planning" be the Vernon Memorial Lectures course and be funded from the Vernon Memorial Fund. [^96] Professor FE Towndrow from the School of Architecture at the Sydney Technical College gave 24 lectures on the subject in 1949 for a fee of 50 pounds. [^97] These lectures still existed in the town and country syllabus in the 1960s, [^98] notwithstanding broader curriculum changes in the faculty and further discussion on how monies funding the Vernon Memorial Lectures should be best applied.

## Conclusion

Under Winston's drive and enthusiasm, the University of Sydney and the Faculty of Architecture dominated the market for university educated town planners in Sydney until 1966, when an undergraduate program in town planning was commenced at the University of New South Wales. [^99] Under Winston's direction, the faculty introduced a master's degree in town and country planning in 1956 and conferred its first doctorate in 1965. Winston was to go on and establish the Planning Research Centre in 1964 to promote contacts between "town and gown," while enhancing the department's disciplinary capacity and the nexus between policy, practice, and the private sector. Although there was to be further debate in the new millennium about where urban and regional planning was best situated within the university, urban planning as an essential discipline taking a leading role in managing, planning and designing the built environment locally, nationally and globally was now firmly embedded in the university's institutional arrangements.

For many reasons, town planning in the early 20th century emerged much slower as a discipline than architecture, which was embedded in teaching structures in the university from the late 1800s. It took nearly 30 years after the establishment of the Department of Architecture in 1918 for a Department of Town and Country Planning to emerge and be formalised within the faculty's institutional structures. This was the same time it took for architecture to be recognised as a school and have its own chair, distinct from engineering. This time lag in the elevation of the town planning discipline reflects the perceived status of understanding how the city was made and shaped from the perspective of the architectural profession and the university at that time.

The gradual ascendency of town planning into a formal academic educational regime within the university and its emergence as a profession reflects a chequered history influenced by the collation of key factors. This evolution was set among tension and positioned between varying stakeholders and disciplines vying to mark and reassert their spheres of influence so as to be relevant in the evolving professional and educational discourse. These factors include (i) the public and professional interest generated by the Vernon Memorial Lectures and the initiative's high profile lecturers; (ii) town planning being positioned within the curriculum of the BArch and the Faculty of Architecture concurrently taking increasing control of emerging professional offerings in town planning education; (iii) the advent of legislation by the NSW Government that required the training of qualified town planners to oversee planning schemes and the like; and (iv) an increasing appreciation of the role of town planning, especially in the immediate post-war period.

[^95]: Minutes of the Meeting of the Faculty of Architecture (1949), 148.
[^96]: Minutes of the Meeting of the Faculty of Architecture (1949), 146.
[^97]: Minutes of the Acting Registrar, 4 May 1949, Vernon Memorial Lectureship (University of Sydney Archives).
[^98]: See, for example, the *University Calendar* (1964), 258.
[^99]: Toon and Falk, eds, *Sydney – Planning or Politics*, 3.

Cutting across the above response was a growing "coalition of the willing," comprised of advocates and associations promoting the relevance of town planning as both a profession and an academic discipline. This spectrum of participating stakeholders included the university and the State Government, which both responded to the requests of the growing profession, albeit with varying levels of interest, while creating a demand for qualified town planners over time, such as through State legislation requiring suitably "approved" town planners. As is true of many places at the time, key individuals involved in town planning in Australia were primarily from the architectural profession or were, to a lesser degree, engineers or surveyors, with many using the TPA of NSW as a key lobby group. Collectively, the town planning movement made incremental gains and progress, gradually increasing available opportunities for formal town planning education while reinforcing a growing professional identity and vice versa.

The elevation of town planning, including the development of robust educational structures, would not have eventuated without the support of prominent individuals and lobby groups, who advocated for the advancement of town planning in a way that was shaped by the circumstances of the time. In this setting, the most notable influence was exerted by John Sulman, who argued that town planning needed to be underpinned by its own "specialist" educational curriculum and professional identity. Sulman had a parallel influence on architectural education, which culminated in the Faculty of Architecture instituting the inaugural Sir John Sulman Prize in Architecture in 1929. Sulman's impact on the early, formative years of town planning education and a growing professional body cannot be overstated and was without peer.

Finally, what was to become of Brown's 1938 concerns about honouring the legacy of Walter Vernon after the discontinuation of the public Vernon Memorial Lectures in Town Planning? Albeit with diminished visibility, the recognition still lives on, with the school annually awarding a Vernon Memorial Prize in Urban and Regional Planning of approximately $100; the amount varies according to the fund's return. This prize is given to an "outstanding student" enrolled in either the Graduate Diploma or Master of Urban and Regional Planning, who has completed at least 48 credit points, that is, the completion of the Diploma requirements or completion of two-thirds of the Masters requirements. [^100] The citation for the award links the prize to the 1915 gift from subscribers who advocated for the use of such monies "to fund a lectureship in Town Planning" to honour the significant contribution of Vernon. [^101]

The year 2019 will commemorate the centenary of the first Vernon Memorial Lectures in Town Planning by Sulman at the University of Sydney and 70 years since the commencement of the Diploma in Town and Country Planning. The year will also mark the centenary of the inclusion of the town planning subject, by way of university by-laws, in the new Bachelor of Architecture. It would be timely if the circumstances shaping this watershed period and its legacy in the evolution of town and country planning education at the University of Sydney and the wider profession could rise again to prominence in 2019. The genesis of the lecture series at the university represented traits of public outreach and engagement, the elevation of new knowledge, a rise in professionalism, and the changing culture of the university, including a new faculty. The last two were critical to underpinning the growth of a new town planning discipline, as well as the depth and breadth of architectural and built environment professions, all with a shared concern for better quality town and city outcomes.

[^100]: *Awards Ceremony Booklet*, School of Architecture, Design and Planning, University of Sydney, 7 May 2018.
[^101]: *Awards Ceremony Booklet*, 2018.

His drawings of buildings and streets would sometimes annoy the historian, as he has a way of donating trees and ornamental devices where they are often, unfortunately, not to be seen. On the other hand, the impulse to add better settings to his picture would delight the town-planning enthusiast

...

— Sydney Ure Smith on Lloyd Rees (1915)

**Figure 1** — Stephen Walker, *Lloyd Rees*, 1988. Photograph by Simon Weir.

# Chapter 3: The Arts of Architecture
— Simon Weir

## Lloyd Rees in Wilkinson's Courtyard

Entering the Wilkinson Building through the courtyard on City Road, you pass through the fixed metallic gaze of Lloyd Rees. [^1] Rees' oversized bronze bust, sculpted by Stephen Walker, sits on a plinth against the western wall of Wilkinson's courtyard [Figure 1]. The placement along the wall aligns with the southern boundary of the Tin Sheds Gallery. [^2] Locating Rees' portrait in Wilkinson's courtyard, on the boundary of its famously contentious art gallery, was doubtless deliberate. It is, in a way, emblematic of the school's fundamental conflict with its founder.

Soon after the School of Architecture was founded in 1918, Professor Leslie Wilkinson gave his inaugural address. The expectations on Wilkinson at the time of the address were considerable. He was Australia's first architectural professor, the first Chair in Architecture, then first dean. He was entrusted with the university's masterplan and the completion of its founding building, the Gothic-revival Main Quadrangle.

When Colonial Architect to New South Wales, Edmund Blacket, began the Main Quadrangle in 1854, Sydney had a growing workforce of skilled masons. Up until the First World War, they produced all of Sydney's sandstone buildings, but Wilkinson travelled to Australia in the final months of the war as masons became increasingly rare. Wilkinson designed the brick exterior faces of the Main Quadrangle and their northern and western ranges, mostly concealed by trees, including the Vice-Chancellor's courtyard. Sandstone was reserved for the Main Quadrangle's remaining inner faces and western cloister. [^3]

For the university's Chemistry Building in 1923, instead of designing a new stone facade as his predecessor would have done, Wilkinson sliced the stone facade off John Hilly's 1854 Commercial Banking Company Building on the corner of George and Barrack Streets. [^4] The facade was reassembled beside the chemistry laboratory, which enclosed the Vice-Chancellor's courtyard. For the Physics Building in 1926, he used his "Mediterranean" style, a long rendered brick building facing the sun. Only the neo-classical entries were sandstone.

The school's curriculum, Wilkinson said in his address, should mix the American and French styles: the clear-headedness of the American schools and the searching graduation tests of the French academies. Architecture was "an Art, a science, a profession and a business," and it was important for students to be "thoroughly equipped in all respects … on the one hand, a thorough grounding in scientific principles and the details of modern work [were] necessary; on the other, the encouragement and development of artistic sense." [^5]

Although Wilkinson's vision for the well-equipped architecture student was a union of construction technique and artistic power, his preference for the artistic is evident in his emphasis on visual representation. He intended to give students "a power of

---

[^1]: The Wilkinson Building has been home of the Sydney School of Architecture, Design and Planning since Eric W Andrew's smaller Wilkinson Building was completed in 1959, but the McConnel Smith and Johnson brutalist Wilkinson building opened in 1976.
[^2]: A similar bust is in a garden on the north eastern corner of Sydney's Town Hall.
[^3]: T Howells, *University of Sydney Architecture* (Boorowa, NSW: Watermark Press, 2007), 48.
[^4]: Howells, *University of Sydney Architecture*, 62.
[^5]: [F Taylor], "Architecture and Australia: The Inaugural Address of Professor Wilkinson, of the Chair of Architecture, University of Sydney," *Building* 24, no. 145 (September 1919), 55.

draughtsmanship which would embrace the skilled technical accuracy of the engineer and the fine feeling of a painter." [^6] Wilkinson arrived in August 1918; the first Bachelor of Architecture students had commenced in March. [^7] The first years' curriculum was assembled from the existing architecture courses operated by the Faculty of Science's Bachelor of Engineering program. John Francis Hennessy was appointed temporary lecturer of architecture and Norman Carter temporary instructor of freehand drawing. [^8]

In Carter, Wilkinson found someone who carried his ideal of educating in the French manner. Carter was born in Melbourne, where he became an apprentice stained-glass maker. Moving to Sydney, he became an acclaimed portraitist. Encouraged to show his work internationally, his *Portrait of Mlle X* was awarded a bronze medal at the Salon des Artistes Française in 1913. As a stained-glass artist, Carter contributed windows to St Andrew's Cathedral and to St Stephen's Church in Sydney, the All Saints Cathedral in Bathurst, and the Teachers' College in Armidale. In 1921, the university's Professor John Anderson commissioned Carter to paint two murals—one with Socrates, Plato, and Aristotle, the other with Descartes, Bacon and Spinoza—in the Main Quadrangle's philosophy lecture rooms. The following year, Wilkinson hired Carter permanently to teach art history.

Wilkinson's philosophical and artistic temperament was inevitably both his strength and weakness. When the 1922 students went into the profession in 1926, Wilkinson took sabbatical leave and travelled back to England. While away, he received a letter from one of his part time lecturers, Alfred Hook. [^9] By all accounts, Hook was competent both with architectural structures and professional politics. In 1922, Hook began lecturing for Wilkinson part time and presided over the Architects' Association of New South Wales, a rival group to the Institute of Architects of New South Wales. He oversaw their merging in 1924 and was elected the institute's president in 1926. To unify national standards, in 1929 he founded the Royal Australian Institute of Architects, which published his textbook for passing the Board of Architects' registration examinations, *A Little About Structural Mechanics*, in 1943. During the months of Wilkinson's sabbatical, Hook complained that graduates had too little technical knowledge. The institute had some sway in the university's performance in this regard since they had lobbied the government to fund a Chair in Architecture at the university years earlier. [^10] Thus, without Wilkinson's consultation, Hook was installed as Assistant Professor of Practice and Construction. [^11] Hook, Carter and Wilkinson worked together for more than 25 years. With Hook's technical expertise and Carter's French style, Wilkinson delivered both sides of his intended curriculum, giving the school a distinctive, even extreme, artistic and philosophical edge. [^12]

In 1946, Wilkinson appointed local artist Lloyd Rees to teach drawing alongside Carter. In 1947, the final year of both Wilkinson's and Carter's tenures, Rees replaced Carter lecturing art history. Rees was 53 years old and had no formal architectural training, but Wilkinson was making an astute choice. Rees' early artistic reputation was based on his drawings of buildings. An almost ideal opportunity for Rees, he taught for 40 years, stretching Wilkinson's personal influence on the school into seven decades.

[^6]: [Taylor], "Architecture and Australia," 55.
[^7]: JM Freeland, *The Making of a Profession: A History of the Growth and Work of the Architectural Institutes in Australia* (Sydney: Thames and Hudson, 1971), 219.
[^8]: C Turney, U Bygott and P Chippendale, *Australia's First: A History of the University of Sydney*, vol. 1, 1850-1939 (Sydney: Hale and Iremonger, 1991), 394. After Wilkinson arrived, Hennessy became a lecturer in building construction, and Alfred Coffey was added as instructor of freehand drawing.
[^9]: Freeland, *The Making of a Profession*, 221; R Johnson, "The Hook Address: Hook/Wilkinson—the architectural mix," *Architecture Australia* 75, no. 2 (March 1996): 42.
[^10]: Freeland, *The Making of a Profession*, 84.
[^11]: Freeland, *The Making of a Profession*, 89, 221; C Lucas, "Wilkinson, Leslie (1882–1973)," *Australian Dictionary of Biography* 12 (1990), http://adb.anu.edu.au/biography/wilkinson-leslie-9104, accessed 31 August 2018; R Broomham, "Hook, Alfred Samuel (1886–1963)," *Australian Dictionary of Biography* 14 (1996), http://adb.anu.edu.au/biography/hook-alfred-samuel-10535, accessed 31 August 2018.
[^12]: Freeland, *The Making of a Profession*, 220.

# Our First Master

Information about Rees' life, his artistic influence and reputation outside the university, can be found in anecdotes about another Sydney painter, Brett Whiteley. In 1934, Rees, his wife Marjory and his son Alan had moved to Northwood, a leafy suburb on the Lane Cove River, a tributary of Sydney Harbour. [^13] A few years later, the Whiteley family moved to neighbouring Longueville. The Whiteleys' son Brett was the "the wild child over whom the district's mothers tut-tutted, worried—and fed." [^14]

After moving to Northwood, Rees slowly moved towards painting landscapes, beginning a beautiful tonal style that would peak a decade later and that increasingly focused on imaginative compositions. The year Rees started lecturing, 1947, he painted possibly his most famous work, *The Road to Berry*. This tiny picture, begun under a copse of trees in Gerringong, prompted Rees to write years later: "I just remember a small canvas and sort of rhythmical movement that just happened… I was never able to repeat that little picture… I was always amazed at the attraction it had." [^15] Rees' reputation as an artist was growing. A regular finalist in the annual Art Gallery of New South Wales' (AGNSW) Wynn prize for landscape painting, he won in 1950 with *The Harbour from McMahon's Point*. Rees would travel to the university on the ferry from the Longueville wharf. In the 1950s, the young Whiteley would also alight on his journey to and from school. Whiteley's sister wrote: "when Lloyd Rees caught the ferry, Brett would stare and admire him from a distance. He would say, 'I wish I could paint like that'." [^16]

In his high school years, Whiteley began to meet the local artists, including the Northwood Group of painters, who would meet each Thursday evening to draw from life in the home of John and Mary Santry. [^17] "Regulars included Lloyd Rees … Rees' weekly contribution was a large billy can of milk coffee made on a splendid Swedish espresso percolator with high-grade, freshly ground beans." [^18] Whiteley later said that, in Rees, he "instantly found a panoply of other painters and a more worldly visual language emanating from Europe." Free continues: "The landscapes had struck him as encapsulating both… European terrain and the invention of Rees' creative adventure which included naturalistic depiction and the decisions and revisions Rees made while painting." [^19] Whiteley's career blossomed after he won the Italian Government Travelling Art Scholarship and left for London via Venice in 1959. Before he left, he visited Rees in Northwood. At the end of the visit, returning to his car, Whiteley turned to Rees and said: "Do you know I'm scared of you?" [^20]

After decades working through expressionism and pop, at the beginning of the 1980s, Whiteley's style was returning to the style of his youth and growing especially toward Rees'. [^21] In 1985, Whiteley completed *Road to Berry, Homage to Lloyd Rees*, which Rees saw soon after in Terry Clune's Potts Point gallery. "I went there and saw a landscape that touched me at once because it was a sort of twilight… then I went up to it and the title was *Homage to Lloyd Rees*… That endeared me to that young man." [^22]

[^13]: R Free, *Lloyd Rees* (Melbourne: Lansdowne, 1979), 47.
[^14]: J Wilson, "Hanging with Brett Whiteley: A Boyhood Idyll," *Australian Financial Review*, 5 May 2014.
[^15]: L Rees and R Free, *Lloyd Rees: An Artist Remembers* (Seaforth, NSW: Craftsman House, 1988), 53.
[^16]: F Hopkirk, *Brett: A Portrait of Brett Whiteley by His Sister* (Sydney: Knopf, 1998), 96–97.
[^17]: L Rees, *Peaks and Valleys* (Sydney: Collins, 1985), 183; L Rees, "Foreword," in *Artists of Lane Cove*, ed. J Washington (Lane Cove, NSW: Lane Cove Public Library, 1989), v; A Rees, "Memories of my Father," in *Lloyd Rees: Painting with Pencil 1930-1936* (London: Michael Nagy, 2015), 170–71.
[^18]: M Hilton and G Blundell, *Whiteley: An Unauthorised Life* (Sydney: Macmillan, 1996), 21; Rees, *Peaks and Valleys*, 183. Rees also met Roland Wakelin in the Northwood group, and Wakelin would join Rees teaching art at Sydney University in 1953.
[^19]: Free, *Lloyd Rees*, 24.
[^20]: Hilton and Blundell, *Whiteley*, 39.
[^21]: Hilton and Blundell, *Whiteley*, 171.
[^22]: L Klepac, *Lloyd Rees, Brett Whiteley—On the Road to Berry* (Melbourne: Beagle Press, 1993), 8.

At Rees' funeral in 1988, Whiteley was unusually silent and subdued. Weeks later, speaking about his current exhibition, Whiteley reiterated his affinity for Rees' broad expressionistic landscapes and natural beauty.

> My new exhibition is the most exacting in terms of beauty. Serenity, peace, order are the most difficult states to aspire to. There is so little beauty around us these days. All that turgid, depressing dogshit school of art at the Biennale is not for me. [^23]

Rees' large "landscape expressionist" paintings of the 1950s and 60s, including the full development of ideas in *Road to Berry*, are among the highlights of his oeuvre. [^24] About these, Whiteley wrote:

> You can't just look at a Rees picture, you have to milk it ... one foot in a monastery established purely to worship mood ... if Hybridism is to be our contribution to evolution, and that looks like what will happen in this section of the globe, for the Asian Western mix, the avoidance of a polar situation, is well in the air ... then Lloyd Rees, in painting terms, is our first Master. [^25]

## Rees Before 1947

Rees' arrival at his expressionist landscapes, which Whiteley labelled a form of hybridism and which earned him the title of first Master, was the result of a long personal progression from the partially informed choices made in childhood through the opportunities of his early life. By middle age, he could articulate his position precisely. It was both Rees' ease and fluency in describing art and his skill in rendering buildings that would have given Wilkinson confidence. Rees wrote an essay for *Art in Australia* in 1940, rather self-consciously titled "What is Good Drawing." Rees called visual realism "depictive art." The representational fidelity, which may easily be called *quality*, that arrives as a result of technical competence is obvious and remains one of visual art's most objective criteria. Yet, as Rees wrote:

> If a drawing is exceedingly like the accepted appearance of an object, it is usually considered to be a good drawing; and if it diverges from that accepted appearance, it is considered a bad drawing ... although the need for exact representation in the fine arts has to a great degree passed, the standards of judgment it set up are still with us, and are still operating *against* a proper understanding of the true function of drawing ... good drawing is expressive drawing. It reveals what the artist is thinking and feeling concerning his subject, and is a creation separate and apart from the subject which inspired it. [^26]

For Rees, the aspiring visual artist should spend years, decades, learning this craft, learning how to see. By reproducing these perceptions with the simplicity of pencil on paper, attending to every square millimetre with equal intensity and fidelity, the artist learns what they see and thereby what is there, building a cycle of awareness; Rees wrote, "when one really observes and analyses natural objects, they become part of you and what is even more important, you become part of them." [^27] The simple and profound process of depictive drawing inherently values honesty and a detailed, high resolution sensitivity to the visual world. Through this sensitive process, not through the objects themselves, artistic beauty emerges; as Rees said succinctly, "Beauty lies in the treatment, not the subject." [^28] He continued:

---

[^23]: Hilton and Blundell, *Whiteley*, 219.
[^24]: Free, *Lloyd Rees*, 80.
[^25]: Free, *Lloyd Rees*, 92; also, Hopkirk, *Brett*, 359, "Brett said that Lloyd Rees didn't look at landscape he 'milked' it."

[^26]: L Rees, "What is Good Drawing," *Art in Australia* 3, no. 78 (23 February 1940): 27. Emphasis added.
[^27]: Rees, *Peaks and Valleys*, 167.
[^28]: Free, *Lloyd Rees*, 65.

My life at Smith & Julius was very much concentrated on work. I did very meticulous pen illustrations by day, and nights at home were spent doing great dark pen drawings of my own imaginings.

— Lloyd Rees (1985)

> It is my own personal belief that depictive art will remain wedded to natural appearances, that drawing will continue to be the link binding them together, and that just as human freedom achieved its greatest scope within the framework of the law, so too will artistic freedom be similarly enlarged. Bounded only by the laws of natural appearances, Art will continue to expand into the realm of visible creation—a realm boundless in interest and extent. [^29]

Craftsmanship's connection to sensitivity, ethics and aesthetics underpinned Rees' approach to architecture, but it was inevitably where he deviated from realistic depiction that most excited architects. When depicting buildings, Rees corrected them. He made them a little more beautiful by working as a designer moving windows into plausible alternative positions, adding or removing ornamental details, or stabilising proportions by stretching and repositioning walls.

This architectural impulse was a recurrent feature in Rees' work. Renee Free, Rees' first biographer, described the first work "he framed and hung at home," which was completed when Rees was 17, as a "hallucinatory drawing of Notre Dame, Paris." [^30] The hallucinatory quality Free described emanates from the formal resonance Rees emphasises between the stone arcs of the church's three rose windows and the bifurcating curves of tree branches in the foreground. Rees accentuated these formal rhythms by adding his own line of planters and shrubs in the foreground, again reflecting the rhythm of the rose windows.

Rees drew from childhood. At school, he "traded drawings for help with arithmetic," a decision with an impact more profound than he imagined. [^31] Completing high school in Brisbane, Rees excelled in drawing, ranking second in the State. "A girl from another high school came first," Rees wrote, "I used to think of her and want to meet her. When I did years later, she informed me she had no interest in art at all! The fascinating twists of life." [^32] When Rees and his father agreed that his skills with the pencil meant that a suitable vocation would be architecture, he applied to Brisbane's best architects. They informed him, however, that the younger Rees' weak grades in arithmetic prevented him entering the profession.

Barred access to architecture, Rees began work as a clerk in the Union Bank of Australia, where he began on "a reasonable salary for those times—fifteen shillings a week," amounting to a little less than 40 pounds per year. There, and soon after, Rees encountered astonishingly harsh labour practices delivered against working men: "no member of staff was permitted marriage until he was on the 200 pounds a year level … To break this ruling led to dismissal." Yet "progression was slow… The bank seemed reluctant to raise its staff to this necessary level." [^33]

As a junior, Rees worked in a basement with cold damp air. The bank's horrid physical and social environment left Rees seriously ill, but he received no firm diagnosis. The months of convalescence afforded hours of drawing time, during which he produced "illustrations of King Arthur's Court, with its Knights and ladies" and Indian ink reproductions of John Constable paintings. [^34] Then, through a former headmaster's unsolicited recommendation, Rees was offered a job as a junior artist in the Government Printing Office; "it was a turning point in my life … The atmosphere of the printer seemed to me far more wholesome than that of the bank." [^35]

For the Government Printing Office, Rees produced four sets of postcards of the city's buildings and a large lithograph of the Government Printing building, adding watercolour to several of the prints. [^36] At the time, some cases of small pox and

[^29]: Rees, "What is Good Drawing," 30.
[^30]: Free, Lloyd Rees, 16.
[^31]: H Kolenberg, Lloyd Rees: Paintings, Drawings and Prints (Sydney: Art Gallery of New South Wales, 2013), 155.
[^32]: Rees, Peaks and Valleys, 64.
[^33]: Rees, Peaks and Valleys, 65.
[^34]: Rees, Peaks and Valleys, 76.
[^35]: Rees, Peaks and Valleys, 78–79.
[^36]: L Klepac, "Lloyd Rees: Draughtsman," in Lloyd Rees: Painting with Pencil 1930–1936 (London: Michael Nagy, 2015), 19.

rumours of the bubonic plague were about, so Rees accepted a vaccination which left him bedridden again due to complications with his previous illness. Taking a vacation to recover, Rees travelled north to Bundaberg on a boat hauling bags of sugar. There he witnessed the whole sugar production process and recalled again seeing men as the victims of punishing labour practices. "When I saw that the three men sewing bags were all hunchbacks I said, 'At least management had the decency to give those crippled men jobs'," but his companion quietly explained "they were not crippled when they began." [^37]

After Rees returned to Brisbane, his father encouraged him to get artistic training in Brisbane's Technical College, where he continued to draw buildings. By 1917, his consistency with architectural subjects led to Rees working for a commercial art firm in Sydney, Smith & Julius. Rees recalled: "My life at Smith & Julius was very much concentrated on work. I did very meticulous pen illustrations by day, and nights at home were spent doing great dark pen drawings of my own imaginings." [^38] The firm's principal, Sydney Ure Smith, an accomplished artist, had just founded the arts journal *Art in Australia*, and wrote insightfully about Rees' works, recognising his architectural impulse:

> **He is not a realist … His drawings of buildings and streets would sometimes annoy the historian, as he has a way of donating trees and ornamental devices where they are often, unfortunately, not to be seen. On the other hand, the impulse to add better settings to his picture would delight the town-planning enthusiast, and if it makes a better picture—why not?** [^39]

The next year, Rees completed a small pencil and ink drawing, *House in the Valley I*, which combined the view of a house in Bondi with the background of Bellevue Hill. It was purchased by the AGNSW from the Society of Artists' Annual Exhibition. It was reviewed by Bertram Stevens in the *Bulletin* as an example of Rees' "tendency to weave fact and fiction with compositions that are partly fancies." [^40]

In his work for Smith & Julius, Rees was engaged largely because of his architectural skills. In advertisements, Rees drew the buildings, and another artist, Percy Lawson, added the living figures, people and horses. Rees described "his most interesting commercial art work" for Smith & Julius as two drawings for the *Daily Telegraph* in 1919: one of the great Sydney peace march and the other of the victory celebration on Armistice Day, *Celebrating the Birth of a New Era* and *Macquarie Street at Night*. [^41]

When, in 1922, Smith & Julius made "the suggestion for a series of drawings of the university," he was "most enthusiastic and … set to work with keen interest," producing the images for the small book, *Sydney University —Drawings by Lloyd Rees*. [^42] The book was conceived as a deluxe edition but was instead released in a smaller format for students.

Rees' paintings at this time were landscapes influenced by the French painters Claude Lorrain and Jean-Baptiste-Camille Corot and the Australian Arthur Streeton. [^43] Rees attributed his affinity to French painting to his half-Mauritian, half-Cornish mother, Angèle Burguez. Travelling around Europe in 1923 and 1924 with his fiancé Daphne Mayo, Rees painted some street scenes, houses and ecclesiastic interiors: "in the winter it was so cold that I spent months in St Paul's Cathedral because, if I stayed in my room, I used to freeze. I couldn't afford the bob after bob for the gas meter." [^44] However, he returned to landscapes when returning to Sydney and ended his engagement with Mayo, explaining "my work in those years lost direction … I was rejected by the Society of Artists, both as an exhibitor and as a member." [^45]

---

[^37]: Rees, *Peaks and Valleys*, 81–82.
[^38]: Rees, *Peaks and Valleys*, 111.
[^39]: S Ure Smith, "Lloyd Rees," *Art in Australia* 1, no. 2 (1917).
[^40]: Free, *Lloyd Rees*, 25.
[^41]: Free, *Lloyd Rees*, 28.
[^42]: B Burdett, "Lloyd Rees," in *Sydney University: Drawings by Lloyd Rees* (Sydney: Smith & Julius Studios, 1922).
[^43]: L Rees "Foreword," in *Lloyd Rees: A Tribute to Sydney* (Sydney: Macquarie Street Galleries, 1979), 3.
[^44]: Rees, *Peaks and Valleys*, 122, 147.
[^45]: Rees, *Peaks and Valleys*, 150.

Within a year, Rees married Dulcie Metcalfe and was widowed. Grief, persistent anxiety, and physical health problems brought Rees to his lowest ebb, and he did not approach oil painting for almost a decade. Instead, Rees found solace in the long hours working purely in pencil, producing a series of drawings of Sydney from 1930-36, which are among his most celebrated works. The subjects of these years are natural rather than architectural, focusing on coves and trees, but buildings almost always occupy the background. Free's writing on these drawings applies to earlier architectural drawings as well: "Observation of nature is the central quality of these works, but they are not realistic entirely. Their impact is of greater detail than that which the ordinary eye can see." [^46] In his autobiography, Rees reiterated his sensitivity as a fundamental element of his character, frequently recalling early instances of this sensitive side contrasting with the rawness of country life and his school's sadistic corporal punishment. After receiving the gift of an air gun as a child, he enjoyed dallying in the predators' craft. Although he relished the challenge of marksmanship, he regretted its consequences. After taking aim at a white duck with a bow and arrow, Rees recalled piercing its back:

> ... not seriously thank heaven, for it simply waddled a bit faster, but I saw the stain of blood upon its feathers and such a feeling of remorse and compassion swept over me that I wanted to comfort the gentle bird. But it had sensibly waddled out of sight, out of reach of small destructive boys. [^47]

A few years later, recalling a Victorian religious song with lyrics about an orphaned girl, who, on "a relentless and stormy night," died in the cemetery where her mother had just been buried, Rees reflected, "I used to wonder why it never seemed to occur to anyone to help the orphan girl at her mother's tomb." [^48]

In each of these anecdotes, as well as many others, Rees described his sensitivity and empathy as separating him from his peers, giving him access to emotions of which others were scarcely aware.

After these years focused on drawing, Rees returned to landscapes in oil. The new compositions were increasingly distributions of detail around the canvases rather than coloured line work. The "recording" aspect of landscape painting was progressively abandoned. Rees wrote, "when painting I would sometimes realise—with a sense of shock—that, in a whole morning's work, I had scarcely been aware of the landscape before me, all my attention being concentrated on the canvas itself." [^49] This is the style Rees kept for the rest of his career. His failing eyesight, which Whiteley wrote only allowed Rees "inspired guesses at his canvas," [^50] would prohibit fine line work, but would not interfere with tonal paintings.

## Rees Follows Carter

When Rees began working in the university in 1946, class was held "on the top floor of the unfinished western tower of the main quadrangle." [^51] The tower had been designed by Wilkinson 20 years earlier, but it would be without its upper floors and turret stair for another 20 years. By then, architecture classes would have already moved to a 1959 version of the Wilkinson building designed by Eric Andrew, one of Wilkinson's earliest Bachelor of Architecture graduates. [^52]

In 1946, Rees taught the first-year drawing class alongside Carter. At 73, Carter was 20 years older than Rees, and he gave his replacement a smooth transition into the position. In their first year together, Carter led. They taught their students "studio work, including freehand drawing from the cast, antique and life,

---

[^46]: Free, *Lloyd Rees*, 44.
[^47]: Rees, *Peaks and Valleys*, 15–16.
[^48]: Rees, *Peaks and Valleys*, 49.
[^49]: Free, *Lloyd Rees*, 51.
[^50]: Hopkirk, *Brett*, 389.
[^51]: Rees, *Peaks and Valleys*, 192.
[^52]: Howells, *University of Sydney Architecture*, 48, 124.

sketching from nature." [^53] The next year, Rees led with Carter supporting. That year, Rees took the fifth-year lecture course, "The History of Painting and Sculpture," which had been part of Wilkinson's original curriculum since 1919:

> A course of lectures on the schools and their characteristics; the world's masterpieces and their authors. Attention will be directed to the decorative value of Sculpture and Painting and the importance of collaboration between painter, sculptor and architect. [^54]

Rees' lectures gave more of a personal view than the handbook description conveys. In one lecture, recorded near the end of his career, he interrupted a description of Spanish Golden Age painters and explained: "it falls naturally into place that the type of lectures I'm giving will often be lopsided because I am telling a story rather than a very formal history." [^55] Rees' descriptions were largely guided by Élie Faure's 1921 *History of Art*, which divided artists into nationalities and described painters' national character and individual idiosyncrasies. [^56] He showed his audience slide after slide of paintings, explaining their virtues, always mentioning the national character and the technique, yet he also added something of the image's emotional value. In response to each image, Rees would say how he felt. The emotional value of images was paramount and, in his lectures, Rees guided students through a range of emotional experiences, calmly and sensitively describing every mood.

After Wilkinson retired, Rees continued his roles as lecturer in "The History of Sculpture and Painting" and part-time instructor of drawing under subsequent deans.

> My week is rather happily regulated, with the University taking all Tuesday, Wednesday and half [of] Thursday, thus leaving 4 clear days for my painting & which I try to keep clear. A complication has been my election [in 1962] as Dean of the Faculty of Architecture, whilst Professor Ashworth is in Europe, but with rather amazing good fortune nearly all my duties have come within the Tuesday–Thursday period. [^57]

As the years progressed, the architectural instruction that had been justifiable in the earlier years eventually came under question, not from his fellow teaching staff but from students' own observations. Robert Hughes enrolled there in 1957, approaching a decade after Wilkinson had retired, but the course had changed too little. Hughes wrote:

> It was modelled closely on the French degree course at the École des Beaux-Arts in the nineteenth century, and was presided over by a self-declared conservative, Professor H Ingham Ashworth, who had scarcely heard of Bucky Fuller and regarded Le Corbusier (this being decades after the Villa Savoye) as rather an upstart and of uncertain value. [^58]

Like all enrolling students, Hughes began with basic art instruction, which consisted of learning to render the light and shadows on a series of standardised objects. In first year, one would begin with cubes and cones and niches. "The conventions for this were strict and absolute because there was no room whatever for 'inter-pretation' or 'expression'." [^59] While Hughes reported that students seemed content to develop these skills, the problem emerged progressively as students entered their final years, because

[^53]: *University Calendar* (University of Sydney, 1946 supplement), 438.
[^54]: *University Calendar* (1947 supplement), 444, 447. Thereafter this course was delivered to fourth year students.
[^55]: L Rees, *AR 065 Lloyd Rees: A Personal View, The Importance of Islands of Crete*, unpublished video (Sydney: Sydney School of Architecture, Design and Planning, University of Sydney, 1986).
[^56]: Free, *Lloyd Rees*, 53; Rees, *Peaks and Valleys*, 152.
[^57]: J Rees and A Rees, *Lloyd Rees: A Source Book* (Sydney: Beagle Press, 1995), 29.
[^58]: R Hughes, *Things I Didn't Know* (Sydney: Random House, 2006), 198.
[^59]: Hughes, *Things I Didn't Know*, 199.

... the students who did them best were the very ones who, when it came to designing their own buildings, did worst ... the problems we were set tended to be remote from the world in which we actually lived and [were] rarely described in terms of use .... But when, as we were in third year, you are presented with the task of designing a monastery on a mountaintop, without any indications of whether the thing is to be a cave or a cathedral, for Catholics or Buddhists or, if for Catholics, whether the order that will use it is contemplative or active, or what the monks' daily routines and ritual requirements may be, the task of design becomes somewhat generic and pointless. (One thing was guaranteed: nearly everyone's design had, somewhere in it, some sort of airfoil roof awkwardly adapted from Corbusier's chapel at Ronchamp, because that was the one modernist building that had been featured in all the architectural magazines we were likely to see in Australia.) [^60]

A similar critique could be made of Rees' art as well. Having risen to prominence across the century, Rees remained aloof from almost all of its artistic innovations. Although he described cubism, surrealism and abstraction as evidence of "that spirit of inquiry without which mankind would lose its port of invention and discovery," [^61] his work and the architecture school proceeded as if they had not occurred. It was not solely Rees' doing. Explaining that the Australian art establishment was "parodically hostile to the new," Hughes reflected that it took Australian culture a long time to "pay for the conservatism and xenophobia of the men who installed themselves as its cultural directors after 1910." [^62]

Australia's cultural isolation began to change at the end of the 1960s. The University of Sydney's Fine Arts Department was set up in 1967. Then, for his weekly drawing classes in 1968, Rees moved away from Wilkinson's western tower of the Main Quadrangle to a carpenters shop on City Road. Rees left plaster busts and panels there, and it was made available as a studio for fifth-year architecture students. [^63] This space was later named the Middle Shed, one of the Tin Sheds' three buildings. [^64] Toni Robertson, the Tin Sheds' first historian, wrote that Tin Sheds began on 11 January 1969, when a group of staff and students broke the padlock on the Top Shed, "a direct and illegal act to attain a particular end that was seen as necessary at the time." [^65]

They had intended to use the Top Shed as a workshop but found cyanide contamination from the electro-plating previously carried out there, so they moved into the Bottom Shed. The Top Shed was decontaminated over the coming months and then used as a ceramics and sculpture studio. [^66] The next decade brought a profound change in the artistic activities around the university. In *Under a Hot Tin Roof*, Therese Kenyon wrote:

> The election of Gough Whitlam's Labor Government in 1972 affected the lives of many artists who came from working-class families ... not having to pay fees meant that there were artists who defined themselves by disputes with the cultural status quo ... [They were] political activists first and artists second ... The more theoretical discussions about art were sacrificed to working politically for change at a domestic level.

[^60]: Hughes, *Things I Didn't Know*, 199–202.
[^61]: Rees, "What is Good Drawing," 28. Here Rees asserted that the principal abstract values of form, colour and design "will always have a higher significance when allied to recognisable objects than they have when related to objects drawn from the mind of the artist himself."
[^62]: Hughes, *Things I Didn't Know*, 211.
[^63]: T Robertson, "Botulism or Preservation: The Question of the Tin Sheds" (unpublished diss., Department of Fine Arts, University of Sydney, 1979), 9.
[^64]: T Kenyon, *Under a Hot Tin Roof: Art, Passion and Politics at the Tin Sheds Art Workshop* (Sydney: State Library of NSW Press, 1995), 11, 25.
[^65]: Robertson, "Botulism or Preservation," 1979, 10–12.
[^66]: Kenyon, *Under a Hot Tin Roof*, 26–27.

As these students entered the university, the art practices they pursued in the environment of the Tin Sheds was primarily non-objective art, assemblages, installations, and collective art, not depictive. Painters and sculptors employing traditional techniques to produce art alone were dismissed and discounted as an irrelevancy. [^67]

Rees' technique undoubtedly belonged to this newly disenfranchised group, but his experience with, and sympathy for, the plight of oppressed workers aligned him with the former politically. Thus, as Kenyon reported, he "often sat around with the students and artists loving the activity and the vibes." [^68] He remained connected yet separate, somehow escaping their often judgmental views. Indeed, when the university decided to cut funds for the art classes, Rees donated his work to a raffle, funding the term's teaching. [^69] Sitting outside the artistic concerns of this generation of artists, but sympathetic and appreciative, Rees encouraged these artists to explore. The 1969 students' report on his teaching noted that "he has earned the respect of every student that has passed through his hands." [^70]

Aside from his pictorial conservatism, Rees internalised some of the Tin Sheds' radical experimentation, accepting the value of critical and experimental practice while retaining more enduring values. After seeing Christo and Jeanne-Claude's 1969 wrapping of Little Bay, assisted by the school's architecture students, Rees described to a journalist possibly the most intense Sydney installation piece imaginable: "I have an idea myself: to fill Sydney Harbour with petrol and drop a match—it would be a magnificent spectacle, but that is all." [^71] Gentle critique nested within his imagining, Rees adding "we must underscore the perman-ence of life rather than the transitory." [^72]

# Rees in Wilkinson's Courtyard

Parting words should perhaps begin with Rees'. His autobiography, completed just a few years before his death at 93, concluded by reflecting on his great fondness for the Faculty of Architecture and all that it had given him:

> Whatever my present standard may be, the foundations of it began with this University appointment. And here I must correct any impression of a division between my professional and personal life as both strongly intermingled. Life friendships were founded in [Smith & Julius] and so they were in the University of Sydney, both among staff and among students. The student links coloured those early years and have continued to do so up to the present, and among my happiest European memories [is] meeting former Sydney undergraduates in Architecture in London, Cambridge, and in such places in Europe as within the Basilica of St Peter's in Rome or on a bridge in Venice. [^73]

A century after Leslie Wilkinson attended his interview with the selection committee in London wearing top hat and tails, Rees' bust on the western wall of the courtyard in the 1976 Wilkinson building looks upwards slightly, towards the morning sun. A science and technology library now stands where the Tin Sheds used to be. Tin Sheds became a gallery integrated into the City Road façade of the Wilkinson building. To the left of Rees' bust, a tall, narrow glass wall shines up to the roof, a rare interruption to Wilkinson's otherwise grim exterior. To the right is a brick panel, the same height as the glass wall. A pattern of steel rods and absent bricks once enabled plants to be hung and housed in the wall, but the watering system concealed behind the wall is irreparable. The wall is untended; no plants grow there anymore.

[^67]: Kenyon, *Under a Hot Tin Roof*, 22.
[^68]: Kenyon, *Under a Hot Tin Roof*, 27.
[^69]: Kenyon, *Under a Hot Tin Roof*, 65; Robertson, "Botulism or Preservation," 27.
[^70]: Kolenberg, *Lloyd Rees*, 157; E Duyker, "Remembering Lloyd Rees," *SAM* (Autumn 2008), 32.
[^71]: Kolenberg, *Lloyd Rees*, 11; *Australian*, 7 May 1970, 24.
[^72]: Kolenberg, *Lloyd Rees*, 11; *Australian*, 7 May 1970, 24.

[^73]: Rees, *Peaks and Valleys*, 241–42.

Most people who enter Wilkinson from City Road do not know that architects McConnel, Smith and Johnson wanted plants on that sunny brick wall, nor whose bust sits there, nor that the Tin Sheds' founders dismissed Rees' depictive art. Indeed, that the Tin Sheds community defined themselves as separate from Rees and what he was doing. Rees' bust on the edge of the Tin Sheds reminds us that Wilkinson's adherence to art was not to one particular style. As he said in that inaugural address, the school "was not intended to foster the development of any particular style of design. This has been attempted in some schools. … This will not be our aim." [^74]

The exploratory discipline of design thrives with what Rees called a "spirit of freedom and inquiry," indicating the "burning desire to wring new secrets from the mystery of life." [^75] Although not practising the same artistic exploration as the Tin Sheds, Rees valued and encouraged them. Broader in taste than younger and more contentious students, he valued both the experimental and the traditional. Nonetheless, on balance, he was more of Wilkinson's era than Christo's. Rees' choice of a project to personally support is most telling. He gave an initial donation then arranged a subscription to pay for the minimalist waterfall fountain that adorns Sydney's Martin Place, and he led the campaign to restore one of Sydney's sandstone masterpieces, the 1898 Queen Victoria Building. Although Rees' predecessor, Carter, was commissioned to leave his mark on the Main Quadrangle with his philosophy murals, Rees himself commissioned Tom Bass to complete a pair of sculptures for the sides of the Great Hall's entrance, the grandest pathway into the Main Quadrangle.

[^74]: [Taylor], "Architecture and Australia," 56.
[^75]: Rees, "What is Good Drawing," 30.

It envisaged a future profession that was "intelligently aware of the full implications of science considered not only as a laboratory affair but as a method of thought and action."

— Daniel Ryan, quoting from the JRIBA (1940)

**Figure 1** — Portrait of Alfred Hook from *Architecture* 18 (1 October 1929), 228.

# Chapter 4: Architects in White Coats: The Development of Architectural Science at the University of Sydney
— Daniel J Ryan

Science is presumed to advance a rational, predictable world. Yet the history of science, in what was long called the Faculty of Architecture at the University of Sydney, is a story as much about power as it is about reason. Rarely were debates about science's role in the faculty predictable. Instead, attitudes to science have been informed by moments of crisis within the faculty and by anxiety within the architectural profession as to the competencies required of architects to deal with a changing world. This chapter explores how the interests of the profession's guardians, both local and international—the Board of Architects of New South Wales, the Institute of Architects of New South Wales (IANSW) and the Royal Institute of British Architects (RIBA)—shaped debates about the balance between art and science in architectural curricula, the relationship between architects and other technical consultants, and the emergence of scientific research in architecture in the immediate post-war era of 1945 to 1960. It tries to answer why the technical and scientific education of architects could generate such controversy and explores the contingent factors that enabled the University of Sydney to establish the first Chair of Architectural Science.

Some of this ground has previously been covered by Australian researchers: Max Freeland, in his seminal 1971 book, *The Making of a Profession*; Richard Blythe's 2006 study of post-war attitudes to science in architecture; and British academics Mark Crinson and Jules Lubbock in their careful research on English battles between traditionalists and modernists for control of the academy from 1930 to 1960. [^1] More recently, Jiat-Hwee Chang has updated Crinson and Lubbock's work by carefully examining the links between debates about the scientific education of architects in England and the post-graduate training of architects for post-colonial development work in the tropics. [^2] This chapter expands and reframes a number of aspects of Freeland and Blythe's studies by returning to the archival sources. It accepts Freeland's general argument that, by the mid-1920s, the design-focused education that Leslie Wilkinson instituted at the University of Sydney created problems with the State's regulating body, the Board of Architects of NSW. However, it suggests that the intervention of the board to install Alfred Hook as a lecturer, as well as the board's attempt to regulate the curriculum, were driven as much by Hook's personal ambitions as by the board itself [Figure 1]. It upholds Blythe's thesis that the arrival of new deans of architecture from Britain from the late 1940s helped institute a modernist curriculum. In the case of Sydney, however, rather than crediting Dean Henry Ingham Ashworth for the changes in scientific attitudes sustained in that school across the 1940s, this chapter argues that Henry "Jack" Cowan's prior training in England, institutional connections, capacity for organisation, and institution building were of immense importance, not just to the technical education of architects in Australia, but also more broadly throughout the English-speaking world.

[^1]: JM Freeland, *The Making of a Profession: A History of the Growth and Work of the Architectural Institutes in Australia* (Sydney: Angus & Robertson, 1971), 218–30; R Blythe, "Science Enthusiasts: A Threat to Beaux-Arts Architectural Education in Australia in the 1950s," *Fabrications: The Journal of the Society of Architectural Historians, Australia and New Zealand* 8, no. 1 (1997): 117–28; M Crinson and J Lubbock, *Architecture—Art or Profession? Three Hundred Years of Architectural Education in Britain* (Manchester: Manchester University Press, 1994).
[^2]: J Chang, *A Genealogy of Tropical Architecture: Colonial Networks, Nature and Technoscience* (Abingdon: Routledge, 2016), 203–44.

The curricula, journals, research training pathways, laboratories and students that Cowan helped shape created the capacity for a network of scientific researchers in architecture to form in the 1950s, 1960s and 1970s, making Sydney an international hub in the exchange of knowledge and scientific practice. This expands the work of Crinson and Lubbock and that of Chang by suggesting that scientific exchange did not occur just from periphery to centre—from London to the former British colonies—but that, with the emergence of Australia as a centre for post-war scientific research in architecture, knowledge exchange flowed in many different directions, enabling the export of an Australian model of scientific research in architecture.

## Art, Science, Education and the Registration of Architects

From the end of the 19th century to the start of the Second World War, architects in Britain and Australia attempted to elevate the status of the profession by emphasising architecture as both a cultural and technical pursuit. In part, this was a response to the increased importance of engineers in the design and procurement of buildings. [^3] For the architectural profession in NSW, from the late 19th century until 1921, better professional organisation, the regulation of professional title, and the admission of architecture into the academy were three key pillars to improve the public standing of the profession. [^4] In Sydney, between 1910 and 1917, the architectural profession actively petitioned the NSW Government to fund a Chair in Architecture. Two visions of architecture were present in this ambition. [^5] One vision, that of IANSW president George Sydney Jones, placed greater weight on the experiential qualities of architecture and saw art as the solution to the industrial city. The other vision, advocated by Jack Hennessy, the Peter Nicol Russell Lecturer in Architecture at the University of Sydney from 1912 to 1918, emphasised technical competence and hygiene as key to improving buildings. [^6] Both approaches, the artistic and the scientific, were embedded in the curriculum of the Bachelor of Architecture (BArch) as it developed from 1917 onwards.

Registration of the profession was premised on better educated and more competent architects. The public benefits of registration were argued less on technical grounds than on aesthetic ones. In 1911, an editorial in the *Sydney Morning Herald* argued in favour of registration of architects on the basis that "more competent architects would soon make their presence felt on the architectural beauty of our cities and the comfort of the inhabitants." [^7] In part, this reaction may be seen in light of the growing pains of rapid urbanisation. Sydney's population in 1901 was 538,800. [^8] By 1921, it was 899,099. [^9] Concrete-framed buildings over 40 metres in height, such as Culwulla Chambers (Spain and Cosh, 1910–12), began to sprout up around the city at the turn of the century, and the acceleration of modern life and construction practices seemed to threaten the cohesion and appearance of cities. Architecture curricula responded to these perceived threats by emphasising architecture's ability to make cities and buildings more beautiful or else to control the means with which they were made.

## Science, Engineering and Architecture During the Inter-War Period

When Wilkinson commenced his appointment at the University of Sydney in 1918, architecture was embedded within engineering, and the

---

[^3]: Freeland, *The Making of a Profession*, 79.
[^4]: Freeland, *The Making of a Profession*, 84. On this point, see also Andrew Leach's chapter in this book.
[^5]: "Sydney Architecture," *Sydney Morning Herald*, 16 March 1912, 20; "Chair of Architecture," *Sydney Morning Herald*, 24 September 1912, 17.
[^6]: "Teaching Architecture," *Sun*, 5 February 1912, 10.
[^7]: "Architects and Registrations," *Sydney Morning Herald*, 16 June 1911.
[^8]: *Year Book of Australia* 1 (1908), 158.
[^9]: *Year Book of Australia* 14 (1921), 1149.

degree content was weighted towards science and technology. This was partly pragmatic, as there was only one other architect, Jack Hennessy, lecturing in architecture at the university, but it also reflected the degree's origins as a course within the Bachelor of Engineering (BE). [^10] In 1920, the university restructured from four to 10 faculties, with engineering and architecture each gaining faculty status, both separating from the Faculty of Science. While this enabled the new faculties to chart their own destiny, many courses were shared between the new BArch and the BE, particularly in the foundation year of 1918, when the first students could pursue a degree in architecture. In 1920, half of the courses in the first years of the BArch and BE were common to both. [^11] Students all took mathematics, descriptive geometry, and either physics or chemistry together. With the exception of descriptive geometry, offered by the Faculty of Engineering, the three other courses were offered by the Faculty of Science. At the same time, architecture students were also expected to take a course from the Bachelor of Arts (BA) degree, with Latin, Greek, English, French or history among the recommended offerings.

While this made for efficient staffing of the course and gave architecture students an inter-disciplinary grounding, it created two problems. Firstly, it meant that shared courses were not tailored to the specific needs of architecture students, with little connection made between fundamental theories in physics or chemistry, for example, and their application in the design or analysis of buildings. Secondly, it created the perception within the profession that graduates of the University of Sydney were not adequately prepared for the technical challenges of architectural practice.

For much of the 1920s, the architecture faculty did not have the in-house expertise to develop its own courses in applied science or structural design, nor could it rely on other faculties to develop courses tailored

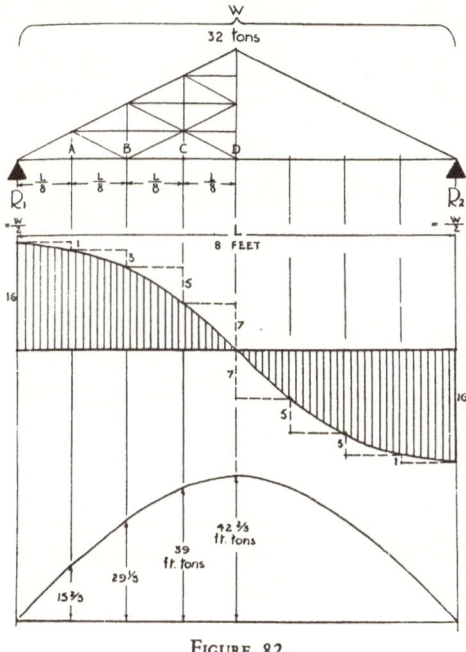

**Figure 2** — Hook's drawing of a shear force diagram and bending moment of a truss. A Hook, *A Little About Structural Mechanics*, 2nd ed. (Sydney: Royal Australian Institute of Architects, 1947), 65.

to its students. Wilkinson, who took over from Hennessy at the university, emphasised architecture as a civic art, bringing in lecturers in town planning (R Keith Harris), freehand drawing (stained glass artist Norman Carter), and even medieval art (architect JL Berry), as well as one for construction (Hook). At Sydney, Wilkinson acknowledged there was a role for science to solve material, structural and environmental problems, but he did not think that this helped with the development of architecture. "Size, costliness, even practical utility, are insufficient," he argued in an address to the Australasian Association for the Advancement of Science in 1924. Instead, the main component of architecture, as he saw it, was taste, and architectural education had to cultivate this. [^12] Under Wilkinson's stewardship, the scientific and technical content in the architecture degree continued to

[^10]: *University Calendar* (University of Sydney, 1926), 305. All subsequent references to the *University Calendar* refer to this serial source, held at the University of Sydney Archives.
[^11]: *University Calendar* (1920), 144–47, 154–55.

[^12]: L Wilkinson, "Modern Tendencies in Australian Architecture," in *Report of the Australasian Association for the Advancement of Science* (Adelaide: REE Rogers Government Printer, 1924), 17, 570.

be provided largely by the Faculties of Science and Engineering. With Hook alone responsible for teaching construction across the degree, but employed from 1922 on only a part-time basis, students received limited tuition from architects in construction and practice. In general, what contact they had with architects during their studies occurred in design studios and drawing tuition.

Had Wilkinson's chair remained within the Faculty of Science, as it was when he arrived in 1918, or been acquired by the new Faculty of Engineering, it seems likely that the course would have continued to place greater emphasis on scientific content. At the University of Melbourne, where architecture was part of the engineering faculty until it gained autonomy as a faculty in 1931, proposals for diploma and degree courses during the 1920s all heavily emphasised science subjects. [^13] At Sydney Technical College, the diploma course was integrated with an apprenticeship and emphasised the practical aspects of architecture and building. [^14] In contrast, the early graduates of the Faculty of Architecture were not, upon graduation, considered technically competent, which created trouble with their registration. Architects who graduated from the faculty were entitled to be registered, but the NSW Board of Architects, as the statutory registration body, was unhappy with the class of graduates being admitted to their ranks. [^15]

Figure 3 — The architectural science workshop on City Road with the McConnell, Smith and Johnson extension to the faculty in the background (after 1976). University of Sydney School of Architecture, Design and Planning.

## An Associate Chair of Architectural Practice and Construction

The Board of Architects of NSW could not formally regulate the curriculum offered by the university but instead used its financial power, prizes and access to government to leverage change. From 1924 onwards, the board offered a travelling scholarship to the value of £400 to one student from both the University of Sydney and the Sydney Technical College. A huge amount, equivalent to half of an associate professor's annual salary, the prize was meant to encourage "the advancement of Architecture," and the members of the board, particularly the president, George Godsell, took the selection of its recipients very seriously.

Difficulties between the university and the board became clear in 1925, when Wilkinson took a sabbatical to return to England. Wilkinson, as Professor of Architecture, was an ex officio member of the eight-person board. At its monthly meeting on 24 August of that year, he reported that his colleague at the university and fellow member of the board, Alfred Hook, would become acting dean. [^16] However, this is not what Wilkinson had arranged with the University Senate when applying for leave. Instead, Wilkinson had proposed that Sir Henry Barraclough, Dean of the Faculty of Engineering and a member of the Faculty

---

[^13]: M Lewis, "The Development of Architectural Teaching in the University of Melbourne," in *Report to the Committee to Consider all Aspects of the Teaching of Architecture and Building in the University* (University of Melbourne, 1970), 111.
[^14]: Freeland, *The Making of a Profession*, 210.
[^15]: Corr. D James to Mr Wood, 20 April 1951 (University of Sydney Archives).

[^16]: Minutes of the 15th Meeting of the Second Board, Sydney (24 August 1925), Minute Books of the Board of Architects of New South Wales. All Board of Architects of NSW documents are sourced from the New South Wales State Archives.

of Architecture, would in fact act as dean in his absence, Hook ultimately being ineligible for this role because he was not a full-time member of the university's staff. When the board learned that an engineer and not an architect would be directing the faculty and potentially joining the board, overlooking their colleague, Hook, they protested to the university in the strongest possible terms. [^17]

Letters were exchanged between the board, the University Registrar, and Vice-Chancellor Mungo MacCallum. Within three months, what had started as a disagreement over faculty representation had become an inquiry into the state of teaching, the tenure of Hook, the quality of architectural graduates, and the appropriate weighting of design and technical teaching in the curriculum. At the board's meeting on 23 November 1925, the President, George Godsell, vented his frustration:

> ... the President expressed as a result of his inquiries the astonishment and disappointment he felt regarding the inadequate provisions existent at the School of Architecture of the University for the education and the training of the students. This of itself did not particularly concern the Board, but when it was remembered that the Board was giving a yearly scholarship of £400 to enable the best graduate of the University to go Home, and that student should be equal to that of the man who passes the final of the RIBA, it was time the Board looked into it, and it was the Board's bounden duty to see that the students generally were receiving proper attention and the Medallion Winners especially were of such a standard that there would be no regrets on the Board's part in having sent them abroad. [^18]

Without a formal requirement to regulate courses in architecture, the board instead sought to protect its prized scholarship, which was only awarded to men at that time, and used this as a pretext to reform the way courses were taught and the faculty staffed. [^19] When the board reviewed the school in December 1925, it expressed its satisfaction with the curriculum but thought there was insufficient instruction and staffing in "General Construction and Office Practice." [^20] To rectify this, they lobbied the Minister of Education and, in 1926, helped secure an additional government grant of £1000 to cover the cost of an Associate Chair of Architectural Building Construction and sought changes to the structure and content of the architecture degree. This change was only partially successful as what initially appeared to be the Board of Architects holding the university to account was also a carefully crafted manoeuvre by Hook (1886-1963) to secure a full-time position at the university.

Hook, an English-born graduate of the Royal College of Art in London, had joined the Faculty of Architecture at the University of Sydney as a part-time lecturer in construction in 1922. As president of the Architects' Association of NSW, he was appointed to the inaugural Board of Architects of NSW that same year. By 1926, the Architects' Association had merged with the IANSW and Hook was elected President of the IANSW. With this new position, Hook remained on the Board of Architects, but, at the Faculty of Architecture, Hook was still subservient to Wilkinson. The criticism of the architecture degree by the Board of Architects occurred in 1925 and 1926, while Wilkinson, also a board member, was absent and after Hook had found out that he was ineligible to act in his stead

[^17]: Minutes of the 16th Meeting of the Second Board, Sydney (14 September 1925).
[^18]: Minutes of the 20th Meeting of the Second Board, Sydney (23 November 1925).
[^19]: Many members of the board were firmly of the view that women were not suited to architecture and actively sought to prevent the award of the scholarship to a woman when Sydney University nominated Marjorie Hudson in 1927. While the board acknowledged it admitted women to their ranks, it also argued that "the future services of a woman architect were not assured in the profession. The practice of architecture in all its phases could not be carried out by a woman. There may be phases where a woman could take her part but architecture was essentially a man's job." Minutes of the 57th Meeting of the Second Board, Sydney (11 July 1927).
[^20]: Minutes of the 22nd Meeting of the Second Board, Sydney (7 December 1925).

at the university. Hook used the Board of Architects' influence to lobby for state funding for a new Chair in Architectural Practice and Construction. With the initial funding secured and no other candidates interviewed, Hook was appointed. In the process, he gained temporary control of the main professional and educational bodies for architects in New South Wales. However, for Hook, his leadership in the Faculty of Architecture was truncated by Wilkinson's return.

The attempts to restructure the degree and to make science courses more directly relevant to architectural education only further distanced the course from science. After the criticism by the Board of Architects in 1926, Wilkinson asked the Faculty of Science to consider offering a composite science course covering the "Chemistry of Building Materials; Botany—the Structure, Growth and Diseases of Timber; Geology of Building Stones; Entomology—insect pests; Physics—acoustics." [^21] The proposal was rejected by the science faculty; instead architecture students were offered the choice to take either a course from the Bachelor of Science (BSc) or a course from the BA. In effect, this further reduced the scientific content of the degree as students could take a course from the humanities rather than the sciences. It was only in late 1927 that Wilkinson sought to control the teaching of construction and structural mechanics, shifting the responsibility to architecture staff, thereby reducing the Faculty of Architecture's previous reliance on the lecturers and rooms of the Faculty of Engineering. [^22] In so doing, the architecture course gained further independence from the Faculty of Engineering, which allowed Wilkinson to enact his vision of architectural education as an education in taste. While Hook's appointment enabled the Faculty of Architecture to develop more technical content in its courses, this came at a cost to the relationship between the university and the profession, as well as to the internal dynamics of the Faculty of Architecture itself.

For the rest of the 1920s and 1930s, as architects struggled with the Great Depression, there was little change in the teaching of construction and no research in this area in the faculty. Building science as a field was largely confined to research at the Building Research Station (BRS) in Britain. The first course in building science was only delivered in 1933, as a collaboration between the BRS and Imperial College of Science and Technology. [^23] In 1939, as Australia entered the war, Wilkinson once more attempted to revive the idea of a composite first year applied science course, but this was curtailed in 1940 due to war-time funding cuts. [^24] Hook produced a textbook, *A Little About Structural Mechanics*, in 1943, but it could hardly be considered innovative and served only to introduce problems of a structural nature to a non-mathematical audience. [^25] As Peter Johnson later reflected on this period, "a scientific approach to architecture was subordinated to an approach based on a general philosophy in which design was predominant." [^26]

Figure 4 — Exhibition of models and scientific apparatus in the architectural science workshops, n.d. University of Sydney School of Architecture, Design and Planning.

[^21]: Minutes of the Meeting of the Faculty of Architecture (9 November 1926), 36. All minutes are held in the University of Sydney Archives.
[^22]: Minutes of the Meeting of the Faculty of Architecture (9 August 1927), 42, 46.
[^23]: "Advanced Course in Building Science," *Architects' Journal* 77 (5 April 1933): 465.
[^24]: Minutes of the Meeting of the Faculty of Architecture (14 October 1939), 100.
[^25]: A Hook, *A Little About Structural Mechanics* (Sydney: Royal Australian Institute of Architects, 1943).
[^26]: RN Johnson, "The Work of the Department of Architectural Science," in *Special Publication on the Occasion of the Twentieth Anniversary of the Department General Report GR6* (Sydney: Department of Architectural Science, University of Sydney, 10 December 1973), 25.

If anything, Hook's legacy was institutional; he was instrumental in forming the national Royal Australian Institute of Architects (RAIA) and in securing a second chair in the faculty. Having side-stepped Wilkinson to become Associate Professor of Architectural Practice and Construction, he failed to gain promotion until 1945, at which point both he and Wilkinson were close to retirement. Hook's definition of his associate chair highlighted the pedagogical and personal schisms that had opened up between the two key staff within the school. He set out the differences between the cultural and technical sides of professional education at the faculty meeting in April 1945:

> The Chair of Architecture is concerned, essentially, with the aesthetic side of the profession; with History, Planning and Design. The Associate Chair of Architectural Practice and Construction is concerned, essentially with the scientific and legal sides; with the construction of buildings, with their mechanical and other equipment, and with Building Law and the Law of Arbitration. It is manifestly essential that an architect should be trained in both sides of the profession, and it is undesirable (as leading to a false set of values) that there should be any material differences in the status of the Chairs concerned. [^27]

It is worth noting that Hook's definition emphasised the chairs' roles in training architects. There was no question of how either chair advanced new knowledge, though this occurred in the same meeting in which the faculty was considering introducing a new research degree, the Master of Architecture. It is also clear that Hook defined the remit for each chair very broadly, touching on all that an architect might need to know a little of but with little sense of specialisation. Instead, Hook argued for the elevation to Chair in Architectural Practice and Construction on economic and service grounds; that is, that he had successfully obtained government funding for his position that would more than cover the cost of any salary increase and that he had been in the same position for 19 years. [^28] Hook's petition was successful, and the faculty recommended upgrading Hook's position to a full chair. This was passed by the University Senate on 12 August 1946. Hook's victory would be short-lived in one sense; within four years, under a new dean, his chair would be under threat once more. However, what did endure, through his promotion and strident defence of the chair he helped create, was a formal commitment by the faculty in the years that followed to a more thorough technical education for its graduates. It was a commitment that was aided by debates within Britain and Australia, during and immediately after the war, on the role of science in architectural education.

## The RIBA and Architectural Science

Whereas at the turn of the 20th century leading architects believed that the profession would gain power by presenting itself as a cultural pursuit, by the Second World War, architects in Britain (within the RIBA) and a number in Australia thought that science held the key to professional standing. As Chang has noted, this period saw building science become more integrated with architecture, a move that was catalysed by the formation in 1939 of the Architectural Science Group (ASG) in Britain, a gathering of key architects and engineers set up by the RIBA in close cooperation with the BRS. [^29] The group was tasked with understanding how to apply the scientific method to the planning and design of buildings. [^30] Of its four committees—Economics, Sociology, Planning and Design, and Education—it was the Education Committee that had most influence on the post-war future of architecture at universities.

[^27]: Minutes of the Meeting of the Faculty of Architecture (17 April 1945), 113.
[^28]: Minutes of the Meeting of the Faculty of Architecture (17 April 1945), 114.
[^29]: Chang, *A Genealogy of Tropical Architecture*, 228.
[^30]: "Research and Planning for Reconstruction," *Journal of the Royal Institute of British Architects* (hereafter *JRIBA*) (18 November 1940): 4.

Rather than just recommend changes to building design, the Education Committee of the ASG believed the profession's "scientisation" could only happen by reforming the training of architects. It envisaged a future profession that was "intelligently aware of the full implications of science considered not only as a laboratory affair but as a method of thought and action." [^31] The committee considered that, while tradition had allowed all members of the building industry to communicate easily, the rapid changes in the composition of the industry and the nature of the problems to be tackled meant that this was no longer the case. Instead, the scientific method, in the eyes of the committee, was the main solution to the problem of preparing architects for an uncertain future.

Its criticism of tradition and its emphasis on science as a modern mode of thought and action closely aligned the ASG with the modernist camp within the RIBA. At this time, as Crinson and Lubbock have shown, the beaux arts system of education was being challenged by a group of hard-line modernists centred on the Modern Architecture Research Society (MARS) and on students aligned to EAA Rowse at the Architectural Association (AA). Terms such as "science" and "research" were used liberally, to the point of vacuousness, as the historian Andrew Saint has argued. [^32] Research, Saint points out, could mean a return to first principles, social studies, an examination of a construction junction, or simply sourcing and collating information from printed sources. [^33] Yet the development of a scientific outlook and the inculcation of research practices were both seen as important means to produce an architect more able to deal with the increasing complexity of building in a post-war society. In addition, science applied to building, with its thermal, visual, acoustic, structural and sociological approaches, was considered by many within these circles to be overly fragmented. A number of commentators argued that architects were best placed to coordinate and integrate scientific knowledge from the early stages of a design's development.

**Figure 5** — Demonstration model of bending in a frame structure. University of Sydney School of Architecture, Design and Planning.

The ASG's committee produced three reports and instituted a series of lectures to inform the public of the latest developments in science applied to architecture. *The Place of Science in Architectural Education*, published in June 1941, was its first and most influential report. It set out problems and opportunities in the application of science to architectural education. It then offered an educational framework that sought to raise scientific knowledge among students by making the study of science mandatory prior to their arrival at the university. It also recommended the development of undergraduate scientific knowledge, preferably through a new course in building science. [^34]

[^31]: "Science and Architectural Education," *JRIBA* 48 (June 1941): 131.
[^32]: A Saint, *Towards a Social Architecture: The Role of School-Building in Post-War England* (New Haven, CT: Yale University Press, 1987), 11
[^33]: Saint, *Towards a Social Architecture*, 11.
[^34]: "The Place of Science in Architectural Education: The First Report of the Education Committee of the Architectural Science Group of the RIBA Research Board," *JRIBA* 48, no. 8 (1941): 135.

Within the architectural press, the work of the ASG and debates about the "correct" relationship between art and science filled up many an issue of the *Architect's Journal* throughout the 1940s and 1950s. While the journal firmly advocated for an increased place for science in architectural education and practice, its editorials clearly show that not all members of the profession were convinced. Some architects worried that they had to master all the scientific facts and could only at best gain a potted knowledge of science. Others feared that science would negatively impact design. In 1946, discussing the impact of the adoption of a more scientific outlook in curricula, Cecil C Handisyde pointed out that it was "evident that a number of architects, including quite a lot of teachers, are apprehensive about this change. They fear that architectural teaching may become a matter of formulae and that the finer points of design will be lost." [^35] It was this fear of science's impact on design that saw traditionalists, some of whom were members of the RIBA's Board of Architectural Education, resist the ASG's report on architectural education. By 1946, when the Board of Architectural Education produced its own report on the matter, the ASG's ideas about architectural education were rejected in favour of a vision of architecture centred on the profession as an art. It would be another 12 years until the Oxford Conference of 1958 saw ASG's ideas enacted and science placed at the centre of architectural education in British schools.

## Constructing a Chair in Architectural Science

As the role of science in architecture was being rethought, debated, and in some cases advocated in schools and in the architectural press in Britain, a similar interest in scientific research applied to architecture was emerging in Australia. The difference was that, prior to the Second World War, there was little in the way of building research infrastructure in Australia, and many of the debates and proposed solutions were indebted to what was happening in Britain. However, war changed Australian practice, bringing what Philip Goad and Julie Willis have termed a "circumstantial modernism," [^36] in which Australian architects came into contact with American engineering practice. Many were tasked with detailed research on specialist military requirements for construction.

Building research was formally instituted in Australia in 1943, when a number of modernist architects such as Walter Bunning and Leighton Irwin, who were active in education and government, convinced the Commonwealth Government of the need to fund scientific building research as part of the post-war housing program. The result, the Commonwealth Experimental Building Station, saw architects and engineers attached to the Commonwealth Housing Commission working together to test material assemblies, develop and test prefabricated building systems, and produce new guidelines for climate sensitive design. [^37] Building research during the immediate post-war era was valued by the government as a means to accelerate and manage the large-scale post-war housing program. Australia was not alone in this regard, its program joining nationally funded building research programs in South Africa, the United States and, to an extent, Israel, which were all closely linked to research and experimentation in post-war housing. [^38]

While architects in Britain debated the role of science in architecture during the war and in its immediate aftermath, in Australia this did not occur in earnest until 1948 and 1949, when the RAIA organised its first Architectural Education Conference. The conference proposed that architects be trained, not just in planning and design, but also structural engineering and architectural

[^35]: CC Handisyde, "The Relation of Science to Architectural Teaching," *Architects' Journal* 104, no. 2705 (28 November 1946): 401.
[^36]: P Goad and J Willis, "Invention from War: A Circumstantial Modernism for Australian Architecture," *Fabrications* 8, no. 1 (2003): 41-62.
[^37]: DJ Ryan, "Settling the Thermal Frontier: The Tropical House in Northern Queensland from Federation to the Second World War" (PhD diss., University of Sydney, 2017), 30.
[^38]: O Aleksandrowicz, "Appearance and Performance: Israeli Building Climatology and its Effect on Local Architectural Practice (1940–1977)," *Architectural Science Review* (hereafter *ASR*) 60, no. 5 (2017): 374.

engineering, and it suggested the establishment of post-graduate courses in building science. Blythe credits Frederick Towndrow, the newly appointed Head Of Architecture and Building at Sydney Technical College, for much of the institute's embrace of science at this time. [^39] Towndrow had come from England and, during the war, was British Controller of Experimental Building Development at the UK Ministry of Works and served on the Building Research Committee. [^40] In 1949, he drafted a proposal for postgraduate education in architectural science for the NSW Board of Architectural Education, which was ratified and promoted by the RAIA as a model for other states to follow. [^41] However, by July 1950, an editorial by Stella Tottenham in the IANSW's journal, *Architecture*, argued against postgraduate courses in favour of better undergraduate training. The RAIA's president from 1946 to 1948, William R Laurie (himself one of Sydney's first graduates in architecture), firmly believed in early specialisation, later arguing that "it is very seldom that a member of our profession is guided from the earliest moment in which he commences his studies towards a definite aim in the practice of architecture, either with regard to the type of building with which he hopes to be associated, or to the technical aspect of our work in which he hopes to be competent." [^42]

The Heads of Schools of Architecture in Australia and New Zealand did not agree with Laurie though, and, in 1950, they firmly stated their "strong disapproval that undergraduate training should be subdivided into specialist fields." [^43] In principle, there was enthusiasm for science within the institute, but the mechanisms to bring architecture and science together, whether through undergraduate training or postgraduate specialisation, were the source of considerable debate. However, despite the interest in science applied to buildings among modernists and within government

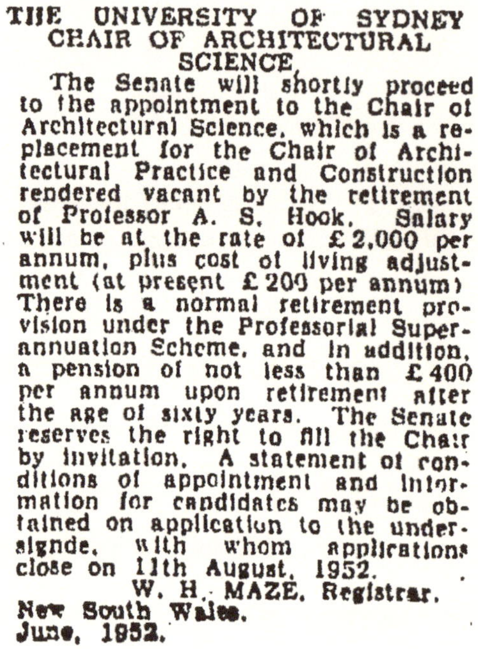
THE UNIVERSITY OF SYDNEY
CHAIR OF ARCHITECTURAL SCIENCE.

The Senate will shortly proceed to the appointment to the Chair of Architectural Science, which is a replacement for the Chair of Architectural Practice and Construction rendered vacant by the retirement of Professor A. S. Hook. Salary will be at the rate of £2,000 per annum, plus cost of living adjustment (at present £200 per annum). There is a normal retirement provision under the Professorial Superannuation Scheme, and in addition, a pension of not less than £400 per annum upon retirement after the age of sixty years. The Senate reserves the right to fill the Chair by invitation. A statement of conditions of appointment and information for candidates may be obtained on application to the undersignde, with whom applications close on 11th August, 1952.

W. H. MAZE, Registrar.

New South Wales.
June, 1952.

**Figure 6** — Newspaper advertisement for the Chair in Architectural Science. *Sydney Morning Herald*, 21 June 1952.

during the war, the Faculty of Architecture at the University of Sydney maintained its conservative outlook across the 1940s. Instead of turning outward to engage with the post-war problems of the state, Wilkinson and Hook, both close to retirement age, were caught up in internecine rivalry. Hook had managed to get the University Senate to establish a full Chair of Professional Practice, but this further antagonised Wilkinson. Both professors stopped communicating with each other up to Wilkinson's retirement in 1947, after which Hook briefly took over as dean. Wilkinson's successor as Chair of Architecture, the English-born architect, Ashworth, joined the faculty in 1949 and replaced Hook as dean in 1950. Unbeknownst to Hook, Ashworth and the Vice-Chancellor planned to terminate the Chair of Architectural Practice and Construction upon Hook's retirement. [^44] Ashworth argued that "two chairs of equal standing in

[^39]: Blythe, "Science Enthusiasts," 124.
[^40]: "NSW University of Technology Foundation Chair in Architecture," *Architecture* 37, no. 3 (July 1949): 69.
[^41]: Blythe, "Science Enthusiasts," 122.
[^42]: *Architecture* 40, no. 1 (January-March 1952): 12.
[^43]: "Heads of School Conference," *Architecture* 38, no. 4 (October-December 1950): 121.

[^44]: Ashworth later alluded that, at his own job interview in London in 1948, the university already planned to end the Chair of Architectural Practice and Construction on Hook's retirement. Memo. H Ingham Ashworth to the Vice Chancellor, 11 November 1951 (University of Sydney Archives).

the same subject (Architecture) are certain to create dissension and divided control" and instead proposed to the Vice-Chancellor that the Professor of Engineering take a more active role in teaching student architects in later years of the course. [^45]

Ashworth's attempt to shore up power early in his deanship was only partially successful. He ensured that he was the only Professor of Architecture for the rest of his time at the university but he lost the argument to abolish the Chair of Architectural Practice and Construction. Although the University Senate initially supported Ashworth and passed a motion not to fill the chair at the end of 1950, it reversed its decision at the end of 1951 after a concerted campaign by Hook and the architectural profession. The profession's representative bodies, the RAIA and the Board of Architectural Education, wanted to keep the chair and feared that its loss would damage the profession's status. The NSW chapter of the RAIA supported Hook. They reminded the Vice-Chancellor of their role in securing government funding for the chair in 1926 and the continuing relevance of technical education. "The increasing complexity of modern building," the chapter's secretary wrote, "is tending to demand a higher degree of specialised teaching in our schools than heretofore, and the whole subject is a complex one." [^46] The chair was saved, but would be retitled the Chair in Architectural Science, a reference to the RIBA's discussion about the teaching of science in architecture during the war and more recently within the NSW chapter in 1949.

Naming the chair provoked considerable discussion over its perceived status, purpose, and faculty affiliation. The Vice-Chancellor, Stephen H Roberts, drew up a committee comprised of himself, the Registrar, the Dean of the Faculty of Architecture, and relevant heads of department such as the Professor of Town and Country Planning (Denis Winston), the Professor of Civil Engineering (JW Roderick), the Dean of the Faculty of Arts (Ralph B Farrell), and the Professor of Aeronautical Engineering (AV Stephens). He also consulted with members of the architectural profession, including Laurie, past president of the RAIA (1946–48), and Cobden Parkes, the NSW Government Architect and Chair of the Architects' Registration Board of NSW. A number of names were considered by the committee, among them Chair in Architectural Science, Chair in Structural Design, Chair in Structural Design and Equipment, Chair in Building Science, and Chair in Architectural Technology. [^47]

Ashworth believed that the title should have both clarity and brevity and firmly supported naming it the Chair in Architectural Science. He rejected the second and third options as he felt they would cause confusion as to which faculty the chair belonged, implying that people would more likely associate a Chair in Structural Design with the Faculty of Engineering rather than architecture. The fourth and fifth options also were not deemed worthy of university status, showing the snobbery that still resided over the inclusion of building and technology in the academy, noting that "both savour of a technological institute." Not only that, the title had to sound proper; he noted of the last options that it "is not a euphonious title." [^48] On the other hand, Laurie thought it should be named the Chair in Applied Science in Architecture, a title Ashworth rejected as too cumbersome. However, not everyone was convinced that the chair should be named a Chair in Architectural Science. Laurie was against such a title as he thought that it did not capture the applied nature of the teaching or the connection with building construction. [^49] Cobden Parkes agreed with Laurie, suggesting that "'Science' may be considered too confusing as associated with 'Architecture' and should be termed 'Applied

[^45]: Memo. Ashworth to the Vice-Chancellor via the Registrar, 28 November 1950 (University of Sydney Archives).
[^46]: Corr. JD Storrie of the Royal Australian Institute of Architects to the Registrar, 28 February 1951 (University of Sydney Archives).
[^47]: Corr. Ashworth to the Vice-Chancellor, 26 March 1952, Title of the Second Chair in the Faculty of Architecture (University of Sydney Archives).
[^48]: Corr. Ashworth to the Vice-Chancellor, 26 March 1952.
[^49]: Corr. WR Laurie to the Vice-Chancellor, 15 February 1952. Applications for Chair in Architectural Science (University of Sydney Archives).

Science'." [^50] Yet in the end, though leading architects were not convinced, Ashworth's argument prevailed with the Vice-Chancellor, and the chair was named the Chair in Architectural Science.

In both Britain and Australia, the concern for technical education masked a widespread anxiety, particularly among those in the modernist camp that, as buildings became more technical, the architecture profession could lose its leading role on construction projects. There was the risk that architects would have to consult engineers rather than the other way around, as was the general practice at this time. [^51] Rather than other professions taking power from architects, the general strategy through the 1950s and 1960s was, instead, for architects to expand their own knowledge, if not their role, by bringing more professionals into their field as educators. While before the Second World War, the architecture faculty at the University of Sydney had been staffed solely by architects and a stained glass artist, by the end of the 1960s, engineers, geographers, town planners, social scientists, and artists all found a home teaching future generations of architects.

## "Scientising" Undergraduate Architectural Education

When the Chair in Architectural Science was advertised in 1952, the information sheet given to candidates betrayed how unclear the university was about what exactly a Professor of Architectural Science would do and should know. Its future occupant, Cowan, did not think it was particularly informative and after his appointment had to research exactly what the field might entail. [^52] Candidates were told simply that the professor would be expected to teach "structural design, equipment of buildings and properties of materials." [^53] There was no information given about research expectations, although, at this time, professors in architecture schools were known more for their contribution to teaching than research per se. As Cowan later noted, for such an unusual chair, the first to be called "architectural science," more effort was spent explaining how the position could be terminated than suggesting the qualities and experience of an ideal candidate. [^54] Given the fraught process involved in creating the chair and the university's desire to avoid the internal discord that had characterised the end of Wilkinson and Hook's time at the faculty, the vague description allowed the university to gather a wide range of candidates and ensure that the future chair was capable but unlikely to cause discord [Figure 6].

Nine architects and two engineers applied for the position. Among the rejected candidates was the Canadian architect and educator Frederic Lasserre, who played a leading role in developing the School of Architecture at the University of British Columbia in Vancouver. However, Ashworth had an engineer in mind rather than an architect and was wary of candidates overstating their suitability. "I am not looking for an Architect with an 'interest' in these subjects," he wrote of Lasserre, "but an 'expert' in the fields referred to and who would supplement the Architectural course in these specific aspects." [^55] Having tried to end the Chair in Architectural Practice and Construction, it would seem Ashworth was loath to have another architect as a potential rival. Instead, he sought an engineer.

The committee unanimously chose Cowan, the youngest applicant [Figure 7]. He was the only one with teaching experience in the field,

[^50]: Corr. C Parkes to WH Maze, 6 March 1952, Applications for Chair in Architectural Science, 32 (University of Sydney Archives).
[^51]: Emeritus Professor Jack Cowan interviewing members of the Institution of Engineers Australia, Sydney Division, 26 May 1992 (State Library of New South Wales).
[^52]: HJ Cowan, *A Contradiction in Terms* (Sydney: Department of Architectural and Design Science, University of Sydney, Hermitage Press, 1993), 73–74.
[^53]: "The University of Sydney, Chair in Architectural Science— Conditions of Appointment," May 1952, Applications for Chair in Architectural Science, 32 (University of Sydney Archives).
[^54]: Cowan, *A Contradiction in Terms*, 73.
[^55]: Corr. Ashworth to WH Maze, 6 August 1952 (University of Sydney Archives).

gained at Cardiff University and the University of Sheffield, and a doctorate, also gained at Sheffield, which was on "Reinforced Concrete in Combined Bending and Torsion." [^56] Born in 1919, in Glogau (Silesia), in what had become East Germany by 1952, Cowan matriculated and received his university education in England, having moved there as a Jewish refugee in 1933. He completed his undergraduate and masters degrees in engineering at the University of Manchester before being upended once more due to war. Despite his family background, in 1940 he was interned in Liverpool and then sent to Quebec. He returned to fight with the British Army, first in the Pioneer Corps and then the Royal Engineers, which he considered "a moral obligation." [^57] After being discharged for medical reasons, he gained some industry experience, working on aluminium homes before returning to academia; at Cardiff and Sheffield, he developed courses in soil mechanics (among the first in Britain) and taught architects about concrete using models and laboratory testing [Figures 4 and 5].

When Cowan arrived in Australia, he brought with him experience in implementing the type of technical education the RIBA's Architectural Science Board (ASB) had proposed. At Cardiff, he had worked under one of the ASB's members and former deputy director of the Building Research Establishment, Norman Thomas, and had proven himself an able organiser. [^58] Afterwards, at Sheffield, he showed that he knew how to engage architecture students in engineering problems. [^59] Although much of his education was British, he did not

**Figure 7**—Professor Henry J Cowan, 1984. University of Sydney Archives.

place London at the centre of his intellectual milieu. He had a deep knowledge of European culture and languages and an interest in the latest engineering developments in the United States. On accepting the chair, he reviewed the ASB's report and was aware of the debates and some of the perceived difficulties of a hybrid and emerging field like architectural science. He actively sought out key figures in academia and building research, among whom was the Director of the BRS, Sir Frederick Lea, who informed him of the BRS's then unsuccessful attempts to institute chairs of building science at the universities of Edinburgh and Liverpool. He visited the Professor of Architecture at Liverpool, RJ Gardner-Medwin, who gave further insight into the departmental politics of creating a chair of building science and the issues for architects of having such a chair located in engineering. Later, Cowan called on the Head of the Architectural Association School of Architecture, who famously told him that architectural science was "a contradiction in terms." [^60] After an eight-month period of reading key reports and talking to prominent figures, Cowan came to Australia well aware of the state of his emerging field and determined to take a leading role in shaping it.

Starting at the University of Sydney in 1953, Cowan was effectively a department of only one person. The part-time lecturers who taught construction, such as Eric Andrews, all reported to the Chair of Architecture, Ashworth. Cowan was not impressed by the state of technical teaching in the architecture degree, and, over the course of 1953 and 1954, he consulted widely with leading members of the architecture profession in Australia. [^61]

[^56]: HJ Cowan, "Reinforced Concrete in Combined Bending and Torsion" (PhD diss., University of Sheffield, 1952).
[^57]: Cowan, *A Contradiction in Terms*, 33.
[^58]: Cowan, *A Contradiction in Terms*, 55–57.
[^59]: Cowan, interview, 26 May 1992.
[^60]: Cowan, *A Contradiction in Terms*, 75.
[^61]: Cowan, *A Contradiction in Terms*, 83.

In 1953, only 123 hours of the whole undergraduate course in architecture were dedicated to teaching scientific content at the University of Sydney. This was only 14 percent of what undergraduates at the NSW University of Technology received. [^62] There, with Frederick Towndrow in charge, the degree was heavily weighted in favour of lecture courses, with students in the first three years taking courses in building science, physics, chemistry, and geology. The scientific emphasis was reinforced for students at the end of their degree (in their fifth or sixth year), when they were expected to produce a thesis in "Architectural Science and Research." [^63] In contrast, the University of Sydney degree, like its Melbourne counterpart, had fewer lecture courses, placing greater emphasis on studio instruction. [^64] Cowan sought to radically overhaul the architecture course, proposing new lecture courses and laboratory courses in natural science, structural design, soil mechanics and building science in the first three years. However, his colleagues in architecture were initially resistant to such radical change.

Although Cowan had the support of Professor Denis Winston in Planning, Ashworth and a few of his colleagues in the architecture department initially vetoed the course's implementation. The University Senate approved the new courses, but Cowan did not receive funding for new teaching positions to implement them, in effect quashing his initial proposal. Cowan recounts that Ashworth advised him afterwards to "relax and accept the status quo," that way he "could have a pleasant life on a good salary if he did not rock the boat." [^65] Richard Blythe suggests that Ashworth helped introduce a scientific outlook to architecture at the university, but, in Cowan's early years, he did not always have Ashworth's backing, having to fight to gain his support. [^66] However, by the end of 1955, Cowan had managed to table a new course in architectural science and to organise a committee to look at the teaching of a new course in building materials. By 1956, this resulted in over 600 hours of scientific content in the architecture course, a considerable shift from three years prior. [^67]

## Developing a Cadre of Building Scientists

As the only Chair in Architectural Science, Cowan was determined to build up the field. Initially focused on Australia, he also communicated his efforts abroad by creating a journal with an international readership and regularly lecturing overseas. While trying to effect change in the undergraduate course, Cowan also sought to educate practising architects and engineers in architectural science. Taking a leaf out of the Vernon Memorial Lectures in Town Planning and lectures in London during the war, Cowan gathered together many of the leading local experts in scientific building research and practice to give a course run by the Sydney University Extension Board in "Some Recent Developments in Architectural Science" in 1954. [^68] The lectures were jointly hosted with the NSW Institute of Technology but took place at the University of Sydney's Law School in the central business district. They covered everything from the "Design of Buildings in Relation to Fire" to "Design of Concrete Mixers." [^69] The speakers included JW Drysdale of the Commonwealth Experimental Building Station, who had directed the station's Climate and House Design Program after the war, and William Laurie, one of the key advocates for the chair Cowan now occupied. [^70] The lectures were successfully

[^62]: HJ Cowan, "The Place of Science in Architectural Education," *ASR* 3, no. 3 (1960): 2.
[^63]: *University of Melbourne Calendar* (Melbourne: Melbourne University Press, 1953), 196–97.
[^64]: *University Calendar* (University of Sydney, 1953); NSW Institute of Technology Calendar (Sydney: NSW Institute of Technology Press, 1953), 121–25.
[^65]: Cowan, *A Contradiction in Terms*, 85.
[^66]: Blythe, "Science Enthusiasts," 122.
[^67]: Architectural Science from years one to five consisted of a total of 246 lectures and 252 hours of practical hours, while Natural Science consisted of a total of 85 lectures. The total number of hours assume one hour per lecture. *University Calendar* (1956), 1046–51.
[^68]: See Paul Jones' discussion in Chapter 2.
[^69]: "Sydney University Extension Board," *Construction* (18 August 1954): 4.
[^70]: "Sydney University Extension Board," 4.

Figure 8 — Pamphlet for the second series of Sydney University Extension Board lectures on architectural science, 1955. From the Baldwinson papers, Mitchell Library, State Library of New South Wales.

attended, with delegates including the architect Neville Gruzman and students such as Richard Aynsley, who would go on to gain an international reputation in architectural aerodynamics [Figure 8]. [^71]

The lectures also formed the basis for the launch of a new journal in architectural science. Through Cowan's strategic management, the lectures expanded beyond the requirements of a local audience and helped establish an international audience for his efforts in Sydney. In the process, awareness of the teaching, facilities and debates about architectural science in Australia grew overseas, and by 1960 figures such as the German-born tropical housing expert Otto Koenigsburger and the British lighting engineer RG Hopkinson were contributing to the journal. [^72]

The journal emerged when local architects and engineers asked Cowan for a permanent record of the extension course. Cowan was approached by a commercial publisher who was willing to fund its publication through advertising. After the first two series of the extension board lectures, Cowan identified the need for a journal to allow scientists and architects to communicate with each other, thus *Architectural Science Review*. Cowan used the term scientist rather broadly, with meteorologists, physicists, materials scientists, public health doctors, and civil, mechanical and lighting engineers all published within two years of the journal's inception. Architects like Harry Seidler and Karl Langer and the architectural historian David Saunders also contributed articles in 1959 and 1960. [^73] Through the journal, the department not only became a clearing house for the latest ideas in architectural science, but was also able to build up the faculty's library by exchanging copies of the journal for technical reports from overseas research institutions. His experience with this journal also meant that Cowan was called on to help set up the journal *Building Science* and later *Energy in Buildings*, both of which continue to the present day.

Although the undergraduate training of architects was always important to Cowan, he also saw a need for research in architectural science. In 1960, he argued that it was not enough to have building research organisations but that somebody needed to train future research scientists. He believed this was best done in a university. [^74] The university provided laboratory space for architectural science in a former broom factory on City Road.

[^71]: Architectural Science Course, 1993 (University of Sydney Archives).

[^72]: O Koenigsburger, JS Millar and J Costopolous, "Window and Ventilator Openings in Warm and Humid Climates," *ASR* 1, no. 2 (1959): 82–96; RG Hopkinson, "Subjective Studies of the Efficiency of Buildings, with Special Reference to Lighting," *ASR* 3, no. 2 (1960): 48–51.

[^73]: K Langer, "Architectural Planning in Relation to Radiation," *ASR* 3, no. 2 (1960): 73–77; H Seidler, "Sunlight and Architecture," *ASR* 1, no. 1 (1959): 47–48; DAL Saunders, "The Reinforced Dome of Melbourne Public Library, 1911," *ASR* 1, no. 1 (1959): 39–46.

[^74]: HJ Cowan, "The Place of Science in Architectural Education," *ASR* 3, no. 3 (1960): 7.

The move gave Cowan, aided by Technical Officer John Dixon and Lecturer Day Ding, the space to make demonstration models, run tutorials, and test materials. [^75] A proposal for a Master of Building Science was rejected by the faculty in 1956. [^76] Instead, Cowan used the Master of Architecture to develop the research skills of a number of promising students, including Peter Smith and Bill BP Lim. Students took advantage of the model workshop and research in shell structures that Cowan was advancing. After completing their masters degrees, both Smith and Lim would go on to undertake doctoral studies. Smith was the first and Lim the second in the faculty to be awarded a PhD, in 1963 and 1965, respectively. [^77] They were joined five years later by Carolyn E Mather (also of the Department of Architectural Science), who was the first woman in the faculty to be awarded a PhD. [^78]

While Cowan was aware that undergraduate specialisation was a contentious issue, having been debated by the Australian heads of schools in 1952 and having created difficulties when implemented in Britain, he still believed that some specialisation was necessary to deal with the increasing complexity of building. It was an approach he thought necessary for both architects and engineers. [^79] While he had sympathy for the integration of architecture and engineering, he recognised that any undergraduate course in architectural engineering (as the field was known in the United States) or building science (as it was known in Britain and, to an extent, in Australia) could create difficulties obtaining professional recognition. Instead, Cowan suggested that it would be better to create a postgraduate degree with entry restricted to those who were already entitled to more general professional registration. He believed that, in this way, architects could gain better technical understanding and engineers would gain the training required for practice in the building industry. [^80] Recast thus, the Master of Building Science (MBSc) degree first took enrolments in 1963 and allowed him to put his ideas into practice. [^81]

The MBSc provided the fledgling Department of Architectural Science (still only three people: Cowan, Ding and Clarke) a focus at a time when relations between the departments of architecture and architectural science had distanced. Cowan suggests that the department's move into the architectural science laboratory improved research but undermined collegial bonds as there was less time and chance for daily encounters between the two departments, and architecture students resented having to traipse from the architecture rooms in

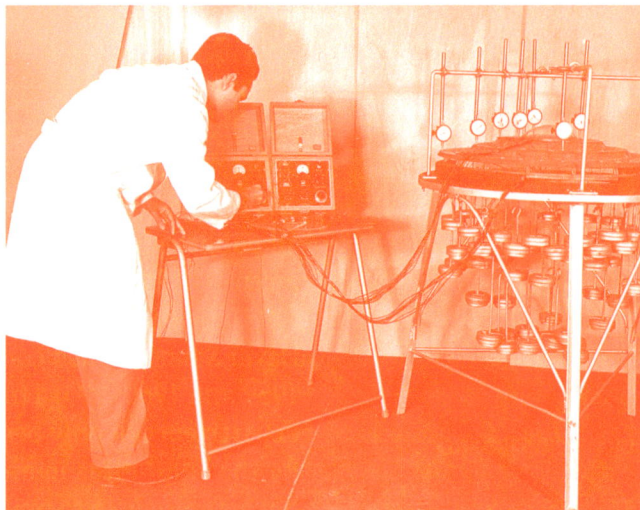

Figure 9 — A researcher testing a model folded plate dome for Granville Returned Servicemen's League Club, early 1960s. University of Sydney School of Architecture, Design and Planning.

[^75]: Cowan, *A Contradiction in Terms*, 98.
[^76]: Minutes of the Meeting of the Faculty of Architecture, 3 August 1956, 234 (University of Sydney Archives).
[^77]: PR Smith, "The Use of Precast Structural Elements in Major Architectural Projects: with Particular Reference to the Application of Prestressing to Three-Dimensional Structures" (PhD diss., University of Sydney, 1963); BP Lim, "The Use of Shallow Concrete Domes in Architecture" (PhD diss., University of Sydney, 1965).
[^78]: CE Mather, "Some Aspects of the Aircraft Noise Problem in the Vicinity of Sydney (Kingsford-Smith) Airport" (PhD diss., University of Sydney, 1970).
[^79]: HJ Cowan, "The Place of Science in Architectural Education," *ASR* 3, no. 3 (1960): 5–6.
[^80]: HJ Cowan, "An Enquiry into the Post-Graduate Training of Architects and their Technical Consultants," *ASR* 5, no. 3 (1962): 100.
[^81]: *University Calendar* (1963), 255–56.

the Quadrangle to the architectural science laboratory on City Road. [^82] The degree, which was offered on both part-time and full-time bases, consisted of courses in "Functional Efficiency of Buildings," "Building Services," "Architectural Structures," "Building Materials," "Scientific Methods in Building," "History of Building Science" and either "Natural Science" or "Building Construction," with the optional courses allowing architects to obtain fundamental scientific knowledge, and engineers fundamental construction knowledge. [^83] The broad coverage of aspects of building science seems very general today, but initially most architects considered it to be a very specialised course. [^84] It is worth noting the inclusion of a course in history, which derived from guest lectures Cowan developed when on sabbatical at MIT and Cornell in 1961 and 1962. [^85] In attempting to bridge architecture and science, Cowan attempted, not only to get architects to adopt experimental methods in the laboratory, but also to use familiar approaches by using historical precedent to consider scientific problems. As with *Architectural Science Review*, Cowan hoped that an historical awareness of environmental design and industrialised building might bridge the gap between architectural and scientific worldviews.

The MBSc degree was a useful training ground for architects and engineers, attracting students from both professions. In its first 12 years, 67 students graduated. Of those, 31 were engineers, with the remainder of the students mostly having a previous degree in architecture. The predictions made by Stella Tottenham, that few would take up a masters degree in building science, were only partly true. After an initial surge of interest, where firms paid the fees for their employees, enrolments tapered off. This was partly offset by the enrolment of students from Southeast Asia and Africa sponsored by the Australian Government's Colombo Plan, as well as others from Singapore, Hong Kong, the United States and Great Britain. [^86] The degree created a small cadre of building scientists, facilitating a steady supply of assistants and future lecturers for the Department of Architectural Science and a number of graduates who would gain leadership positions in both industry and academia.

This development over a decade or so allowed the field to grow its numbers and foster a particular outlook towards architecture and science, one that the research architect Mather described as teaching her to "think of building production as a system," conversing with other building professions and working within financial, regulatory and manufacturing constraints. [^87] Graduates gained key positions at a number of universities around the world. Day Ding and Jens Pohl, for instance, moved to Cal Poly San Luis Obispo, while Lim became Professor of Building Science and Dean of the Faculty of Architecture at the University of Singapore, setting up a similar architectural science laboratory to that in Sydney. [^88]

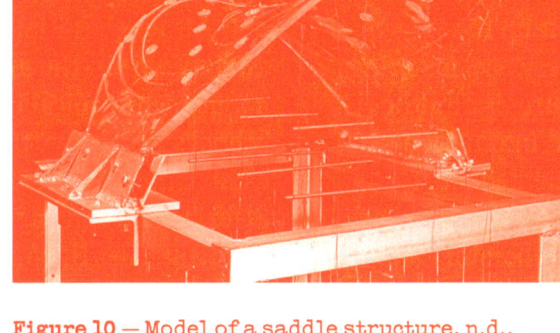

Figure 10 — Model of a saddle structure, n.d., University of Sydney School of Architecture, Design and Planning.

[^82]: Cowan, *A Contradiction in Terms*, 98–99.
[^83]: *University Calendar* (1963), 256.
[^84]: Cowan, *A Contradiction in Terms*, 133.
[^85]: Cowan, *An Historical Outline of Architectural Science* (London: Elsevier Publishing, 1966), vi.

[^86]: Cowan, *A Contradiction in Terms*, 132.
[^87]: Mather, "Comments from Former Students," in *General Report GR6: Special Publication on the Occasion of the Twentieth Anniversary of the Department* (Sydney: Department of Architectural Science, 1973), 36–37.
[^88]: BP Lim, "Putting Science into Buildings: A Review of the Work and Development of the Department of Building Science, University of Singapore, 1970–75," *Singapore Institute of Architects Journal* 76 (May/June 1976), 6–13.

Many of the students who undertook the MBSc, such as Smith, John Gero, Warren Julian and Mike Rosenman, later joined the Department of Architectural Science as it expanded during the 1960s and 1970s.

When Cowan arrived in 1953, there was uncertainty about the nature of his role and the impact it could have. By 1973, he had put in place the institutional basis for his field, with a laboratory, journal, more technical content at undergraduate level, a postgraduate course, a network of alumni in Australia, and consulting roles on some of the major building projects being developed in Sydney at the time. Cowan's chair emerged out of a rivalry between two people with competing visions of architecture: Wilkinson, who saw design as the cultivation of individual taste for the benefit of society; and Hook, who emphasised professional and technical competence. Where Hook helped build up the institutions of architecture, enabling federation of the profession, Cowan built up the institutions of architectural science, fostering its dissemination through journals and the research training of local and international students. He carefully documented most aspects of his department, publishing articles on every development at the laboratory and on the projects on which it consulted, from the Siding Spring Observatory telescope support frame to the MLC tower.

He accepted the gradual decline in research activity in his own area of expertise, while recognising and fostering emerging areas long before many in the architectural profession fully realised their potential. As he presciently noted on his retirement to the Vice-Chancellor, John Manning Ward, in 1983:

> The demand for a more natural environment in air conditioned buildings will, in my opinion, also increase, as will the demand for more daylight, unadulterated by heat-absorbing glass ... There is a distinct possibility that computers in the foreseeable future may be used not merely for working drawings but also for presentation drawing ... Decision-making is the most important new development in architectural computing. [^89]

Fast-forward 35 years and the School of Architecture, Design and Planning continues to lead research efforts in the areas of indoor environmental quality, coding and architectural design that Cowan sketched out. Although initially driven by a local anxiety within the architectural profession about the technical competencies of the school's graduates, the events that led to the establishment of the Chair in Architectural Science, and the appointment of Cowan in particular, set the path towards an influential discipline. Architectural science, through the efforts and persistence of many, both within and beyond the institution, came to contribute significantly to a century of debate about the future challenges of architectural practice and education. ▥

---

[^89]: Cowan, *A Contradiction in Terms*, 233.

# The Inaugural Wilkinson Lecture

**Introduction —** The University of Sydney School of Architecture, Design and Planning has had a long tradition of engaging with politics and policy. Recent examples include the Planning Research Centre's regular invitation to the Planning Minister of the day to provide their vision for the city. In 2013, the night that the Minister of Planning, Brad Hazzard, defended his draft Planning Bill in front of a raucous full house on campus, was a great example of democracy in action. However, the most significant political address given in the faculty was probably the first Wilkinson Lecture for the Sydney University Architecture Society. Named after the university's founding Professor of Architecture, Leslie Wilkinson, the lecture was organised by students Michael Dickinson, Rod Hayes and David Turner. Its purpose was to recognise Wilkinson's contributions to Australian architecture and to increase understanding between architects, planners and the general public. The students invited the federal opposition leader, Gough Whitlam, to deliver the inaugural lecture, titled "An Urban Australia," in the university's Great Hall. In the July 1969 speech, delivered three years before it was "Time", Whitlam provided a detailed criticism of city making in Australia up to that point and provided a rich vision of how his party would tackle important urban issues. [^1]

What is intriguing about the speech is that a number of the issues Whitlam discussed at length still trouble our large cities today, including:

— the power of private interests versus the public interest;
— the need for metropolitan governance;
— the high costs of servicing urban land;
— the problems of too much development in Warringah when the costs of development, especially transport, are so high (new tunnel under the harbour anyone?);
— the need for Commonwealth involvement in cities;
— the problem of the political selection of infrastructure projects, and;
— the need for good research.

You could only imagine how different our cities would have been if the Commonwealth Government had maintained its interest in cities rather than the on/off interest it has displayed since the end of the Whitlam Government.

The following transcript of Whitlam's lecture was printed by the Sydney University Architecture Society (SUAS) in response to "steady demand" for the full text. It is reproduced here courtesy of the School of Architecture, Design and Planning.

— Peter Phibbs

[^1]: Gough Whitlam was leader of the Australian Labor Party from 1966 to 1977 and Australia's Prime Minister from 1972 to 1975. During its 1972 election campaign, Labor campaigned under the slogan "It's Time".

SYDNEY UNIVERSITY ARCHITECTURE SOCIETY

AN URBAN NATION
FIRST ANNUAL LESLIE WILKINSON LECTURE
E.G. WHITLAM

In answer to a steady demand, the Sydney University Architecture Society has released the full text of Mr. E.G. Whitlam's paper, "An Urban Nation", delivered as the inaugural Leslie Wilkinson Lecture in July, 1969. The lecture was named to recognise Professor Wilkinson's profound influence on Australian architecture, and presented in an effort to lessen the mutual lack of understanding between architect/planners and the general public. The foresight of Mr. Mike Dickinson in calling for such a desirable communication was borne out by the significance placed on Mr. Whitlam's remarks by the press, and by the continued interest shown in the lecture, which has culminated in this publication.
It is to be hoped that this, and subsequent publications of the S.U.A.S., will further the expressed aims of the Leslie Wilkinson Lecture.

---

Australians live in an affluent society at a time when levels of education and sophistication are said to be rising rapidly. Yet, as the most distinguished and perceptive of all Australian critics of the Australian way of life Mr. Robin Boyd, has pointed out, half our factories, nine-tenths of our small suburban shops and ninety-nine in every hundred of our private houses are built without the services of an architect. Townplanners are able to influence the development of our cities and regional centres in only the crudest sense. It is a mark of foresight and enterprise on the part of this university that its Chair of Architecture was established 48 years ago in an era less affluent and more philistine by far than our own. It is a mark of courage and determination on the part of the man for whom this lecture is named, Professor Leslie Wilkinson, that he left a country in which the influence and prestige of architects had been established for generations to teach in one where architects were held to have more in common with artists than with engineers or doctors of medicine and to be only marginally less expendable than artists. It is a mark of some failing on the part of architects as a profession that Australians still so readily and in such great numbers choose not to avail themselves of the skills with which their houses could be transfigured and their cities transformed.

Architects, like some governments, are myopic. They have difficulty in seeing the wood for the trees. Their preoccupation with the design of individual buildings too often precludes an equal concern for the design of the cities of which individual buildings are components and the communities of which citizens need to feel a part. The masterpieces of Karnak, Paestum and Angkor Thom were left to stand in a desert, a swamp and a jungle. It is no longer satisfactory for architects to think of themselves primarily as artists or to seek the seclusion of the penthouse eyries which are the modern equivalents of ivory-towers. Our cities increasingly need the skills of architects and townplanners as sick men require the skills of doctors. Architects and planners must now fulfil a curative as well as a creative function. Those who seek to cure the ills of our cities must deploy their skills in conjunction with the power and resources of the Commonwealth government. As I pointed out 4 years ago in the first of my public addresses on the problems of Australian cities: "Architects and townplanners must learn to lobby Commonwealth authorities as assiduously as they lobby municipal and State authorities and as effectively as industrial and commercial interests lobby Commonwealth authorities."

## LOST OPPORTUNITY

There has never been so great an expansion in the population or the parameters of Australian cities as the expansion which has occurred during the post-war period. We have never before in our history lost an opportunity more singular or significant than the opportunity which could have been seized in that period to reshape our existing cities and undertake the development of new regional centres and which the Chifley government intended should be seized. We have never seen a sight more sorry than that of Australia's cities increasingly coming to exhibit all the problems of America's cities except the overtly racial problem.

## MOST URBAN OF ALL NATIONS

Australia is the most urban of all nations. In 1961 our urban areas contained 81.9% of our population, whereas Britain's urban areas contained 80%, America's 69.9%, Canada's 69.6% and Japan's 63.5%. Between the census of 1911 and the census of 1966, our degree of urban concentration rose from 57.8% to 83.2%. In the space of 5 years, between 1961 and 1966, it rose by 1.3%. Clearly the trend to city dwelling as a way of life is a continuing one. Cities are the place where most Australians choose to live. Increasingly they are the place where Australians find themselves obliged to live by government policy and the economics of primary production, whether they choose to do so or not. The Minister for Primary Industry, Mr. Anthony, said at Warragul on 20 September 1968 that the Commonwealth government could see no solution to the problem of the low-income farmer but for him to leave the land. He should have added that Australia's rural population cannot be fully employed or fully retained unless and until the Commonwealth helps to create some large cities outside the State capitals. We should not seek as some advocate, to prevent the exercise of free choice or perpetuate the myth of a bucolic utopia, but to make our cities and regional centres places where life can be lived with maximum advantage, pleasure and happiness.

## URBAN CHALLENGE

Australians who are able to travel overseas observe at first hand the rewards of enlightened urban development. Others less fortunate can scarcely imagine the beauty of new towns in Scandinavia, Britain and the United States or the standard of amenity which is being brought to established communities in those countries through programmes or urban renewal. The Director of the Canadian Institute of Urban Research, Mr. Humphrey Carver, told the inaugural meeting of the Australian Institute of Urban Studies that: "Building cities is far the most difficult, complex and majestic thing that men do. In this we come nearest in scale to what God does in creating the stars, the hills and the forests." Australians must learn to appreciate the direct and intimate relevance of Mr. Carver's vision to their daily lives. As the Head of the City of Stockholm Finance Department, Mr. Richard Carlgren, has asserted: "We feel that if we aim for the sky, we may be able to hit the treetops." Australians cannot afford in developing their cities to aim lower than the people of Stockholm.

Stockholm was cited in 1961 by the International Union of Architects as "an example to all other cities because it shows foresight in land policy and intelligent co-ordination of the many problems confronting the modern city." In addition to the basic urban services, Stockholm is able to provide its 800,000 citizens with 15 hospitals having 9,200 beds, 71 medical care centres for children under 7 years of age, 137 day nurseries for children of working mothers, 9 children's theatres, 62 youth centres and 5,000 flats for pensioners. It provides institutional care of the highest quality for 3,900 chronically ill aged persons and free hot lunches for all school children. Australian cities which equal or exceed in size the City of Stockholm cannot win comparable honours or provide comparable facilities because they can neither tax adequately in their own right nor secure adequate subsidies from State governments or from the Commonwealth government.

## COMMONWEALTH NEGLECT OF CITIES & REGIONAL CENTRES

Despite Australia's uniquely high level of urbanisation, State and Commonwealth governments pay far less attention to the problems of the nation's cities and regional centres than they pay to those of its rural areas. Australia's urban electorates have always been under-represented in every mainland parliament, and last year's distribution of electoral divisions in the House of Representatives was deliberately designed from the outset to leave them more grossly under-represented than ever before. At a time when the American legislatures are implementing for the first time under pressure from the Supreme Court the ideal of equal representation for equal numbers of people, Australian legislatures are drifting still further away from that ideal. As a result, Commonwealth expenditure for rural research and the more readily identifiable forms of rural subsidy each year exceeds $130 million, but urban research and the development of urban services receive from the Commonwealth government only a fraction of that amount. Until recently, the Commonwealth allowed the States to spend more than 80% of its grants under the Commonwealth Aid Roads Act on roads in rural areas, and less than 20% on urban roads which carry about 80% of the nation's traffic, Not even the Labor Party's success in compelling the government to appoint Mr. Justice Nimmo's committee of inquiry into health insurance or the committee's confirmation of every significant aspect of Labor's criticism of the voluntary health insurance system has given me such satisfaction as our success in obliging the government to recognise in the new Commonwealth Aid Roads Act the claims of roads in urban areas. If Labor's long advocacy of the rights and the interests of those Australians who live in cities and regional centres had achieved nothing else, I would think in the light of the transformation of the Commonwealth Aid Roads Act that it had been worthwhile. The Liberal government's belated and begrudging transformation of a single Act of Parliament precedes and foreshadows transformation of the cities themselves under a Labor government.

## INVESTORS MAKE THE DECISIONS

Virtually uncontrolled decisions by private investors govern most of the development of Australia's urban areas. In deciding where to build factories, shopping centres and housing estates, private investors need take into account neither the capital cost of those services which public authorities provide nor the social cost which communities incur as a consequence of accumulated urban blight and unplanned urban sprawl.

Residents of the Warringah Shire are doubtless convinced that their presence in that large and attractive area of broken country — originally zoned Rural and Green Belt in the Cumberland County Planning Scheme — harms nobody. Yet it was predictable from the start that these residents would become an effective pressure group for the provision of urban services. It was predictable, too, that they would be commuters, imposing new demands upon road systems and public transport already operating at full capacity. These things have come to pass. Water has been reticulated at great cost through Warringah's stony soil and sewerage pipes are being laid. Two expensive bridges in quick succession have been thrown across Middle Harbour, and one and a quarter miles of expressway have been constructed for $21 million. At current construction rates, further expenditure approaching $400 million will be required to link that expressway with the areas it is intended to serve and yet another crossing will need to be built over Middle Harbour. Nor is that all.

If development continues at the present rate, the Harbour Bridge itself will need to be duplicated. Duplication will cost some $200 million, including about $80 million for the actual crossing. Moreover, in order to complete the system and accommodate traffic flowing from it, a distributor road will be required along the western side of the city. Provision of access for the Warringah Shire threatens to become an open ended commitment rivalling in its demands the Opera House and the F-111.

Since funds for the development of urban services are limited, the cost of roads serving the Warringah Shire will be met by road users in better located areas, whose road construction programmes are deferred while the Shire's accessibility is improved and the investments of landholders in Sydney's central business district are protected. Reticulation of water supply and sewerage for the Warringah Shire will be financed by citizens who for years have lived in unsewered homes and dutifully paid a water rate in which the costs of expensive areas are averaged, Residents of Balmain Greenwich, North Sydney and Willoughby will make a contribution to Warringah when their homes are uprooted for a new harbour bridge and new freeways to serve it.

Townplanners estimate that in existing cities the cost of providing buildings, engineering works and utilities for each additional resident ranges as high as $10,000, while similar facilities in new cities and regional centres would cost for each additional resident only about $7,000. In other words it would be possible to build new cities and regional centres for a capital outlay certainly no greater than that required to settle new residents in existing urban areas and very probably less.

Moreover, building new cities would allow Australians to avoid not only the direct capital cost of urban sprawl but its social costs and the economic burden imposed in existing cities by facilities which increasingly are inadequate, outmoded and inefficient As the Vernon Committee noted in its report: "The growth of the cities leads to ever-increasing strain on transport and other facilities, which become more and more costly to maintain. If such facilities are under less strain in non-metropolitan (or can be made available there at comparatively low cost), there is an obvious argument for diverting industries to the locations concerned … "

Clearly, unlimited expansion of existing urban areas is profitable from the point of view of the private investor alone. Were such investors required to recompense public authorities for the cost of bringing schools and hospitals to the areas in which they have their interests; to finance the acquisition of adequate public open space; or to make up the deficits which public transport inevitably incurs under conditions of urban sprawl, the developments of Australia's cities might follow entirely different lines. In these circumstances, investors themselves might voluntarily take their factories, shopping centres and housing estates right away from existing cities and into new ones. I am convinced that, given the availability of private capital, a Dusseldorp, a Jennings or a Strasser would find greater rewards in developing new cities than in tinkering with the problems of any existing city. Establishing new cities seems to (be) much more costly than permitting existing cities to expand only because the calculations on which investors base their decisions reflect a mere fraction of the real cost of such expansion. Laissez-faire economics and traditional market mechanisms are not giving us the information we require in order to devise rational solutions to the problems of accommodating an expanding population in an acceptable urban environment.

## DECLINING URBAN AMENITY

In these circumstances it is not surprising that a great majority of the Australians who exercise their right to live in urban areas are obliged to do so under conditions of declining urban amenity. The destruction of Australia's flora and fauna and the spoliation of the countryside are frequently the subject of public controversy, yet it is in our cites that the overthrow of our environment is permitted to proceed with greatest abandon and greatest pace. As a community, we seem to lack the discernment required to identify the source of this destruction and the will to call a halt. We loudly condemn the teenagers who for want of better employment in an urban wilderness, uproot the saplings planted 10 days ago; we softly chide the aldermen who uproot the trees they wrongly sited 10 years ago; we accept without protest the defoliation produced by new commercial enterprises. The real vandals in the community are those who lay a landscape waste and make an environment ugly in the name of government or commerce.

Again, differences in the standard of living which Australians enjoy arise increasingly from their access to government services such as hospitals schools, recreation facilities, sewerage and public transport. Under present arrangements, these things are provided with a growing geographical discrimination against those who live on the expanding perimeters of cities and regional centres.

Sewerage is the most basic and essential of urban services, yet the proportion of our population which is served by sewerage has declined over the past 20 years in Perth from 72% to 47% and in Melbourne from 95% to 85%. Half the population of Brisbane and a quarter of the population of Sydney still live and work in premises which are unsewered. No other western nation has cities in which the incidence of urban sanitation is so primitive or so ludicrous as in the cities of Australia. Liberals neglect sewerage services because they are a socialist undertaking. We are the most effluent (sic) nation in what Liberals call the free world.

## PREMATURE DEVELOPMENT

All our shortages of urban services are artificial and unnecessary. Residents of Blacktown, for example, are rightly proud of the homes which they have gained through hard work and financial sacrifice. Yet hard work and financial sacrifice cannot sewer those homes or pave the streets on which they stand; modernise a drainage system more primitive than drainage systems built in Rome before the birth of Christ; provide adequate schools, public transport and shopping facilities; or reduce in length, duration or discomfort the journey between homes and work places and create jobs for women who seek them locally.

These are things which can be achieved or provided only if governments exercise foresight and plan ahead. The privations which Blacktown residents must endure are direct result of failure by governments to exercise foresight or to plan ahead. Blacktown was developed prematurely, at a time when there was still Metropolitan area of supply of vacant service blocks sufficient to meet Sydney's building land requirements for at least 7 years. Premier Brand's Commission on Land Taxation and Land Prices in Western Australia — the McCarrey Commission — recommended that holding metropolitan land vacant should be made unprofitable by the use of selective taxation measures. Had the government of New South Wales used such measures, there would have been no need to develop areas such as Blacktown in advance of the services required to support them. Five years of population growth would have been absorbed in the existing metropolitan area. An additional $100 million would have been available to upgrade services in that area and to prepare Blacktown for development. Scarce resources of serviced land would not have been allowed to lie idle. Scarce resources of developmental capital would not have been spread thin to the point of ineffectuality.

## DILATORY REDEVELOPMENT

Again investors who shrink from the challenge of building new cities are equally deterred by the prospect of redeveloping the inner suburbs of existing cities where so much of the best residential land is occupied by low density and sub-standard housing. There are at least 125,000 sub-standard houses in Australia. Estimates of the area of slums and sub-standard housing in Melbourne alone vary from 1,000 acres to 5,000 acres of which the Victorian Housing Commission is able to clear at the most 20 acres a year. At this rate, the present stock of sub-standard housing will not be replaced for at least 50 years, in which time at least as many more dwellings will have become sub-standard. Land in our cities which is occupied by older houses and slums is close to the central business districts. It is serviced by water sewerage, electricity telephone and transport facilities, all of which must be provided anew for development in outer areas. It should be possible to replace the sub-standard housing in Australian cities without at the same time destroying the priceless architectural heritage which contributes so greatly to their grace and character. The Commonwealth's failure to make available finance to redevelop inner-suburban land is a significant factor in forcing Australians in increasing numbers to make their homes on the urban perimeter, further from the centre of the city than in any other city in the world except, perhaps, Los Angeles, and a prey to poor roads and public transport, inadequate or non existent recreation facilities, deferred sewerage and telephones and a mounting incidence of neurosis, delinquency and vandalism.

## FAILURE TO DEVELOP COMMUNITIES

The austerity and inconvenience of outer suburban life is aggravated and exacerbated by our excessively statistical approach to housing. The Commonwealth Government, the State governments and private entrepreneurs are all preoccupied with squeezing from available capital the greatest possible number of dwellings. A great number of the attendant problems stem from our failure to develop housing estates in which there is a focus for community activities. They stem from our obsession with providing row after row of housing units instead of housing communities. The NSW Housing Commission's Annual Report for 1962-63 asserted that in the Commission's Green Valley estate: "Special attention has been given to the public sector and adjacent community buildings, which will comprise a post office, medical centre, public health clinic, library, public hall and the Commission's administrative offices." Yet 3 years later, in July 1966, a research team from the Department of Social Work the University of Sydney reported that "A list of what else one might expect to find in an outer suburb of this size reveals some of the lacks. There was no library, no pre-school centre or kindergarten despite the size of the eligible population, no playground supervised all the year round, no drama, arts or craft group except what the church groups provided, no dance hall or other specifically teenage facility and no picture show … There is a very slender provision in the social and recreational amenities for a population of over 25,000 judged not by ideal standards but by the simple application of what normally the Australian population can expect."

Similar structures could be applied to the work of any other State housing authority. Most private developers and now required to dedicate land for recreational purposes, but preparing that land use is the responsibility of municipal authorities which are already embarrassed by the demand which developers have generated in a dozen other directions. Erection of the shopping centres which private developers frequently include in their estate prospectuses lags years behind the erection of their houses. Not one private developer in 10,000 had heard of the Radburn plan, much less applied it in his sub-divisional activities. Indeed why should he have done so when the relevant local government authorities have failed to bring Radburn to his attention, and when public housing authorities in their own sub-divisional activities are equally ignorant neglectful?

Far from establishing communities in any meaningful sense of the word, we are moving in the opposite direction. Sydney and Melbourne, the cities in which the most Australians choose to live or are obliged to live, are becoming less and less communities and more and more conurbations — agglomerated, sprawling masses of houses, inhabited by people whom the pattern of urban growth forces to travel further and further to work; taking a longer and longer to get there; sharing less and less in common with their fellow citizens; knowing and wishing to know less and less of the common problems and interests of those around them. Hundreds of thousands of Australians in each of our major cities today could not answer, even in its most literal sense, the typical question: "Who is my neighbour?" As Ms. Caroline Kelly pointed out in a most perceptive 1966 Australian Planning Congress paper: "… these people are in fact migrants. We get very concerned about migrants from overseas and we organize groups to befriend them, but who ever gave thought to the uprooted Australian family and how it fared in new and strange surroundings?"

## LIMITS OF URBAN RESOURCES

And to what purpose is for this endured? Australians prefer to live in cities because they value the variety of social contact, entertainment, employment, cultural opportunities and recreational opportunities which cities are best able to provide. The availability of these seven resources is limited, however, by transport facilities, by transport costs and by the number of persons seeking to share them at any given time. In Sydney and our other capital cities neither transport facilities nor transport costs encourage Australians to take advantage of the art galleries, picture theatres, concert halls, zoos and museums to which theoretically they enjoy access. Our supply of beaches, rivers, harbour waters and open space is not so extensive as to offer an unlimited welcome to all those citizens who might wish to make use of them if they were able to do so. There are very real limitations on the resources of all our cities.

Moreover, as Professor Galbraith pointed out in "Architectural Town" 2 years ago, "Economists and politicians still measure accomplishments by indices relevance to the popular concern of 30 years ago … If the gross national product grows adequately and unemployment declines, this, pro tanto, means success. If our cities, at the same time, become unlivable in part as the product of this growth and the smoke, sewarage, trash and traffic that spawns, that is unfortunate but not highly relevant." Australian politicians exhibit in varying degrees precisely the indifference to which Galbraith refers. Increasingly our cities exhibit the consequence of that indifference.

## COMMONWEALTH RESPONSIBILITY

It is high time that the goals of urban development were made explicit. It is high time that a national framework of urban planning was established, and specific and appropriate planning responsibilities assigned within that framework to the Commonwealth government, to state governments and to regional government. It is high time the Commonwealth accepted a proper share of the financial responsibility for urban redevelopment in all its forms. Australian federalism should not be less vigorous in these matters than the federalism of the United States and every other federal system with which we compare ourselves. A Labor government would not emasculate federalism as it has been emasculated under successive Liberal governments. A Labor government would not deny State governments and local government finance adequate for the functions which they are incomparably best able to perform or by default impose upon them functions better performed at a national level.

In the last 20 years the indebtedness of the Commonwealth has diminished. The debts of state governments have risen 4 times, of local government 9 times and of semi-government authorities 10.5 times. Within 5 years, the combined debts of Australia's 900 municipal authorities will cost more to service than the combined debts of the States. The present crisis in financial relationships is as much a matter of the pressure on the local government and semi-government authorities as the squeeze on the States. While State governments complain that the Commonwealth is indifferent to their problems, the States themselves are no less indifferent to the problems of local government. The Premiers who upbraid the Commonwealth for its parsimony are themselves most parsimonious in their dealings with local government.

More money alone, however, is not a cure-all for the problems of federalism. More money cannot rationalise the 6 State boundaries which were established arbitrarily in London more than a century ago by officials ignorant of Australian affairs. It cannot reduce Australia's grossly excessive proliferation of independent and autonomous local councils. In Victoria, for example, the jurisdiction of inner metropolitan councils extends over areas of from 5 to 8 square miles. The population of these municipalities ranges from 40,000 to 80,000 persons. Many are divided into awards of 1 or 2 square miles and 10,000 to 20,000 persons. With 3 councillors in each ward, individual councillors may represent areas as small as a third of a mile and populations as slight as 3,000 persons.

If we were devising a new structure of representative government for our continent, we would have neither so few state governments nor so many local government units. We would not have a federal system of overlapping parliaments, and a delegated but supervised system of local government. We would have a House of Representatives for international matters and national matters, an assembly for the affairs of each of our dozen largest cities and a few score regional assemblies for the areas of rural production and resource development outside those cities. Vested interest and legal complexities should not discourage or deter us from attempts to modernise and rationalise our inherited structure. Federal countries like the United States, Canada and West Germany are showing much more initiative and enterprise than Australia in adjusting yesterday's forms to today's needs.

Professor Zelman Cowan observed in his 1966 CG Lewis Memorial Lecture: "To speak of the redevelopment needs of Melbourne and Sydney which house more than a third of the population of this country as particularly municipal or state problems does not seem to me to make sense. These are distinctly national problems commanding national attention, resources and energies."

In the absence of "national attention, resources and energies", the burden of new urban development and the provision of basic urban services falls more and more on those least able to support it. Local government, which relies on rates and charges, State governments, which rely on indirect taxes and charges, and land developers, who pass on rising costs in rising land prices, together provide the finance for most of our new urban development and most of our basic urban services. All these indirect taxes and charges are inherently unfair in their incidence. They fall most heavily on Australians with smaller incomes and larger families.

It suits Liberals to assert that urban facilities and urban services are matters for the States. Liberals are appalled by the inevitable increase in government expenditure and planning involved in providing better urban facilities and better urban services. They know that the best way to restrict government expenditure on any activity is to claim that it is one for the States, which have fewer financial resources than the Commonwealth. It would be naïve and erroneous for Australians to accept the proposition that the national government has no responsibility for the cities and regional centres in which the majority of the nation's population make their homes. Indeed it should never again be possible for that proposition to be put forward seriously now that the new Commonwealth Aid Roads Act has passed on to the Statute Book. That Act sets a precedent for Commonwealth involvement in all forms of urban development and the provision of all urban services. Labor believes that efficient functioning and fair financing of urban facilities and urban services can be achieved only by our national government accepting an increasing share of the responsibility for these functions, as all comparable national governments are already doing.

The Commonwealth has a monopoly of direct taxation and most forms of indirect taxation — customs duties, excise duties and sale tax. It floats all government loans. The States depend on the Commonwealth for more than half of the funds for their current expenses and all the funds for their public works. The Commonwealth has the dominant role in deciding the size and nature of the borrowings by semi-government and local government authorities. It has, directly or indirectly, control over 90% of all money spent on housing. It has constitutional power to make grants to the States on such terms as it may stipulate. All these financial and constitutional powers combine to make the Commonwealth the most effective and appropriate instrument for ensuring that proper urban development and proper urban planning are implemented in Australia. The Commonwealth must now accept the responsibilities which its great powers and resources confer. It must reaffirm the prescient injunction of the Commonwealth Housing Commission in 1944 that "Planning is of such importance that the Commonwealth government should not make available financial assistance for housing unless the State concerned satisfies the Commonwealth that it has taken, or is taking, definite steps to erect and implement regional and town planning legislation." It must expand the scope of that injunction to include assistance not only for housing but for all forms of urban development. It must begin to make good the 20 costly years of chaos ushered in by Sir Robert Menzies when he announced that the County of Cumberland Planning Scheme would receive no financial assistance from the Commonwealth because to grant such assistance "could mean the assumption by the Commonwealth of a new and costly responsibility."

In February 1967 I appointed a Shadow Minister with special responsibility for urban affairs. If a Labor government takes office in December it will establish a Commonwealth Department for Urban Affairs. This department will have 4 main functions.

Analysis and appraisal of plans

First the department will take responsibility for analysing and evaluating proposals for urban development received from State governments and from local government authorities. The proposition that public expenditure must be as rigorously justified as private business expenditure is now generally accepted in academic and executive circles. Clearly, if there is a fixed budget available then the public officials who advise ministers must be able to say: "The funds can be spent on projects A, B or C. In terms of a stated set of objectives we can advise you, Mr. Minister, that Project A yields a rate of social return which exceeds the returns available from Projects B and C." This "cost/benefit" approach to decisions on expenditure and investment first gained acceptance in the United States under President Kennedy, with Defence Secretary Robert McNamara as its chief protagonist. Its acceptance in this country was foreshadowed 3 years ago in a seminal Treasury Information Bulletin on "Investment Analysis". In the meantime, the bulk of our public expenditure continues to be disbursed under the traditional formula: "Give each department 5% more than last year and spread what remains among those Premiers and Ministers who make the most noise."

By using the cost/benefit approach, we shall be able to focus urban planning on its ultimate objectives, and to deduce by what precise sequence of steps those objectives can most rapidly and most economically be achieved. For example, in each of our major cities we spend a great deal each year on building and maintaining roads and on operating systems of public transport. The objective of all this expenditure is to improve an urban transport system. The value of spending on any particular project such as a freeway, a ring-road, an underground railway or a new bridge can be determined only by looking at the effect of that particular project on the operation of the transport system as a whole.

In practice, what happens is that each year the main road authority receives funds to build roads and the railways receive funds for certain improvements to rolling stock and the permanent way. In many cases, additional road funds are in the hands of local government authorities, which have their own parochial networks of road to maintain. Nobody in fact has a brief to spend money where it will produce the best return for transport as a total system. Nobody is required to ask himself whether in a given year it would be more advantageous to concentrate the available funds on, say, a rail extension and to hold back on road improvements, or vice versa. As the United States Committee for Economic Development pointed out 3 years ago in its statement on

"Budgeting for National Objectives": "Most spending plans focus on the agencies and their subdivisions, rather than on the functions performed and the programmes projected."

The big problem with urban and regional planning in Australia is that, with the exception of Brisbane and Canberra, the planning organisation is not the organisation which spends the funds and the organisations which do spend them see their responsibilities in terms of running trains, generating electricity, supplying water, building schools and so on. The spending organisations in other words, have instrumental goals which they quite rightly pursue in the way which seems most efficient from their own sectional point of view. They spend the funds allocated to them by the Loan Council in the way which suits their own sub-system best.

Whether the objectives of the main roads authority are consistent with those of the water supply and sewerage authority is a question which no-one in particular is required to examine. Whether their objectives are consistent with those of the local planning agency is, equally, a matter of chance. If there are inconsistencies, it is the spenders not the planners who prevail.

This is the crux of the matter. Choose any city or regional centre. If its population is growing, then surely the objective is to create an urban environment for those people as economically and as effectively as possible. It is to create a total urban environment and not a set of uncoordinated sub-systems. Clearly as the existence of Canberra shows, this is not a utopian goal. In Canberra, Australia is creating urban facilities of a higher quality than are found in the outer suburbs of any of the other capital cities, and there is good reason to believe that their cost to the community is less great. The same facilities can be achieved with the same economy in Melbourne, in Sydney or in any of the smaller cities and centres. The basic requirement is simply that, before a State or local government authority comes to the Commonwealth for funds for urban development, it should prepare an integrated programme budget which covers the total requirements of the area for which it is responsible. The very process of co-ordination required at the local and regional level to construct a total specification of requirements will force planners to take into account the varying interests of the instrumentalities which will construct and operate the sub-systems within their overall design. Armed with such a brief, representatives of the States and of local government could come to Canberra and say: "We have looked at a number of alternative methods of coping with the 5 years' population growth in this capital city or that provincial city. We think that it can best be done in the following

manner, at a cost of so much in year 1, so much in year 2 and so on." The Department of Urban Affairs will appraise all plans and advise the Commonwealth Grants Commission that, for example, "Proposal A is well conceived and appears to be efficient, while Proposal B should be sent back to its originators for reworking." Once a plan has been approved, it will be up to the Grants Commission to enter into a financial commitment, extending if necessary over a period of years. Local planners and instrumentalities will then know what finance they can expect, and within that limit they can proceed to spend as their technical capabilities permit. The Commonwealth will be concerned not with the substance or priorities of particular plans but with their internal consistency. It would be inappropriate and unacceptable for the Commonwealth to interfere with the substance or priorities of any internally consistent State or local government plan.

Conservation of the National Estate

Secondly, the Department of Urban Affairs must act as an initiator, an innovator and a co-ordinator of efforts to conserve Australia's national estate. It is now clear from an abundance of overseas experience that urban man is diminished by any final severance of his links with nature and the countryside, and we should be appalled by the prospect that such a severance may ultimately come about in our own domain of great open spaces, scenic grandeur and abundant wild life. We cannot safely assume that, because our cities occupy less than one half of one percent of Australia's area, the remaining 99.5% of that area can be left to look after itself. We should not suppose that the natural environment of our ancient continent is so tough or so resilient as to withstand without harm the insults and injuries inflicted by its more thoughtless inhabitants. We should not suppose that, because our unique flora and fauna have outlasted a variety of predators in the course of their cloistered evolution, they will also survive unaided the predatory activities of man.

The Department will carry out as a matter of urgency a survey of the Australian countryside designed to identify areas suitable for the expansion of existing cities or the establishment of new regional centres, areas to which mineral deposits, water resources or soil fertility impart a special economic significance and areas which should be preserved for their natural beauty, historic associations or scientific interest. The department will pass on the results of its survey to planning authorities throughout Australia, and thereafter expect its categories and classifications to be taken into consideration in plans submitted for Commonwealth appraisal. It should be a condition of any Commonwealth grant for urban development that proper regard is paid to the economic potential, the scientific potential and the recreation potential of areas for which assistance is sought. The Commonwealth should see itself as the curator and not the liquidator of the national estate.

Research

Thirdly, the Department of Urban Affairs should become the clearing-house and the power-house for urban research and urban planning throughout Australia. It is clear that the Commonwealth Bureau of Census and Statistics requires guidance and advice on the data required for effective evaluation and administration of programmes of urban development; that guidance and advice will be provided by the department. It is clear that the States require additional information and inspiration in planning their urban development programmes; that inspiration and information could flow from the department. The department will commission inquiries by universities and by independent groups into problems which concern all Australia's cities and regional centres and into problems of concern to particular cities and regional centres. It will itself undertake research programmes or undertake them jointly with the Australian Institute of Urban Studies. It will become over a period a centre to which administrators, academics, architects and other persons expert in urban affairs can come on study leave both from within Australian institutions and from abroad. It will provide for such persons a unique setting in which both to draw abreast of the whole field of urban studies and to make a practical contribution to urban development under conditions of challenge and opportunity.

Service

Finally, the Department of Urban Affairs will provide a service organisation with a role in many ways similar to that played in rural enterprise by the Snowy Mountains Authority, the Northern Division of the Department of National Development, the C.S.I.R.O. and the Bureau of Agricultural Economics. This service organisation, consisting of engineers economists, ecologists, townplanners, architects, urban anthropologists, landscape architects and other persons with relevant professional skills, would, on request, advise and assist the States and local government in their preparation of plans for cities and regions. This would not mean as some have suggested, that Collingwood or Cabramatta would necessarily be planned from Canberra, but that local planning authorities with slender resources will have access to a full spectrum of professional competence from individuals or from teams, in Canberra or at home, as their particular needs, circumstances and desires dictate.

DECENTRALISATION

Rational urban development cannot successfully be undertaken without at the same time and as energetically undertaking rational decentralisation or, as I prefer to call it, regional concentration.

Decentralisation hitherto has been a cause commanding lipservice from all political parties and effective action from none. The Country Party is the most vociferous peddler of nostrums for decentralisation and the group with most to lose from the results of decentraliasation. Australia for the past 19 years has been ruled by a Liberal-Country Party coalition government which at all times has resisted taking the initiative in new developments. It has resisted above all taking the initiative in matters such as decentralisation, where little or nothing can be achieved until the Commonwealth assumes the leading role. The Minister for Primary Industry, Mr. Anthony, asserted in his speech at Warragul on 20 September 1968 that "ways must be found to arrest the drift (to the cities) and the Country Party has devoted itself to this problem during the whole of its existence." The efficacy of the Country Party's endeavours may be gauged from the fact that since its formation in 1919 the proportion of Australia's population resident in capital cities has risen from 43% to 58% and in other urban areas from 19% to 25%. As I have already pointed out, Australia's cities and regional centres now contain 83% of our population whereas in 1919 they contained about 62 percent. The Country Party member for Indi, Mr. Holten, told the annual conference of the Victorian branch of the Country Party at Wangaratta on 24 April that the present government's activities in decentralisation are a joke.

Australia's failure to decentralise has moved Sir Alan Westerman to wonder whether Australians by the year 2000 "want threequarters of our population of 25 millions concentrated in 9 bloated cities which between them occupy one-half of one percent of the total area of Australia." It prompted the Vernon Committee to point out the economic consequences "evident in rapidly mounting costs of widening and reconstructing main roads in these cities, the increasing problems of public transport, and steeply rising land values." It led the Director of the Canadian Institute of Urban Research, Mr. Humphrey Carver, to highlight for Australia's newly founded Institute of Urban Studies the fact that "cities are the scene of the highest creative performance in the arts and sciences and in executive talents. But they are also the scene of the greatest poverty and loneliness and the spiritual degradation. The devil and the angel both live in cities and they are close neighbors."

In the face of these doubts and reservations, Australians are witnessing in New South Wales the development of a single urban complex amalgamating with Sydney Newcastle-Cessnock in the north, Penrith in the Blue Mountains in the west and Wollongong in the south. Some years ago I tentatively and somewhat inelegantly dubbed this complex Newsydneygong. In all, 67% of the population of New South Wales already reside in it. New South Wales between 1956 and 1966 increased its population by 650,000. Ninety-five percent of that increase occurred within the boundaries of Newsydneygong.

The Commonwealth could relieve the intolerable strain on Australia's capital cities by enabling State governments and local government authorities to implement a radical and adventurous policy of decentralisation. By this I mean something very different from the Leader of the Country Party, Mr. McEwen, when he talks about decentralisation. Decentralisation for the Country Party is limited to granting tariff protection and freight concessions to investors who establish factories in country towns. Concealed subsidies in themselves cannot enable Australians to make better use of their resources or bring about a significant reduction in urban sprawl and the costs attendant upon it. They are no substitute for the sort of sponsored and systematic development which would establish numbers of factories simultaneously in selected regional centres while at the same time creating the standards of urban amenity necessary to attract additional population to those centres. They are in fact nothing more than an additional form of rural patronage for Country Party ministers to disburse without fear of attracting Labor or Liberal voters in numbers sufficient to upset their party's rural hegemony. This sort of decentralisation was roundly condemned in the recent Report on Selective Decentralisation by the Development Corporation of New South Wales. The Corporation concluded bluntly, unequivocally and unambiguously that "reliance upon the dispersed decentralisation measures which have prevailed to date is unlikely in the future to achieve any significant degree of population growth outside the central coast metropolitan region." No political party has had its policies so devastatingly or so damningly refuted as the decentralisation policies of the Country Party have been refuted by the Report on Selective Decentralisation of the Development Corporation of New South Wales.

For the Labor party, decentralisation has a far more important meaning. For us, it is the beginning of the process of cutting down on the vast social cost of urban sprawl and of making it possible for Australians to develop fully their continent's resources in the regions where those three sources are found. If these aims are to be achieved it will be necessary to bring about really significant shifts in the distribution of Australia's population. Such shifts will not be bought about merely by policies of this dispersed development such as the Country Party at elections intemperately advocates and in government indolently and ineffectually administers. Only the Commonwealth has the constitutional power and the financial capacity to create the conditions in which enough Australians will prefer homes in new regional centres to homes in established areas. The Commonwealth in partnership with State governments and with local government authorities should establish a number of new Regional Development Authorities. It should require and enable these Authorities to implement the policies of regional concentration and forced development through which alone decentralisation can become a reality. The only case so far in which this has happened has been the case of Canberra.

Canberra exemplifies how governments, having taken the initiative, can create pleasant and economically viable cities. The population of Canberra-Queanbeyan already exceeds 100,000. It double between 1950 and 1959, doubled again between 1959 and 1965, and will pass the quarter-century mark by 1981. Yet forward planning and co-ordinated development allow Canberra each year to absorb an additional 10,000 citizens without loss of convenience or amenity. Development costs at the same time are held at an economic level, while rising land values offer through the leasehold system a source of the long-term development funds and an assurance of public investment profitability. Through impetus of growth, associated with a sound choice of site, the establishment of high residential standards and the creation of urban amenity early in the pioneering stage, private capital has been attracted to Canberra in quantities sufficient to ensure a continuing expansion over and above expansion attendant on increasing Government activity.

Canberra, however, at present represents only the first stage of decentralised development as it is envisaged by the Labor Party. In the next stage, the process of the expansion already underway in Canberra must be extended to encompass surrounding areas and their resources. The development of these areas has become feasible through the proximity of a substantial city market and industrial area where previously it could not seriously be considered. Canberra is the fastest growing market in Australia. It is bigger even than population figures suggest. The average level of income in Canberra exceeds by 32% the level for the remainder of New South Wales. Stability of employment in Canberra ensures that a very high proportion of income earned in Canberra is in fact spent.

Studies by the National Capital Development Commission indicate that the area of influence of the Canberra market covers the south-east corner of NSW lying south and east of Young. It embraces some 19 shires and 9 municipalities with a population of about 140,000. The supply of fabricated steel from Young shows how this area can be developed by demand generated in Canberra. Canberra must now be effectively integrated into a pattern of regional development. The city must be outward-looking, seeking ways of drawing upon the production and the skills of the diverse and fertile areas among which it stands. This process would be facilitated by the establishment of a Canberra Regional Development Authority or Regional Council, representing local government authorities, the Commonwealth government and the government of New South Wales.

Australians who once traveled 20 miles for the service of banks, lawyers, medical specialists, hospitals, shops and clubs will now as readily travel 100 miles for a greater quality and variety of services. Even architects can flourish in a large enough provincial city! There is room for another Canberra between Canberra and Melbourne and for another Newcastle between Newcastle and the Gold Coast. There is room too for new industrial cities processing Australian mineral resources to arise at Gladstone and in the region of Port Headland as that Mt. Isa and Whyalla since the war.

New cities will each ultimately provide housing, employment and recreation for up to 500,000 Australians. They will require sites of approximately 90,000 acres, costing between $9 million and $90 million. Their total cost, including the land acquisition, is likely to approach $3,000 million, of which approximately half will be found by governments and half by private enterprise. The Development Corporation of NSW Asserted in its Report that "selective urban growth is the only possible alternative to economic and political stagnation." It asserted that "whatever the economic cost of promoting non-metropolitan urban growth the only alternative is the certain economic liability of continued metropolitan centralisation." The Commission recommended that "certain regional centres with a demonstrable inherent capacity for growth be selected, and that the growth of such centres be accelerated by the exercise of public powers in relation to them and the concentration of public assistance measures within them." It expressed its conviction that financially "the issue is very largely a matter of the reallocation of existing public sector expenditure." These conclusions reached by independent experts under the auspices of a Liberal-Country Party government are wholly in accord with the declaration of the 1967 Federal Conference of my party "That it is the policy of the Australian Labor Party to concentrate on selected centres with a view to raising population in these centres to a size which is recognized as a self-governing point." They effectively give the lie to the recent assertion by the Minister for National Development, Mr. Fairbairn, that's my Party's proposals are "bastardised decentralisation."

Professor Colin Buchan wrote in the London Observer on 21 January 1964 about a reshaped Britain: "Cities, towns and villages would be such that I would be proud to show them off to a foreign visitor. He would be a thoughtful discerning foreigner, not just looking for 'show pieces'. Towns cannot be rebuilt overnight, or even in a decade, but everywhere I took my visitor I would like him to be aware about the importance of the environment was understood."

I would like him to see that danger in the streets was being rooted out, squalor was being eradicated, and that ugliness was being tackled positively. I would like him to see that researches were being undertaken and experiments being tried, and that, when the course of action was clear, changes on a broad scale were being initiated, for he would certainly wish to be satisfied that a major impact is being made on the vast legacy of bad surroundings everywhere now discernible. I would like my visitor to see that the inheritance from the past, so vital to the richness of urban life, was being cherished.

At the same time I think he would wish to be sure that there were no inhibitions about the architecture, in the sense that new solutions to new problems were being trammeled by the insistence of clients and authorities upon outdated forms. Above all, I would wish him to be satisfied that the urban environment was being worked over and redesign with as deliberate an eye to the convenience and delight to the clients for whom he is designing a house. And I am sure my visitor would expect with all the evidence that Britain is wealthy country, that the reshaping of the environment was not being done in any niggling, parsimonious way, but that quality was being sought in everything."

I can imagine no better expression of the aspirations which I cherish for Australia and which I believe are cherished increasingly by all thinking Australians. I can imagine no better summary of the cause with which Professor Leslie Wilkinson fired successive generations of students in the Architecture faculty of this university. In honouring Professor Wilkinson, let us honour all those who, themselves planning today, shape the planners of tomorrow. Let us seek with them to transform a nation.

The collected modern domestic buildings were framed as innovative outcomes of the "Sydney School". As successful adaptations to indigenous circumstances, these examples were submitted as uniquely Australian.

— Catherine Lassen and Julie Willis, "The Sydney School"

**Figure 1** — Foregrounding the Sydney bushland, an image of architect Ken Woolley's own house in Mosman formed the cover of Jennifer Taylor's first book, *An Australian Identity: Houses for Sydney 1953–63* (1972, 2nd edition, 1984). Extending commentary by JM Freeland, Robin Boyd, David Saunders, Eva Buhrich and others, Taylor here amplified claims describing a "Sydney School" of residential architecture, designated as a new national style. Lisa Moore and the University of Sydney School of Architecture, Design and Planning.

# Chapter 5: The Sydney School
— Catherine Lassen and Julie Willis

> Australian architecture [since 1960] has had more than the usual number of nuggets. Many of the recent buildings are equal in architectural quality to their opposite numbers overseas and just as frequently to be found. Numbers of them have a distinctive and unique flavour and give rise to a justified hope that the Architecture in Australia of the future will be a truly Australian architecture. [^1]

Observing 100 years of architectural education in Australia's first university, we might recall a parallel moment in Australia's first comprehensive architectural history, when JM Freeland's parting words focused on the search for a national idiom. *Architecture in Australia: A History*, published in 1968, traced Australia's architecture from the shores of Portsmouth, England, to then-current local developments, highlighting an established style "initiated by a small coterie of Sydney architects." [^2] Freeland described that work as an often brutal, yet crafted, in part romantic reaction to the "anaemic spiritless sophistication and the smooth, transparent emptiness of the work of the preceding decade." [^3] Pointing to the positive international and domestic response following the 1954 publication of Morton Herman's book, *The Early Australian Architects and Their Work*, [^4] he connected such regional developments to the growing interest in Australian architectural history and the final establishment in all states, during the 1950s, of National Trusts to foster and protect that heritage. [^5]

In 1971, Jennifer Evelyn (née Bogle) Taylor commenced her first year of teaching as a lecturer in architectural history at the University of Sydney. In 1972, her first book was published by the university's Department of Architecture, *An Australian Identity: Houses for Sydney 1953-63* [Figure 1]. Catalogue-like, her book amplified Freeland's call, developing an extended commentary on work by the Sydney architects he had briefly mentioned. [^6] From the outset, Taylor historically situated such current projects. In a career as an architectural critic and historian that spanned nearly 50 years—also as an architect, educator, commentator, cultural advocate, and professional mentor—she was arguably the most prolifically published and widely influential historian of Australian architecture of her generation. She profoundly shaped our understanding of post-war architectural history across the region but is perhaps most well-known for her role in the documentation and promotion of a group of architects who were labelled in all her writings the "Sydney School" [Figure 2].

Through and against the framing undertaken by Taylor in *An Australian Identity*, this chapter will consider key figures in Sydney's modernist moment. It recovers the dissemination of a late modernism across the 1950s and 1960s and a generation of graduates whose work shaped the University of Sydney architecture faculty's post-war critical fortunes. Modernism in Sydney was, in this manner, positioned as an embrace of local identity over "tradition" and hence in counterpoint to Wilkinson's tenure as dean (up to 1946). During this period, newly formed relationships with the city emerged through developing

[^1]: JM Freeland, *Architecture in Australia: A History* (Melbourne: Cheshire, 1968), 314.
[^2]: Freeland, *Architecture in Australia*, 305.
[^3]: Freeland, *Architecture in Australia*, 305.
[^4]: M Herman, *The Early Australian Architects and Their Work* (Sydney: Angus and Robertson, 1954).
[^5]: Freeland, *Architecture in Australia*, 311.
[^6]: J Taylor, *An Australian Identity: Houses for Sydney 1953-63* (Sydney: Department of Architecture, University of Sydney, 1972).

urban planning, the high-rise office building, corporate architectural practices, and the emergence of a heritage consciousness.

Taylor's appointment in 1970 was the third of three important new positions established by the University of Sydney in the area of architectural history. In 1968, David Saunders had joined the Power Institute of Fine Arts, followed in 1970 by Joan Kerr. Both Kerr and Taylor held research masters degrees, bringing a new level of scholarly attainment to their positions and activities and heralding the professionalisation of architectural history research in Australia. This was underscored by Saunders' later founding of the Society of Architectural Historians, Australia and New Zealand (SAHANZ) in 1984. Students of architecture typically took courses within their own faculty but were able to cross register at the Power Institute of Fine Arts if they had particular interests in, say, art history. Taylor taught in the design studio program, as well as her history courses. Via Taylor, Saunders and Kerr, an impetus for Australian architectural history was located at the University of Sydney, fed by interest in the city's early colonial heritage and self-consciously positioned modernism. In the relationship between the modernism of the studio and the self-reflectiveness of the lecture hall and library, a process of unfolding local and national identity was located.

As well as the initiation of Taylor's university career, 1971 also registered the untimely loss of Robin Boyd. Arguably, she assumed his mantle as a leading voice in Australian architectural scholarship that was as interested in the contemporary as in the past. Like Boyd, Freeland, and many others preoccupied with Australian architectural identity, Taylor saw the genesis for this in the nation's residential buildings, particularly those examples that suggested adaptations to local conditions. Like Boyd, her observations ultimately spanned a variety of building types. Both figures further made major contributions to architectural scholarship beyond Australia, particularly with their focus on Asian architects and architecture.

Eight months before his death, Boyd had published an article on the state of Australian architecture in the January 1971 issue of the

**Figure 2** — Jennifer Taylor signing copies at the launching of her book, *Australian Architecture Since 1960*. First published in 1986, it became a standard textbook for students studying Australian architectural history and contemporary work around the nation. University of Sydney Archives.

English *RIBA Journal*. Boyd's final missive, "Architecture in Australia," expanded on his previously published views, preoccupied with local architectural developments and the possibility of an "Australian Style." [^7] In particular, he wrote of a folksy craft style in Sydney that had developed in reaction to aspects of the modern movement, recognising Japanese architecture, British brutalism, and the style of the Californian bay region in its evolution. [^8] Boyd belatedly recognised a distinct shift in the sources and ideas of Australian architecture, which was exemplified by the Sydney-based work.

His earlier extensive article "The State of Australian Architecture," published in June 1967 in *Architecture in Australia*, had offered an overarching diagnosis: "All in all… the ordinary Australian architectural scene is uninspiring… because even in much of the best… or most thoughtful work there is little or no clear or consistent sense of a movement, let alone a sense of direction or promise." [^9] Using the term "school" to characterise prevailing architectural tendencies in Sydney

[^7]: R Boyd, "Architecture in Australia," *RIBA Journal* 78 (January 1971): 12–20.
[^8]: Boyd, "Architecture in Australia," 19.
[^9]: R Boyd, "The State of Australian Architecture," *Architecture in Australia* (June 1967), 457.

and Melbourne, Boyd reiterated a comment by Neil Clerehan, claiming that the leadership linked to bold modern architectural production in Melbourne during the first half of the 20th century had shifted to Sydney sometime just before 1960. He described differences in outlook: "The Melbourne school was forward-looking, daring all and damning all aesthetic rules … The Sydney school was … of quite a different character: conservative and aesthetic." [^10] Sydney architects, by looking to a recent past, had "rediscover[ed] in the uninspiring local vernacular … a native cunning with brickwork and carpentry. The Sydney school adapted these qualities of technique to a sophisticated architecture." [^11] Naming Ken Woolley, Russell Jack and Ian McKay as strong proponents, he noted further that work by others had been "watered down… until practically all that was left were the rough dark bricks and the brown creosoted off-saw timber, a tamed Australian romantic kind of brutalism." [^12]

Clearly, he was not an enthusiast: "Local inbreeding of fashion is active all the time; for instance the present passing flush of clinker brick and brown creosote." [^13] Boyd nonetheless noted that there was enough work to form "the nearest thing to a regional style seen in this country for more than a century … [It] was a grassroots movement. Its language could be understood by the spec. builder." [^14] Pointing to subtle romantic allusions and aspects of nostalgia, including the revival of Marseilles-pattern tiles and interest in the Californian bungalow of the 1920s, he described buildings with "earthy colouring and nutty-crunchy textures." [^15] Sydney Ancher and Harry Seidler were incorporated in his discussion, with their distinct commitments to modernism forming more "independent positions". Similarly noted as a discrete participant was the "boldness" up to 1965 of the Sydney Opera House. [^16]

[^10]: Boyd, "The State of Australian Architecture," 459.
[^11]: Boyd, "The State of Australian Architecture," 459.
[^12]: Boyd, "The State of Australian Architecture," 459.
[^13]: Boyd, "The State of Australian Architecture," 454.
[^14]: Boyd, "The State of Australian Architecture," 459.
[^15]: Boyd, "The State of Australian Architecture," 463.
[^16]: Boyd, "The State of Australian Architecture," 463.

At the time of his death, Boyd had circumscribed the popular imagination of Australian architecture for some 20 years. An erudite, witty interlocutor, he had made perspicacious assessments of the moods and modes of Australian architecture from the early colonial period to the present. Equally engaged with the contemporary as with the past, Boyd positioned Australian architecture within an international frame, seeking a local idiom. But his discomfort with the brutalist-inflected Sydney work and his later, begrudging recognition of its importance presaged a generational change in the voice that defined an Australian view of its architecture.

That voice would become Jennifer Taylor's; the locus of contemporary writing on Australian architectural history would be the University of Sydney. There were, of course, differences between Boyd's approach and Taylor's. Boyd's singular commitment to modernism was echoed, yet reoriented, by Taylor in her articulation of more regionally specific adaptations and via a focus on Sydney specific sites and circumstances. Her prolific writing examined a remarkable variety of architects across the globe, many with whom she developed strong friendships and professional relationships. Her commitment to chronicling the history of the present reduced the time gap between the creation of architecture and the writing of its history. Written from within the university's Department of Architecture, her observations relayed the suggestion of institutional endorsement.

## Jennifer Taylor's *Houses for Sydney*

Born in Sydney and brought up in Queensland, Taylor was the daughter of a doctor who did not believe in further education for women. She trained as a nurse and married a doctor, whom she followed to England. More interested in design, at the age of 25 she sought a place at what is now Oxford Brookes University (then a polytechnic) intending to study graphic or interior design. She was instead offered a place in the architecture course, which she described as "the greatest fluke of my life," having previously considered architecture the sole province of men. [^17] Relocating to the United States with her family in 1963, she continued her architectural studies at the University of Washington, Seattle. In 1967, she graduated with a Bachelor of Architecture cum laude, receiving an American Institute of Architects student medal the same year. Taylor graduated from further study at the same university in 1969 with a Master of Architecture in architectural history. Her thesis, "An Inquiry into Some Aspects of Recent Unorthodox Trends in Architecture," was prescient of her scholarship to follow. [^18]

In 1969, Taylor, her husband, and their two children returned to Australia, settling in Sydney. In consultation with Richard "Peter" Johnson, Dean of Architecture at the University of Sydney, Taylor was offered an academic position as a lecturer in contemporary architectural history. Johnson, an architectural graduate of the University of Sydney, was also the Dean of the Faculty of Architecture from 1967 to 1986. A partner in the respected Sydney firm McConnel, Smith and Johnson, he served in wide-ranging leadership roles during his tenure, including as national president of the (then Royal) Australian Institute of Architects from 1981 to 1982 and as a member of the New South Wales Architects Registration Board. Promoting connectivity between the academy and architectural practice, he oversaw an increased research focus at the university during the 1970s and 1980s. Taylor consistently credited Johnson as having given her enormous support; he helped her establish new courses and arranged funding for her programs. She noted he introduced her to people and opportunities, encouraged her to start publishing, and assisted with her books. [^19] Such assistance was to prove critical for Taylor's writing as well as her teaching, and both built on relationships between the university and the profession.

At the University of Sydney until 1998, Taylor's career was marked by a dual commitment to educating tomorrow's architects and chronicling the architectural past. Significant figures in Sydney today recall her lasting impact. Peter Tonkin from Tonkin Zulaikha Greer remembers her teaching a course on modernism in 1971. Later courses such as "The Modern Movement in Architecture," together with its complement "Current Architecture," were to become regular, popular, though non-compulsory, offerings. Students in these classes were oriented via historians such as Reyner Banham, Nikolaus Pevsner and Sigfried Giedion, clearly framed as a series of signposts for understanding early and late 20th-century architecture. Tonkin notes that, in 1972, Taylor also taught studio to all students in second-year design, remembering an ambitious focus on urban attitudes and citywide influences. [^20]

Respected architect, urban thinker and City of Sydney Councillor, Philip Thalis recounts advanced seminars with Taylor during 1983-84 in which Banham presented to a discussion group of approximately 10 students. Influential British architects and theorists such as Alison Smithson and Peter Cook participated in these seminars in 1983; Dutch architect Aldo Van Eyck contributed in 1984. For Thalis, such moments were academically memorable. [^21]

Esteemed architect, educator and urban design manager for the City of Sydney, Peter John Cantrill taught with Taylor in many of her courses from the mid-1980s to the 1990s. [^22] Describing her endless enthusiasm, generosity and personable qualities, he emphasised her strong interest in speaking to architects and seeing their works. Students enrolled in her popular Australian architecture elective were given talks by the relevant architects and taken on numerous local tours to see all the buildings.

[^17]: J Howlin, "Indesign Luminary: Jennifer Taylor," *Indesignlive*, 22 April 2014, https://www.indesignlive.com/people/luminary-archives-jennifer-taylor, accessed 2 March 2018.
[^18]: Taylor's staff profile at QUT records her major achievements. See "Adjunct Professor Jennifer Taylor," Queensland University of Technology, http://staff.qut.edu.au/staff/taylorje/, accessed 12 May 2018. The thesis is also listed in the library catalogue of the University of Washington.
[^19]: Howlin, "Indesign Luminary: Jennifer Taylor."
[^20]: P Tonkin, in telecom conversation with the authors, 15 May 2018.
[^21]: P Thalis, in telecom conversation with the authors, 15 May 2018.
[^22]: PJ Cantrill, in telecom conversation with the authors, 15 May 2018.

… she acknowledged the influence of Frank Lloyd Wright and organic architecture; the influence of Asia, particularly Japan; interest in the natural landscape; and neo-brutalism.

— Catherine Lassen and Julie Willis, "The Sydney School"

Cantrill reported expansive first-hand accounts of buildings and architects by Taylor in her teaching, referring to interviews and personal experiences rather than architectural theory. American architect Peter Eisenman, for example, was presented through Taylor's own slides of his radical houses. [^23] From an era marked by increasing complexity in architectural discussions, numerous former students remember Taylor fondly for her capacity to simplify.

In 1972, Taylor published *An Australian Identity*. Both the creative and institutional milieu in which Taylor found herself had been an impetus for the book. Documenting and offering commentary on recent local architectural production, it showcased a series of key Sydney architects and their domestic projects, including Sydney Ancher, Arthur Baldwinson, Peter Muller, Russell Jack, Bill and Ruth Lucas, Bryce Mortlock, Bruce Rickard, Ross Thorne, Tony Moore, Donald Gazzard, Ken Woolley, Michael Dysart, Peter Johnson, John James and Ian McKay. Harry Seidler's work was also present, yet its commitment to an apparently earlier set of preoccupations associated with the modernism of the International Style was less visible within the context framed by the book.

Many of the included architects had a relationship to the University of Sydney; both Woolley and Johnson were distinguished alumni. Woolley had graduated in 1955 with the University Medal, among other major awards and a prestigious Byera Hadley Travelling Scholarship. Johnson, an Honours graduate under professors Wilkinson, Hook and Ashworth in 1951 had, as dean, appointed Taylor and encouraged her in publishing books. Moore worked for McConnel, Smith and Johnson. Lucas, Mortlock and Dysart were respected graduates. Baldwinson and Thorne were University of Sydney Department of Architecture academics. Also its publisher, the architecture school in which Taylor taught was collectively present within her book.

This select series of Sydney dwellings were identified with the emergence of a new national architectural style. The collected modern domestic buildings were framed as innovative outcomes of the "Sydney School." As successful adaptations to indigenous circumstances, these examples were submitted as uniquely Australian. Taylor's term, first suggested by Milo Dunphy some 10 years earlier, was in some parts tentative, in others more committed. Her use of the stylistic label gave it credence; indeed, she suggested there was "some validity in the term," but she did not attempt to defend or closely define it. [^24]

At the outset, she suggested a provisional position: "The ... material is the result of an exploratory study, intended to provide a [starting] point for further investigation for those interested in this particular development in the history of Sydney's architecture. In many ways it is simple journalism—who did what and why." [^25] The book had three main parts: an introduction that positioned housing, the "Sydney School" and the Sydney scene within an emerging Australian identity; a section titled "The Development of a Regional Architecture 1953-1963," and one described as "After 1963." The subheadings within the regional section offered the kind of treatment that came to characterise Taylor's writing: a neatly organised set of ideas, not necessarily chronologically organised, but corralled as architectural themes presented across multiple projects. In this way, she could promote an encompassing attitude— such as there being something distinctive about Sydney architecture of the period—while allowing the presence of differing inspirations within her narrative. Within the section on regional development, she acknowledged the influences of Frank Lloyd Wright and organic architecture; the influence of Asia, particularly Japan; interest in the natural landscape; and neo-brutalism. All are distinct themes within the fraught and fought term, the "Sydney School." Taylor here demonstrated an approach to writing architectural history that she would carry forth into subsequent publications: a documentary attitude, noting who did what, overlaid with a thematic reading that directed and demonstrated the distinctive variations and architectural inspirations of the time.

[^23]: Cantrill, in telecom conversation with the authors.
[^24]: Taylor, *An Australian Identity*, 67.
[^25]: Taylor, *An Australian Identity*, 6.

**Figure 3** — Max Dupain, Peter Muller's "Audette" House in Castlecrag, NSW, 1953. In *An Australian Identity*, this image appeared (as cropped) heading a section titled "The Development of a Regional Architecture 1953-63." Collection of Peter Muller.

In her brief introduction to *An Australian Identity*, Taylor underlined ongoing appeals for a regionally specific architecture. She referred to Freeland's productive identification of a Queensland country house type well attuned to local climate, technology and material availability, quoting his depiction: "Growing logically out of physical causes, it had a distinctive character that was the closest that Australia has ever come to producing an indigenous style." [^26] Noting the tendency for Australian designers to imitate international examples, she described her exploratory study as concerned with some architects who have attempted a remedy. [^27] Emphasised throughout her illustrated discussion were the particular qualities of a series of Sydney settings, largely steeply sloping sites with natural bushland and sandstone outcrops. Highlighted were dwellings in these locations with roughly textured materials, without applied finishes, suggestive of rustic origins and designed to merge with the natural indigenous environment. Roof forms over platforms that stepped and echoed the terrain, coupled with economical priorities and an interest in slightly rough construction techniques, were all presented as characteristic.

While many of the works were indebted to British brutalism and modern Scandinavian architects such as Alvar Aalto, her descriptions of these houses promoted a deliberately local idiom. Suggesting historical distance, *An Australian Identity* positioned key figures in the development of modern Sydney architecture between historical overview, looking backwards, searching for a regional style, and Johnson's explicitly projective architectural goal, described in Taylor's book as a "self-conscious aim to produce something that was Australian." [^28]

[^26]: Taylor, *An Australian Identity*, 11–13; Freeland, *Architecture in Australia*, 209.
[^27]: Taylor, *An Australian Identity*, 13.
[^28]: Taylor, *An Australian Identity*, 72.

**Figure 4** — Max Dupain, Peter Muller's own house in Whale Beach, NSW, 1954. Muller's self-built home was published in *An Australian Identity*, although not with this image. Collection of Peter Muller.

By emphasising climate specificity, geographic locale and regional history, concerns identified by Taylor as also characteristic in architectural developments in England and the United States were underlined as particular to Sydney.

## Sydney School Reflections

Recently relocated from the University of Melbourne to the Power Institute of Fine Arts at the University of Sydney, David Saunders affirmed in 1969 that Sydney had a "lively architectural theme or style" that he designated "the backward-looking avant-garde." [^29] In a succinct article titled "Sydney," he called this work romantic, linking it to "Griffin's Castlecrag" and the Californian bungalow, as well as brutalism and Mediterranean or "Italian alpine" images. [^30] Gazzard's 1960 Hunters Hill House was included as the earliest example. [^31] Moore's 1961 North Sydney House, Woolley's 1962 Mosman House, and Johnson's Chatswood House of 1963, were all discussed. Saunders' concise overview of this style, not dissimilar to earlier accounts, mentioned clinker bricks and white washed brickwork, as well as "lots of wood" employed with a small range of often hand-wrought materials. [^32] Tricky split-levels, unexpected sources of light, and short structural spans with roofs of "brown terracotta tiles" were customary. [^33] Describing integral gardens, he relayed the emphasis on predominantly native planting that also admitted bamboos and ferns, with water seepage "diverted to Japanese-type ends" and designed incorporation of found Sydney sandstone outcrops. [^34]

When *An Australian Identity* appeared in 1972, Taylor extended such commentary. However, with the exception of a connection to Freeland in her introduction and a minimal mention of Saunders' article in the concluding section, the study was presented without detailed reference to any published context. [^35] Earlier observations had suggested tendencies in the manner of a school; Taylor more vigorously claimed identification of a "Sydney School" style, framing her approach in the acknowledgements: "I have relied almost entirely on conversations with those directly involved. ... In particular I wish to express my gratitude to the many house owners who allowed me to visit their homes." [^36] Taylor's distillation of trends in Sydney's architectural scene, which served to underscore and extensively promulgate the appellation "Sydney School," would be contested by many historians and architects, including those whose work was surveyed. [^37]

A sequence of more current statements from many of the architects in *An Australian Identity* provides conflicting perspectives. Woolley, whose Mosman House formed a key moment for Taylor within the "Sydney School," later questioned the collective endeavour: "A number of times I've said it didn't exist ... In the sense of a group of people getting

[^29]: D Saunders, "Sydney," *Architect* (Melbourne) 3, no. 4 (September-October 1969): 20.
[^30]: Saunders, "Sydney," 20.
[^31]: Saunders, "Sydney," 20.
[^32]: Saunders, "Sydney," 20.
[^33]: Saunders, "Sydney," 20.
[^34]: Saunders, "Sydney," 20.
[^35]: In the concluding section, "After 1963," Saunders' comment on John James' Mosman house as "the most vigorous variation on the theme" is quoted. Taylor, *An Australian Identity*, 74, 76.
[^36]: Taylor, *An Australian Identity*, 6.
[^37]: See, for example, Stanislaus Fung, "The 'Sydney School'?," *Transition* 4, no. 3 (July 1985): 38-43; and Michael Bogle, "Arthur Baldwinson: Regional Modernism in Sydney 1937–1969" (PhD diss., RMIT University, 2008).

**Figure 5** — Max Dupain, Sydney Ancher's own house in Neutral Bay, NSW, 1957. As published (cropped) in *An Australian Identity*. Underlining their "Australian" qualities, two houses designed by Ancher were illustrated in Taylor's book. Both exterior photographs showed a single, horizontal volume, framed between bands of landscape. State Library of New South Wales.

together to form a school or even to recognise that there is one ... it didn't exist." [^38]

In *An Australian Identity*, Taylor framed Gazzard's 1961 project home as of "importance in the establishment of this ethic." [^39] In 2016, he outlined his perceptions of the "movement":

> Some credence perhaps was given to the idea that Sydney houses were special in some way when Lendlease developed a residential estate at Carlingford and chose the young architects in Jennifer Taylor's book to each design two or three houses for sale ... But building these houses designed by a group of these young architects in one place only demonstrated to me that there wasn't much in common between them in a design sense, much less that they formed any sort of coherent "school" ... What these houses did have in common was that they all used the same economically available materials, there was a fashion for clinker bricks, and they were all located in the Sydney suburbs. [^40]

Muller had designed two important modern houses, one constructed at Castlecrag in 1953 and the other constructed at Whale Beach in 1955 [Figures 3 & 4]. Prominent in *An Australian Identity*, they were the first examples in a section titled "The Development of a Regional Architecture 1953-63." [^41] In 2014, Muller reflected: "Academics, scholars and journalists very much need to classify everything, [and] labelled those Sydney architects who use natural materials such as wood and stone, like myself, [as] organic architects and members of the Sydney School as if we were a coherent group. We were site specific to a certain extent but certainly not organic in the sense I've... described." [^42]

[^38]: "Interview with Ken Woolley: The Context of the Melbourne/Sydney Debate," *Transition* 21 (September 1987): 13–22.
[^39]: Taylor, *An Australian Identity*, 59.
[^40]: D Gazzard, "Is There 'a Sydney School of Architecture'?" August 2016, http://dongazzard.com/publications/articles/is-the-a-sydney-school-of-architecture.aspx, accessed 12 February 2018.
[^41]: Taylor, *An Australian Identity*, 24–29.
[^42]: P Muller, "Walsh Bay New South Wales," interview by Michael Bogle, 15 May 2014, transcript courtesy NSW AIA.

James' 1965 Mosman House, the subject of the final section in Taylor's book, "After 1963," was seen as a particular synthesis of the "style." [^43] In 2015, he wrote of the collective endeavour:

> I was part of the Sydney Timber-and-Bush School along with Peter Muller, Russell Jack and others. I suggested to Jennifer Taylor that we all meet and see if we could discover what inspired us. This we did at her house in the summer of 1981 [sic] … It was an extraordinary meeting. We all noted that though we knew of each other, we seldom met; neither socially, nor for business, nor did we spend much time running around looking at each other's houses. Yet together we created a common style, now called the Sydney School. The only things we had in common, and that we all agreed stimulated our creativity, was sandstone rocks and angophoras. [^44]

Projecting strong thematic connections between the architects she discussed, Taylor's 1972 study had framed a sequence of distinguished architectural domestic works in suburban Sydney, for the most part via plans, black and white photographs, and commentary. Presentation formats for each house varied; it was difficult to precisely compare the selected designs. Plans were shown at a range of scales and orientations. Occasionally no north point, photo or plan of a project was present. Isometric drawings rather than plans depicted three of the dwellings, and sections were only included for two houses, designed by Lucas. Respected architectural photographers Max Dupain and David Moore were responsible for many of the black and white photographs. [^45] Such depictions persistently showed buildings surrounded by local landscape. Native bushland, rocks or eucalypts featured prominently in 24 of the 39 total photographs; in most, only a portion of the building was visible. With the Sydney setting as much in focus as the buildings, and lacking sufficient material for architectonic comparison between designs, a collective appearance framed by the indigenous natural surroundings predominated. Seidler's "House in Turramurra, 1949" was included, illustrated in plan alone. [^46] Typically referred to as the Rose Seidler House today, this celebrated modern building was an almost pure translation of the Bauhaus design principles inherited by Seidler, who had studied under European modern masters Gropius and Breuer at Harvard University. Taut and light, machine-like, this house combined standardised construction, strict functional organisation, economy of means, compact arrangements, and minimalism in materials and details with a structural clarity and austere aesthetic elegance. Geometric restraint provided both a contrast and means of engagement with the natural surroundings. Large glazed areas enabled connections between the inhabitants and the landscape. Typically oriented towards the north, such openings were shaded from the summer sun by overhangs. In *The International Style*, Henry-Russell Hitchcock and Philip Johnson's influential 1932 exhibition at New York's Museum of Modern Art, a radical modernism with a global emphasis had been promoted. [^47]

Seidler's house was, in many ways, a textbook example of the International Style. Through publications such as Taylor's, the increasingly international post-war cultural impacts of early modern architecture in Australia were positioned as nationalist and regionalist. [^48] Seidler's first building in Australia had won the prestigious Sir John Sulman Medal in 1951.

Sydney Ancher had also been awarded the Sir John Sulman Medal in 1945 for his own house on Maytone Avenue in Killara. In *An Australian Identity*, his work was framed as a Sydney-specific modernist adaptation. Photographs showed elegant, grounded yet

[^43]: Taylor, An Australian Identity, 74–79.
[^44]: John James, "Architecture 1957–1969," http://www.johnjames.com.au/johnandhilaryjames-architecture.shtml, accessed 12 February 2018.
[^45]: Eleven photographers were listed in the acknowledgements, most for one, two or three images. Max Dupain and David Moore were each credited with nine images. Taylor, An Australian Identity, 6.
[^46]: Taylor, *An Australian Identity*, 22.
[^47]: HR Hitchcock and P Johnson, *The International Style: Architecture Since 1922* (New York: Norton & Co., 1932).
[^48]: WJR Curtis, *Modern Architecture Since 1900* (Oxford: Phaidon Press, 1987), 334.

abstract volumes between bands of local landscape and in horizontal counterpoint to vertical eucalyptus trees. Generous external terraces and sheltered verandahs provided expanded living space, which was sensible in Sydney's temperate climate and protected the long glass walls from the elements.

The painterly aspects of the work were emphasised, together with the suggestion of a relaxed modesty and an informal lifestyle. Taylor stressed the regional particularity of this approach over equally present late-modern preoccupations: "Ancher's modest, almost self-deprecating manner cannot conceal the importance of the idiom he established. The appeal of these houses lay in their beauty, their suitability for the climate, and the new lifestyle they made available. They demonstrated to others the possibilities of a different approach to Australian domestic architecture" [^49] [Figure 5].

Ancher's dwellings had slate roofs coloured to match the local bark and walls painted in the individual pinks and greys of angophoras and other eucalypts. [^50] However, he explored architectural threads leading from well-known examples in England, Germany, Scandinavia, as well as from the United States and Japan. A pioneer in modern domestic Australian architecture, he had spent five years in Europe, travelling extensively, visiting Mies van der Rohe's work in the 1931 Stuttgart Weissenhofsiedlung and in the building exhibition in Berlin. Admiring both Mies and Le Corbusier, he had also been impressed by a series of four lectures given by Frank Lloyd Wright in London and had travelled to Denmark, Sweden and Finland, where he was "bowled over" by some of their

[^49]: Taylor, *An Australian Identity*, 33.

[^50]: S Murray, "Obituary: Sydney Ancher," *Architecture Australia* (February-March 1980): 68.

**Figure 6** — David Moore, Bill and Ruth Lucas' Lucas House in Castlecrag, NSW, 1957.
Two pages from Taylor's 1972 book, in which the Lucas' home was presented.
*An Australian Identity* prioritised the sense of the house immersed in its native bushland setting.
Collection of Lisa Moore, and the University of Sydney School of Architecture, Design and Planning.

**Figure 7** — David Moore, Bill and Ruth Lucas' Lucas House, Castlecrag, NSW, 1957. Contemporaneous with the Lucas House photographs taken by Moore shown in *An Australian Identity*, this image formed the cover to a book published in 2017, *An Unfinished Experiment in Living: 150 Australian Houses 1950–65*. Rather than privileging the locale, this image suggests connections to architectural examples such as the Californian Case Study House No.8 by Charles and Ray Eames in Pacific Palisades (1949). Collection of Lisa Moore.

modern buildings. [^51] In 1939, *Architecture* published extracts of his thesis, titled "The Evolution of Modern Architecture." [^52] David Saunders and Catherine Burke's book on Ancher, published by the Power Institute of Fine Arts at the University of Sydney in 1976, noted his high regard for the Case Study House #8 (Eames House) in California by Charles and Ray Eames. [^53] While acknowledging this background, rather than reading his work as a complex assimilation within the local context of such evolving modern preoccupations, Taylor underlined Sydney-specific aspects of his houses to promote his design mode as uniquely Australian.

As with Ancher's buildings, dwellings by Lucas were presented in *An Australian Identity* to highlight their climatic and site specificity. Six pages of the slim book were devoted to his work. Mentioning his University of Sydney education, Taylor emphasised that, after graduating, Lucas "did not travel overseas to study architecture. He was sure that the solution to Australian architecture was to be found in Australia." [^54] For Bill and Ruth Lucas, in their Castlecrag House, a primary ambition was to retain and safeguard the local bushland and terrain [Figure 6]. Built in 1957 in a simple, frugal manner, it was an elemental platform hovering around a floating courtyard in the treetops. Four minimal steel columns with rough sawn hardwood members in a braced steel and timber frame formed a direct yet delicate assembly. Extremely economical, the house provided the lightest formwork for living, barely touching the sandstone outcrops, eucalyptus and ferns. Glass walls in lightweight frames around the suspended court evoked a sense of the building being almost all void. With no corridors, the rooms, in a three by four grid, were each surrounded by light and air. Their uses could be reorganised over time to suit changing family needs or work arrangements. Throughout, a clear distinction was evident between the assembly and its natural setting. High above a steeply sloping gully, one might have had the sense of floating, finding a life within the trees.

The Sydney suburban context of Castlecrag was unusual. Planned and realised by Frank Lloyd Wright associates Walter Burley and Marion Mahony Griffin in the 1920s, it was an innovative experiment conceived and laid out to celebrate the particular qualities of the indigenous landscape. Legally and materially constructed, it architecturally articulated an ideal social community living in appreciation of the native flora, rock formations and precarious harbour foreshore. Important natural elements and harbour reserves were collectively owned, protected, and enjoyed.

Covenants established by Griffin, aimed at preserving the region's natural character, were in accord with the Lucas' design and ethical attitudes; they sought to reinforce such priorities. [^55] The explicit desire was for an

[^51]: R Apperly and P Reynolds, "Ancher, Sydney Edward Cambrian (1904-1979)," in *Australian Dictionary of Biography*, vol. 13 (Melbourne: Melbourne University Press, 1993), 41–42.
[^52]: S Ancher, "The Evolution of Modern Architecture," *Architecture* (1 December 1939), 244–49.
[^53]: D Saunders and C Burke, *Ancher, Mortlock, Murray & Woolley: Sydney Architects 1946-1976* (Sydney: Power Institute of Fine Arts, University of Sydney, 1976), 12.

[^54]: Taylor, *An Australian Identity*, 38.
[^55]: WE Lucas and R Lucas, "Lucas House, Castlecrag," *Architecture in Australia* (October–December 1958), 63.

architecture that made possible a way of living in that bushland, with minimal disruption to the landscape. Aligned with the Griffins' architectural ideals, engagement with the indigenous terrain had been critical to the earliest conception of Castlecrag. In the Lucas House, a return to first-principles living, in the manner of Thoreau, overlapped with the Griffins' directive.

Interests in the architecture of Japan were also evident; similarly important were material assembly techniques aligned with Alison and Peter Smithson's "brutal" directness. Future-focused technological experimentations that optimised radical lightness were also crucial. Multiple aspects associated with the global dissemination of modernism were present in the Lucas' home. By framing these explorations in terms of Sydney-specific sites and climate, Taylor foregrounded the work's locality [Figure 7].

Connections to Wright were present in a number of the houses in *An Australian Identity*, including three designed by Muller. Castlecrag as a context may have encouraged such interests; architects such as Ancher had expressed admiration for Wright's thinking. Muller's 1953 Audette House in Castlecrag [Figure 3] and his own home at Whale Beach [Figure 4], built in 1955, were described by Taylor as "buildings which clearly exemplified those qualities that were found so desirable in Wright's work. They were contemporary buildings, actually erected in Sydney … built with an understandable and realizable technology." [^56] Muller's house at Whale Beach had been previously described in numerous contexts as Wrightian; a December 1955 issue of *Architecture and Arts* had featured a portfolio of his work, including a plan, photos, and numerous details of that dwelling with the accompanying text:

[^56]: Taylor, *An Australian Identity*, 25.

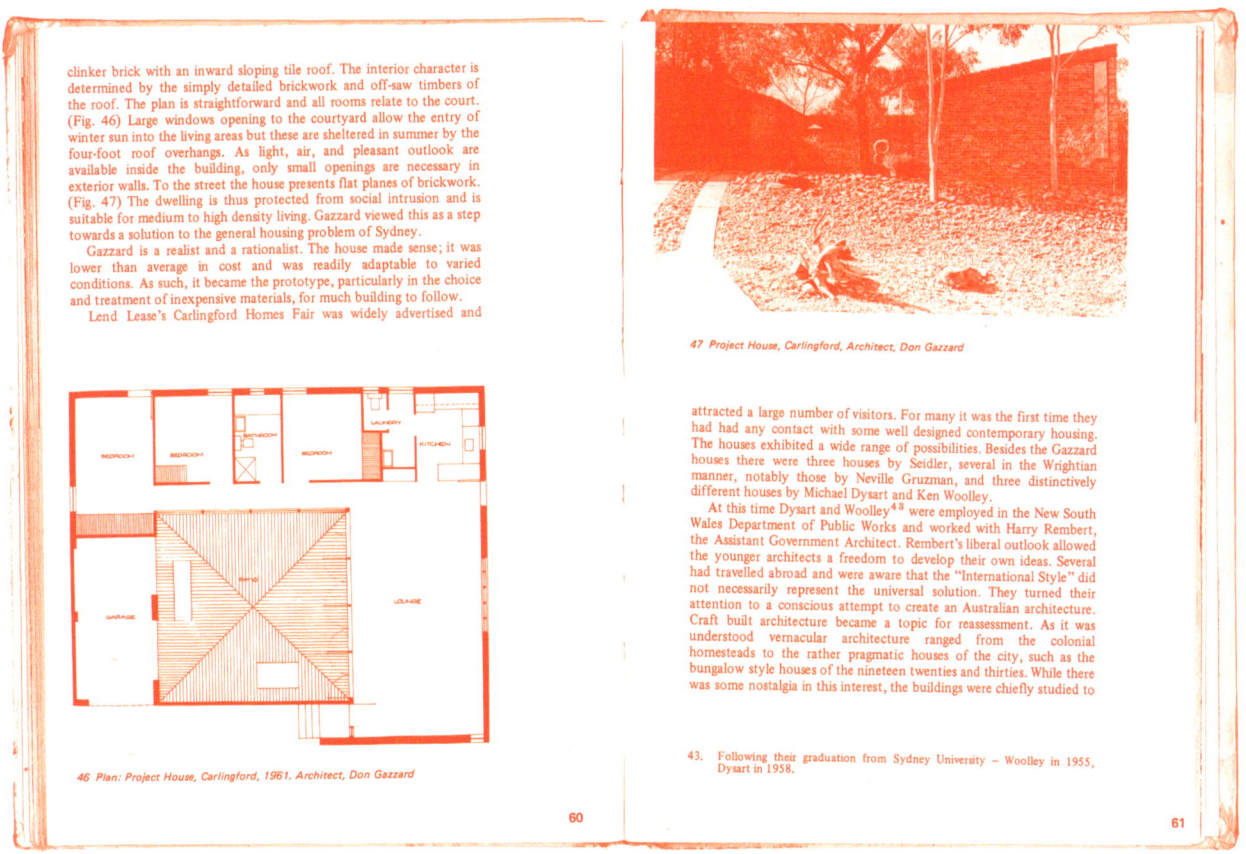

**Figure 8** — Two pages from *An Australian Identity* in the section titled "Builder's Architecture." Using "spotted clinker brick with an inward sloping tile roof," Donald Gazzard designed this economical project home in Carlingford, NSW, in 1961. University of Sydney School of Architecture, Design and Planning.

> Mr Muller, whose work is in the style of famed (87-year-old) American architect, Frank Lloyd Wright, is the second Architect to interpret 'organic' architecture in its true sense in Australia. The first was the late Walter Burley Griffin, who planned Canberra and many fine buildings both in Melbourne and Sydney. [^57]

Wright's principles were locally resituated by Muller. Imaginative re-employment of materials "at-hand" was evident. A batch of prosaic, red, wire-cut bricks, purchased inexpensively by the owner of the Audette dwelling, were, for example, adapted by Muller with a technique he referred to as "snotted brickwork." [^58] Mortar was allowed to escape from between each brick to produce a texture. [^59] Taylor commented on his inventive use of "marine varnish" to protect unpainted exterior hardwood in that house; the building was treated as if it were a timber boat. [^60] At Whale Beach, Muller specified "grey cement bricks to match exactly the colour of the gum tree bark, supplied by 'Monier'." [^61] The found Sydney foreshore was foregrounded. Natural elements such as angophoras were radically incorporated; a native rock outcrop formed the fireplace. Grass-covered, glass and flat roofs lined with water, mirrored the surrounding trees and sky. Daring, spatially interlocked cantilevers and technologies, all used at their current limits, employed technical plywood expertise from Ralph Symonds, later associated with the realisation of Jørn Utzon's Opera House.

The fourth subheading within the "Regional Architecture" section of *An Australian Identity* was "The Natural House," invoking the title of Wright's 1954 book. [^62] Focused on adaptations of a Wrightian idiom, Taylor noted that dwellings by architects such as Rickard "represent a direct implantation in Sydney of those qualities Wright achieved in his 'natural' house." [^63] While Gruzman was mentioned for working with similar priorities, none of his designs were described. His omission was curious, particularly given a more recent description of a house he designed in Sydney's Middle Cove:

> Features included industrialist Ralph Symonds' Copperply panels—plywood panels with copper on the outside and aluminium on the inside... and, significantly, dark stained timbers and natural brick. These make the Goodman House [1956] one of the earliest examples to employ the language of the so-called Sydney School of the early 1960s. [^64]

Taylor did not offer criteria for her selection of architects and buildings; émigré Sydney architects such as Hugh Buhrich, today celebrated, were similarly excluded. Equally absent were architects such as Douglas Snelling. Snelling had won *Architecture and Arts*' best house award in 1955 for his residence in Bellevue Hill, which "displayed influences of Wright's organic architecture in its plan, horizontal roof planes, wide eaves, expressed stonework and wood structure, flowing spaces and the integration of the house with the surrounding landscape." [^65]

Alongside Wright's impact, discussing the simultaneous interest among Sydney architects in brutalism, Taylor recalled Le Corbusier and his vaulted double Maisons Jaoul, adding: "the 'brut' aspect of Corbusier's work reached Australia directly... and indirectly through the 'Neo Brutalism' of the Smithsons and their followers in England." [^66] Placing Tony Moore's work in this tradition, she discussed "builder's architecture" through a series of project homes designed by architects

[^57]: "A Portfolio of the Work of Peter Muller," *Architecture and Arts* 28 (December 1955): 20.
[^58]: S Crafti, "Peter Muller Profile," *Indesign* 59 (2014): 168.
[^59]: Crafti, "Peter Muller Profile," 168.
[^60]: Taylor, *An Australian Identity*, 26.
[^61]: "A Portfolio of the Work of Peter Muller," 21.
[^62]: FL Wright, *The Natural House* (New York: Bramhall House, 1954).
[^63]: Taylor, *An Australian Identity*, 52–53.
[^64]: G London, P Goad and C Hamann, *An Unfinished Experiment in Living: 150 Australian Houses 1950–65* (Crawley, WA: University of Western Australia Publishing, 2017), 206.
[^65]: P Hogben, "Architecture and Arts and the Mediation of American Architecture in Post-war Australia," *Fabrications: The Journal of the Society of Archietctural Historians, Australian and New Zealand* 22, no. 1 (June 2012), 44; "House of the Year by Douglas Snelling, Architect," *Architecture and Arts* 34 (June 1956): 34–39.
[^66]: Taylor, *An Australian Identity*, 56.

**Figure 9** — David Moore, Richard (Peter) Johnson's Johnson House, Chatswood, NSW, 1963. As Dean and Head of School for the Department of Architecture at the University of Sydney, publishers of *An Australian Identity*, Johnson was present in multiple ways in Jennifer Taylor's book. Represented by this distinctive image in a section of the book titled "The Prototypes," his family home came to exemplify the Sydney School style. Collection of Lisa Moore.

such as Gazzard and Woolley [Figure 8]. Accentuated in these latter works was the production of simple, dignified but economical homes, favouring robust, less finished, low maintenance materials. She described these results as:

> a revolution in the standard of new single family project built homes … Through the skilful handling … contained volumes appear larger than they are, allowing minimum square footage, and therefore cost reduction … Materials used directly in the Brutalist sense also lower cost. The "earthy" colours and textures of the selected materials have their roots in the past. They create an atmosphere of homeliness and allow the houses to blend with the undeveloped terrain on which they are often erected. The result has been a house in which the buyer feels comfortable and one that he believes is distinctly "Australian." [^67]

Optimising light, air, outlook and privacy within tight planning pressures, such examples tested modernist ideals to provide well-designed, socially inclusive housing via close engagement with locally inexpensive materials, details, and assembly modes. Here, the regionalist plea was framed by an adaptation to optimise amenity within local circumstances.

Concluding the presentation of *An Australian Identity* with a section titled "The Prototypes," Taylor presented two dwellings, respectively designed by Woolley in 1962 and Johnson in 1963. [^68] [Figure 9] Saunders had discussed each in 1969; both had won Australian Institute of Architects Wilkinson Awards. *Sydney Morning Herald* architecture critic Eva Buhrich had also published articles on these houses. [^69] Introduced by Taylor as "sophisticated expressions of what is basically a folk theme," both buildings were presented as products of "the movement," explicated by Taylor in a footnote: "This movement is sometimes referred to as the 'Sydney School'." [^70] Here, building on extant commentary by Boyd, Saunders, Buhrich and others, *An Australian Identity* more explicitly linked the assembled local architectural works with an impression of unified stylistic goals and a memorable architectural image. Photographs of Woolley and Johnson's own houses framed by bushland were clear examples. By collecting works within a book endorsed by the university in multiple ways, Taylor's overarching narrative gathered parallel institutional support.

[^67]: Taylor, *An Australian Identity*, 63–64.
[^68]: Taylor, *An Australian Identity*, 67–73.
[^69]: From 1963–67, émigré architect and architectural writer Eva Buhrich published a series of detailed articles in the *Sydney Morning Herald* in which she discussed many of the houses published by Taylor in *An Australian Identity*. Offering an early, professionally informed, public, and local perspective on architectural attitudes today largely identified with Taylor, Buhrich located the work in a wider global context with a nuanced account of the "natural." See E Buhrich, "Designing Here 'Bitter Pill' to Melbourne," *Sydney Morning Herald*, 23 May 1967, 18.
[^70]: Taylor, *An Australian Identity*, 67.

# Taylor's Two Sydney Schools

Inventive architectural adaptations to domestic Sydney circumstances presented in Taylor's first book indicated a wide range of broadly late-modernist priorities. Lasting contributions such as Gazzard's project homes emphasised locally produced materials and the economical construction methods of the region. Wrightian works such as those by Muller were extended in relation to the delicate vegetation and precarious topography of the Sydney Harbour basin. Notwithstanding "clinker" brick walls, single pitched dark roofs, vertical windows, heavy oiled timber, natural sandstone, and tall gum trees, architects such as Lucas and Thorne explored discrete attitudes in Sydney's architecture of the 1950s and 1960s. Such figures might be rather better related via connections to another school and their University of Sydney affiliations.

Intertwined in *An Australian Identity* were many threads that connected the book to the Department of Architecture at the University of Sydney. Taylor had noted Johnson's material and moral support as crucial; he in turn benefitted from her critical writings. His own house design was clearly nominated as emblematic of the "Sydney School" mode. As noted, a large group of the represented architects were successful alumni or current faculty members, and some were both. As much a faculty project as her own book, Taylor's positioning of the wide-ranging reactive evolutions of late modern architecture within Sydney as characteristic of a new national style promoted both her institution and the selected architects. It could further be argued that Taylor's most significant "Sydney School" was created via her activities as an energetic mentor and generous architectural educator. Students from her popular history courses and thesis studies gradually formed her architectural community. Many stayed in touch throughout her life, discussing their work as it developed, was published, and often premiated. Most of the architects discussed within her books formed a local circle of professional colleagues and personal friends.

Located between an historical overview and Johnson's projective identification of an Australian style, Taylor was to return to the format employed within *An Australian Identity* in future projects. As a productive combination of her teaching that positioned contemporary architecture within the region, linked with personal friendships, strong connections to practice, and historical writing, the material in her first book was revisited in an expanded later volume, in which a dedicated chapter reaffirmed her commitment to the "Sydney School" style. *Australian Architecture since 1960*, first published in 1986, with chapter three titled "The Sydney School," became a staple textbook for architecture students around the nation during the last decade of the 20th century. [^71] With a foreword by Johnson, Taylor here too thanked the University of Sydney for financial support in developing the project. The courses she taught often became her books. A paper she gave in the 1970s on tall city buildings gave rise to a book on Australian skyscrapers in 2001, *Tall Buildings: Australian Business Going up: 1945-1970*. [^72] Her chapter on Oceania for Banister Fletcher's magisterial history of architecture in 1986 some decades later became a book titled *Architecture in the South Pacific*. [^73] Reiterated throughout her substantial career was a set of professional, personal, teaching and research relationships, interconnected with architectural history as an evolving discipline and contemporary architectural production. Through Taylor, two Sydney schools were interwoven. Her enthusiasm for architectural history could be seen as projective; her students were also to make architectural projects entwined in historical reflections. ≡

---

[^71]: J Taylor, *Australian Architecture Since 1960* (Sydney: Law Book Co., 1986).
[^72]: J Taylor, *Tall Buildings: Australian Business Going Up: 1945–1970* (Sydney: Craftsman House, 2001).
[^73]: J Taylor and J Conner, *Architecture in the South Pacific* (Honolulu: University of Hawaii Press, 2014).

Architecture was experiencing its own identity crisis, in which the fundamentals of architectural education were being challenged and students demanded new kinds of knowledge …

– Lee Stickells, "Pig Education"

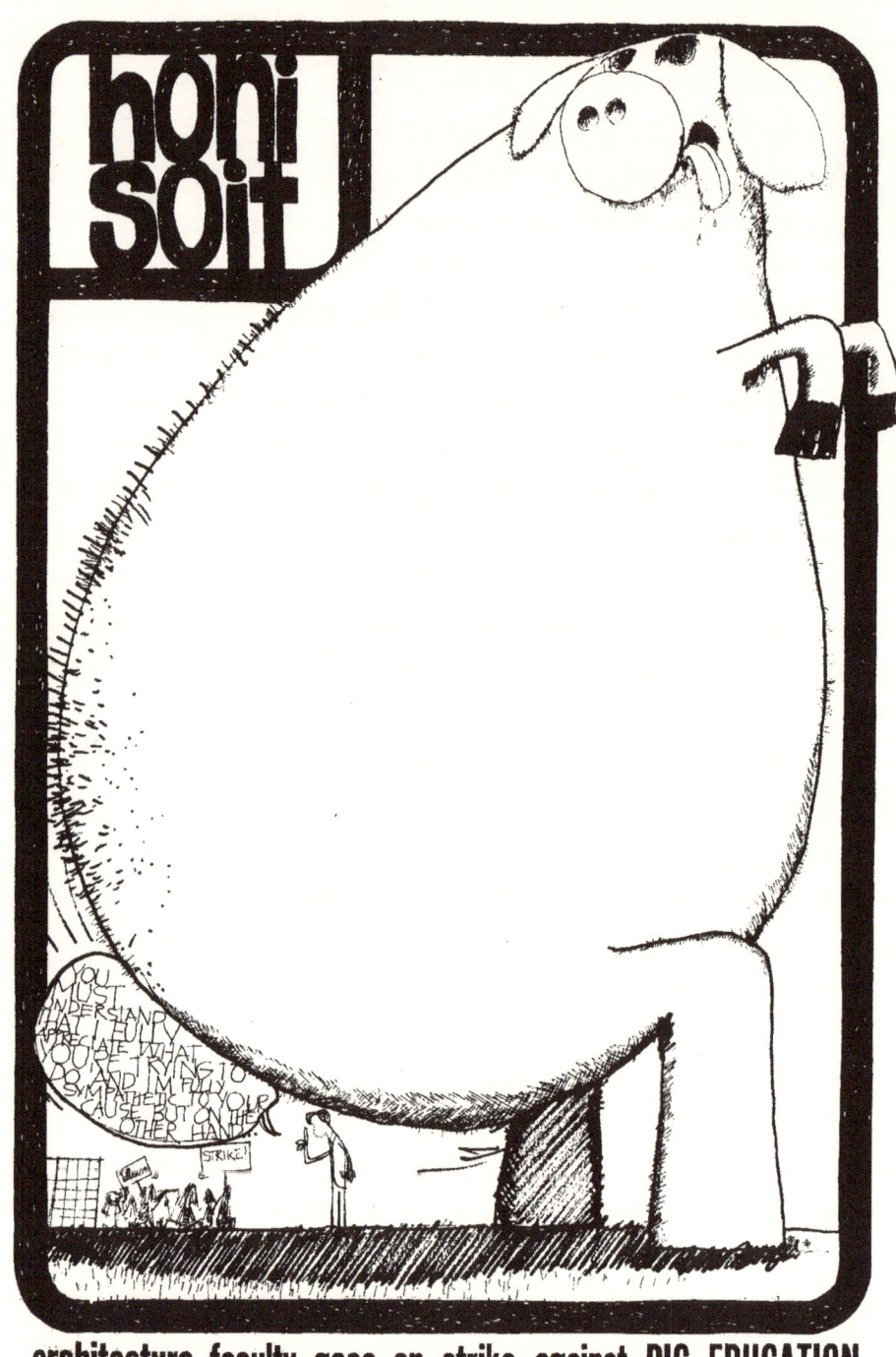

**Figure 1** — The cover for this issue of *Honi Soit* was devoted to an anonymous cartoon depiction of the architecture student strike. The faceless figure positioned precariously beneath the giant pig represents Peter Johnson, the Dean of the Faculty of Architecture at the time. The speech bubble reads: "You must understand that I fully appreciate what you're trying to do and I'm fully sympathetic to your cause but on the other hand." Protesting students bear placards reading "STRIKE!" and "PIG EDUCATION." (*Honi Soit* 45, no. 19, 3 August 1972). Lasse Kaukomaa and the Students Representative Council of the University of Sydney.

# Chapter 6: Pig Education
— Lee Stickells

> The students had long hair, were against capitalism and against architects who designed buildings.
> — Jennifer Taylor [^1]

In September 1972, *Honi Soit*, the University of Sydney's student newspaper, established in 1929, published an article detailing a shutdown of the Faculty of Architecture by students on strike [Figure 1]. Its anonymous authors recalled the scene of Monday 24 July:

> "Pig Education" slogans painted on walls and paths, notices of demands, chalk, rope, uniformed dummy, the odd burning of papers, appeared—the usual trappings, plus a few more. At 11am students went into all lecture theatres and offices, calling for a meeting on the outside lawn to "discuss the failings of the education being offered (read imposed) by the undergraduate course." Electricity to the Faculty was shut off.

Approximately 160 students and 15–20 staff (including the Dean) out of a total of 220 were present at the meeting, and after short discussion, voted overwhelmingly to strike: "to stop for at least a week in order to reassess our present education system in the light of growing dissatisfaction and frustration on the part of students and staff." [^2]

This chapter locates the architecture student strike of 1972 as a pivot point in considering the impact of the 1960s counterculture and protest movements on the professional education being delivered in the faculty. The chapter begins by reaching back into the 1960s to situate the growth of student activism and unrest in Sydney as part of a wider international phenomenon, then articulates the strike as part of that broader challenge to the period's conventional architectural education and practice. It closely examines the questions that the striking Sydney students raised about the role of expert knowledge as a political force, their demands for new pedagogical modes and their redesign of the architecture curriculum. The immediate outcomes of the strike are considered, including some of the educational experiments made possible by a new curriculum, alongside questions about the lasting effects of the student-led changes and their significance.

**Figure 2** — Sit-down protest as part of the Vietnam moratorium march and demonstration in Sydney 1969; the location is likely Broadway. University of Sydney Archives.

[^1]: J Taylor, "In Memoriam: Professor RN (Peter) Johnson 1923–2003," *Archetype* 10 (August 2003): 8.
[^2]: "Faculty Strikes," *Honi Soit* 7 (September 1972): 3. The article also included mention of a student strike at the University of Auckland's School of Architecture and Planning in late July. On the Auckland strike, see B McKay, "The Counter-Culture and its Containment: The Loose Years," in *The Auckland School: 100 Years of Architecture and Planning*, ed. J Gatley and L Treep (Auckland: School of Architecture and Planning, University of Auckland, 2017), 74–100.

# 1968 and All That

The Sydney strike was the product of very specific complaints driven by localised circumstances and personal antipathies, as well as a looser sense of dissatisfaction and outrage, expressed in sweeping demands for an architectural education that fundamentally recast architecture's social responsibility. Such claims reflected the upheavals being fomented by architecture students elsewhere as, after becoming taught as orthodoxy in the early 20th century, modernism was challenged. [^3] The Sydney architecture students' actions can also be regarded as a strand of the larger outburst of late 1960s student radicalism, characterised by strikes and sit-ins and an emphasis on direct, democratic participation. [^4] They appear to be the product of what the social critic (and former *Honi Soit* editor) Donald Horne later characterised as a "time of hope" in Australian society. [^5]

A time of hope, perhaps, but also a volatile, momentous period in which the social and political structures on which post-war affluence had rested became highly contested. The years of reconstruction for much of the world post the Second World War—shaped by the Marshall Plan, the Bretton Woods system, and the growth of the welfare state, which embraced the mainstream Left in Australia as in Europe and the UK—emerged as a long economic boom period, spanning 1947 to 1972. There was near full employment and rising standards of living in countries such as France and the UK, as well as North America, and the growth of increasingly urbanised and suburbanised societies. A similar story can be told in Australia, captured, with a little irony, in the title of Stella Lees and June Senyard's account *The 1950s: How Australia Became a Modern Society and Everyone got a House and Car*. [^6] But, as the 1960s dawned, there was also growing concern about the purpose and impacts of this growth. Outrage and anxiety were expressed over the increasing mediation of social relations through technology and consumerism; the resource depletion and environmental damage of unbridled industrialisation; and the corruption of modern ideals of progress and liberal democracy via the domineering geopolitics of the United States, epitomised by the Vietnam War. Coupled with the anger over societal inequalities, expressed, for example, in the civil rights movement and second-wave feminism, anti-authoritarianism was rife. [^7]

Universities were critical sites in the seismic social and political change that occurred across the globe during the 1960s. The number of university students worldwide grew enormously in the post-war period; between 1950 and 1970 it more than quadrupled, from six million to 26 million. [^8] The swelling of student enrolments and the growth in size and numbers of universities intensified the importance of campuses and their populations as generators of agitation, protest, and political action. [^9] A distinctive aspect of student activism in this period was an exhortation for a large-scale restructuring of society to become more just and equitable. [^10]

---

[^3]: For recent consideration of this phenomenon, see, for example: M McLeod, "The End of Innocence: From Political Activism to Postmodernism," in *Architecture School: Three Centuries of Educating Architects in North America*, ed. J Ockman (Cambridge, MA: MIT Press, 2012); S Sadler, "An Avant Garde Academy," in *Architectures: Modernism and After*, ed. A Ballantyne (London: Blackwell, 2008); B Colomina et. al., eds, *Radical Pedagogies* (Princeton, NJ: Princeton University), http://radical-pedagogies.com/, accessed 31 August 2018; B Colomina, E Choi, I Gonzalez Galan and A Meister, "Radical Pedagogies in Architectural Education," *Architectural Review* 28 (September 2012).

[^4]: In Australia, see G Hastings, *It Can't Happen Here: A Political History of Australian Student Activism* (Adelaide: Students' Association of Flinders University, 2003); K Murphy, "'In the Backblocks of Capitalism': Australian Student Activism in the Global 1960s," *Australian Historical Studies* 46, no. 2 (June 2015): 252–68; J Piccini, *Transnational Protest, Australia and the 1960s* (London: Palgrave Macmillan, 2016).

[^5]: D Horne, *Time of Hope: Australia, 1966–72* (Sydney: Angus & Robertson, 1980).

[^6]: S Lees and J Senyard, *The 1950s: How Australia Became a Modern Society and Everyone got a House and Car* (Melbourne: Hyland House, 1987).

[^7]: T Chaplin and J P. Mooney, eds, *The Global 1960s* (New York, NY: Routledge, 2017); M Kurlansky, *1968: The Year that Rocked the World* (London: Jonathan Cape, 2004); A Marwick, *The Sixties. Cultural Revolution in Britain, France, Italy, and the United States 1958–1974* (New York: Oxford University Press, 1998); D Reynolds, *One World Divisible: A Global History Since 1945* (London: Penguin Books, 2001); TS Brown, "1968. Transnational and Global Perspectives," 1st vers. in *Docupedia-Zeitgeschichte* (6 June 2012), http://docupedia.de/zg/brown_1968_v1_en_2012, accessed 31 August 2018.

[^8]: Reynolds, *One World Divisible*, 301.

[^9]: In the US, the growth in college enrolment in the 1960s and 1970s was 11 times the growth of the general population. M Katz, "Aspects of the 'Embattled University,'" *Proceedings of the American Philosophical Society* 114, no. 5 (1970): 344.

[^10]: J Skolnick, "Student Protest," *AAUP Bulletin* 55, no. 3 (September 1969): 313; N van Dyke, "Hotbeds of Activism: Locations of Student Protest," *Social Problems* 45, no. 2 (May 1998): 208.

**Figure 3** — Christo directing work at Wrapped Coast, 1969. Many of the volunteers who assisted in completing the work were architecture students from the University of Sydney. Photograph by Harry Shunk-Kender. Copyright Wolfgang Volz/laif.

In this sense, Australia was not unusual in seeing its university campuses develop as key territories for challenges to the established order. [^11] The early civil rights movement in the early to mid-1960s shifted in the late 1960s to radicalism and the emergence of the New Left political formations, anti-Vietnam War moratorium marches, draft resistance and anti-apartheid demonstrations, creating a significant upsurge of student protest in Australia [Figure 2]. Alan Barcan has described the emergence of student radicalism at the University of Sydney in the mid-1960s as initially focused on increased "democratisation" and student participation in university procedures, institutions and courses, as well as broader political issues such as anti-conscription and anti-Vietnam War activity. [^12]

From the global student unrest emerged the sense of a prolonged crisis of identity and function in the university. [^13] Mario Savio, a prominent student leader at Berkeley during the Free Speech Movement, was blunt in claiming that universities had become "training camps—and proving grounds—rather than places where people acquire education." [^14]

[^11]: Hastings, *It Can't Happen Here*; M. Armstrong, *1, 2, 3, What Are We Fighting For?: The Australian Student Movement from its Origins to the 1970s* (Melbourne: Socialist Alternative, 2001); G Davison and K Murphy, *University Unlimited: The Monash Story* (Crows Nest, NSW: Allen & Unwin, 2012); D Beer, ed., *A Serious Attempt to Change Society: The Socialist Action Movement and Student Radicalism at the University of New England, 1969–75* (Armidale, NSW: Kardoorair Press, 1998).

[^12]: A Barcan, "The Arrival of the New Left at Sydney University, 1967–1972," *History of Education Review* 40, no. 2 (2011): 158.

[^13]: WF Connell, GE Sherington, BH Fletcher, C Turney and U Bygott, *Australia's First: A History of the University of Sydney, vol. 2 1940–1990* (Sydney: University of Sydney in association with Hale & Iremonger, 1991–1995), 359.

[^14]: M Savio, "Berkeley Fall: The Berkeley Student Rebellion of 1964," in *The Free Speech Movement and the Negro Revolution: A News & Letters Pamphlet*, M Savio, E Walker and R Dunayevskaya (Detroit, MI: News & Letters, 1965), 17, http://content.cdlib.org/view?docId=kt896nb2rx&query=&brand=calisphere, accessed 9 October 2018.

More directly impinging on the mood in the University of Sydney's architecture faculty, members of the Sydney offshoot of the Free University movement were arguing, via the pages of *Honi Soit*, that existing universities "splutter as centres of research, fail as a means of education and march backwards as agents of social change." [^15] Inspired by the Free University of New York, which opened in 1965, the Sydney iteration operated in a

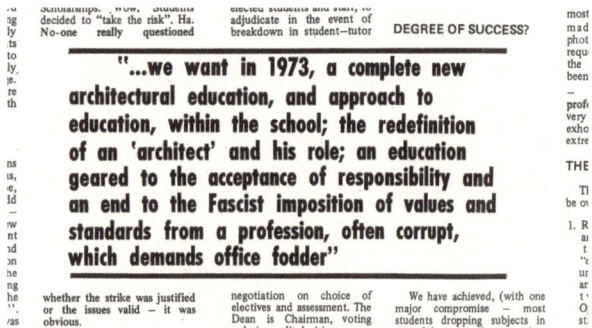

Figure 4 — Detail from an anonymous account of the student strike action in the Faculty of Architecture, published in *Honi Soit* 45, no. 20, 7 September 1972. Students Representative Council of the University of Sydney.

Redfern terrace house from 1968 until 1972, attempting an autonomous, co-operative study and research program.

The broader social and political turmoil of the 1960s profoundly affected architectural education, especially because that education was now predominantly undertaken within the university. In the early 20th century, the academy had taken hold of training architects (see Leach, Chapter One) so that, by the late 1960s, formalised programs within university schools had been the norm for decades. [^16] This meant that architectural schools, like the universities in which they sat, were marked by phenomena such as the fiery anti-Vietnam War protests, the rise of the women's liberation movement, and the critique of the post-war university. Architecture was experiencing its own identity crisis, in which the fundamentals of architectural education were being challenged and students demanded new kinds of knowledge, "educational relevance," and modes of participation. [^17]

In a basic sense, the existing operations of architecture schools around the Western World were disturbed from the mid-1960s to the early 1970s because of the general convulsions of the period. Understandably, a proportion of architecture students and educators were engaged in the wider protests and political action. At Berkeley, in the mid-1960s, they joined other students in the Free Speech Movement. In Paris, the Ecole nationale supérieure des Beaux-Arts was in the centre of the protests of May 1968. Students of Harvard University's Graduate School of Design were among the anti-Vietnam War occupations and class boycotts of 1969. [^18] At the University of Sydney, the Student Action for Aborigines group, established in 1964, was a focus for student activism until around 1966, when the Vietnam War and conscription redirected that activity. [^19] However, there was a concurrent critique of the idea of architectural education and practice on which the Faculty of Architecture at the University of Sydney had been founded. Students demanded that the profession's role in the spatial production of the city be reformed to respond to a rapidly changing society. This flowed, in many ways, from a challenge to the professions presented by the activist movements of the 1960s, particularly a general refusal of the seemingly immutable rule of expertise and the irreproachable status of experts. [^20]

[^15]: R Cahill, R. Connell, B Freeman, T Irving, T and B Scribner, "The Lost Ideal," *Honi Soit* (3 October 1967).
[^16]: See JM Freeland, *The Making of a Profession: A History of the Growth and Work of the Architectural Institutes in Australia* (Sydney: Angus & Robertson in association with the Royal Australian Institute of Architects, 1971), 202–31; Ockman, ed., *Architecture School*, 66–90; M Crinson and J Lubbock, *Architecture—Art or Profession? 300 Years of Architectural Education* (Manchester: Manchester University Press, 1994).
[^17]: For a contemporaneous assessment of such demands, see A Tzonis, "The Last Identity Crisis of Architecture," *Connections* (1969), reprinted in A Tzonis and L Lefaivre, *Times of Creative Destruction: Shaping Buildings and Cities in the Late C20th* (London: Routledge, 2016), 56.
[^18]: Architecture students put their design skills to work devising and manufacturing the "red fist" posters and t-shirts that became a well-known symbol of the student actions of 1969. "The Fist and its Clencher", *Harvard Magazine* no. 7 (1998), https://harvardmagazine.com/1998/07/alumni.fist.html, accessed 9 October 2018
[^19]: CA Rootes, "The Development of Radical Student Movements and Their Sequelae," *Australian Journal of Politics and History* 43, no. 2 (1988): 173–86; J Spigelman, "Student Action for Aborigines," *Vestes* 7, no. 2 (1965): 116.
[^20]: LM Hoffman, *The Politics of Knowledge: Activist Movements in Medicine and Planning* (Albany: SUNY Press, 1989), 1.

Student demands for a change in the identity of architecture were often propelled by a corresponding disillusionment with the profession's social impact. Many students were developing a sensitivity to the profession's contentious role in the shaping of troubled urban environments. At Yale, for example, students were disenchanted by the results of extensive urban renewal projects in New Haven; at Columbia, the University's proposal for an intrusive, segregating gymnasium development in Harlem was a key instigator of student unrest. [^21] More generally, politicised students railed against an idea of the architect as technocratic professional. The XIV Triennale in Milan, curated by the Italian architect Giancarlo De Carlo, opened on 30 May 1968 and was immediately occupied and shut down by student protestors, who demanded greater social responsibility and a more extensive critique of existing power relations from the designers. [^22] In terms of their own education, "irrelevance" became a repeated, dismissive catchphrase among students, and demands for new modes of professional intervention grew. Students and educators experimented with radical new modes of pedagogy and practice. Students in many schools demanded greater autonomy in terms of their influence on curricula and in school governance. They demanded a voice in policy-making (even staff selection) and acted against what were seen as overly bureaucratic, out of touch administrations. They occupied buildings, went on strike, conducted teach-ins, constructed "liberated zones" on and off campus, and developed community advocacy organisations, participatory design initiatives, and design-build projects. Architecture schools began to host radical rethinking about the making of the architect and architectural culture.

# Sydney

The 1972 strike at the University of Sydney emerged from frustrations similar to those felt in architecture schools elsewhere. There were also echoes and parallels in the subsequent demands and the protest tactics that were employed. The students were keyed into existing international networks (for example, through internationally circulating journals such as *Architectural Design* or *L'Architecture d'aujordhui*) but were also developing their own connections. The Australasian Architecture Students' Association (AASA) broadsheet, *INK*, captured the global outlook and relations open to Australian architecture students at the time. In 1970, an issue of the journal reproduced Ché Guavara's address to the International Union of Architects congress, as well as impassioned statements from the students involved in the London-based Architects Revolutionary Socialist Enclave, the 1968 AIA New Haven convention, and the Pratt Institute in Brooklyn, which collectively decried a profession that was ruled by bureaucracy and profit over social benefit. [^23] The AASA student congresses leading up to the 1972 strike also point to Australian students' shifting aspirations for what architecture could be and do. Attendance sometimes outstripped that of the national professional conferences, and the guest speakers were more radical and diverse. Visitors to Sydney included Christopher Alexander, Archigram's Dennis Crompton, and Buckminster Fuller, who gave a series of lectures at the University of Sydney in 1970. [^24] More locally, there was regular correspondence between University of Sydney students and experimental settings such as the Environmental Design program developed at the Tasmanian College of Advanced Education, Hobart, from 1969 to 1979. [^25] The Sydney

---

[^21]: RAM Stern and J Stamp, *Pedagogy and Place: 100 Years of Architectural Education at Yale* (New Haven, Connecticut: Yale University Press, 2016, 350–51; M Gutman and R Plunz, "Anatomy of an Insurrection," in *The Making of an Architect 1881–1981, Columbia University in the City of New York*, ed. R Oliver (New York: Rizzoli, 1981), 183–211.
[^22]: P Nicolin, "Beyond the Failure: Notes on the XIVth Triennale," *Log* 13/14 (2008): 87–100.

[^23]: *INK* 4 (March 1970), 2.
[^24]: B Kinnaird and B Bennett, eds, *Congress Book V1.0* (Melbourne: Freerange Press, 2011).
[^25]: C Owen and S King, "Legend and Legacy: Barry McNeill and a Decade of Radical Pedagogies in Tasmania," (Paper presented at "Educating Architects and Planners, 1917–2017," School of Architecture and Planning, University of Auckland, New Zealand, 8 September 2017).

students' own travels built and extended this interrelation, priming them to make new claims on their education, especially its articulation of the socio-political, cultural and technological transformations of the period.

The mood for curriculum change had been developing during the 1960s, giving strength to the students' actions. As an undergraduate student at the close of the 1950s, the future art critic Robert Hughes found the architecture degree a stultifying experience that largely followed the 19th century École des Beaux-Arts model (see Weir, Chapter Three). [^26] In the embrace of modernist solutions, the students of the early post-war period often chafed at the lack of encouragement they received from the faculty. [^27] The dean at the time was Henry Ingham Ashworth, who had arrived from England in 1949 to take up an appointment as Professor of Architectural Design and History. Ashworth served as dean from 1952 to 1964 before moving to the University of New South Wales. Architecturally conservative and a strong proponent of British culture, Ashworth is reported to have discouraged female students with his very traditional views about the place of women in the workforce. [^28] In this, he did little to win over students. Despite Hughes' impression, though, Ashworth was considered to have at least "modernised" the curriculum during the 1950s, keeping pace with international developments. An accustomed administrator, he oversaw the introduction of a common core course for first years and the inclusion of physics and mathematics subjects, as well as supporting the development of postgraduate studies. [^29] As Daniel Ryan describes elsewhere in this book, Ashworth was influenced by the forceful Jack Cowan, Chair of Architectural Science from 1953, and Ashworth's tenure as dean saw time spent on science subjects in the architecture degree grow alongside the establishment and expansion of an Architectural Science discipline. [^30]

By 1960, though, there was internal concern about a drift in the teaching focus in the School of Architecture. Enrolments were increasing, and students' needs were changing. Central Sydney was beginning to transform through the impact of high-rise development, and the relevance of the school's programs to industry in the preparation of graduates for the demands of contemporary professional practice was questioned by the profession and some of the school's teaching staff. [^31] A faculty committee was appointed to investigate all the existing courses in detail, driven by concern over a reduction in the time allocated to design, a lack of course coordination, and the suspicion that graduates were not prepared with sufficient practical and professional knowledge, worries that seem to echo through the ages. [^32] It recommended that a standing committee be appointed to keep the course under review, to allow it to adapt as required to the needs of the profession, and to coordinate the various aspects of the course overall. Under these pressures, the teaching programs were shifting away from Wilkinson's initial prospects for the training of a gentlemanly, cultured professional.

A more industry-focused orientation and more administrative oversight of programs characterised developments in the early 1960s. In 1963, the Professorial Board recommended that a School of Undergraduate Studies in Architecture be established. [^33]

[^26]: R Hughes, *Things I Didn't Know* (Sydney: Random House, 2006), 198.
[^27]: Reflecting on their education at Sydney Technical College and the University of Sydney, respectively, Russell Jack and Philip Cox have both noted the anti-modernist strain of teaching at the University of Sydney at the time. Jack considered the Sydney Technical College as offering the most progressive architectural education, while Cox observed that, apart from George Molnar, the teaching staff were British-inspired and believed that "the architectural world ended with Lutyens." R Jack, interview, Oral History Project, Royal Australian Institute of Architects, 31 March 1996; P Cox, interview by M Bogle, Oral History Project, Royal Australian Institute of Architects, 4 September 2014.
[^28]: R Lumby, "Ashworth, Henry Ingham (1907–1991)," *Australian Dictionary of Biography* (Australian National University), http://adb.anu.edu.au/biography/ashworth-henry-ingham-15498/, accessed 9 October 2018.
[^29]: Minutes of the Faculty of Architecture, 13 October 1954 (University of Sydney Archives). Ashworth's recorded accomplishments lean towards the administrative. In 1933, he published *Architectural Practice and Administration* through Sir Isaac Pitman & Sons; on moving to Australia, he became involved in a range of professional committees and would eventually chair the jury for the Sydney Opera House competition.
[^30]: On the development of Architectural Science in the faculty, see Chapter Four.
[^31]: Freeland, *The Making of a Profession*, 222, 229.
[^32]: Connell et al, *Australia's First*, 281.
[^33]: Connell et al, *Australia's First*, 277–81.

We came up on a bus … about a dozen students … and designed toilets with alternative technologies, natural saunas utilising steam tents, hot rocks, and creeks with geodesic domes …

– Gary Fiddler, quoted in Caravans and Communes (2011)

However, it was left to Ashworth's successor to take on responsibility as its head. Ashworth had announced he was retiring in order to take up a new position at UNSW. As part of a restructure of the school, prompted by the various review processes, as well as Ashworth's departure, it was determined that his replacement would be both Professor of Architecture and Head of the undergraduate school. In the interim, Ron Meyer, a Senior Lecturer in Architecture, who had studied under Wilkinson, was appointed as Acting Head of the Department. Although only in an acting position, Meyer responded to the students' own concerns for the reshaping of their education and instituted regular formal staff-student consultations. [^34]

4.3 Is practical experience necessary. What alternatives?
4.4 Distinction between two degrees. NOZZANOZZANOZZA??

5.1 Educational/faculty problems:

LIST OF YOUR YEAR'S GRIPES AND FRUSTRATIONS — Lectures, Staff, Subjects, Learning methods, Assessment, Weighting/work load, Others...

5.2 Use of Building: Services-office, phone, typewriter, communication devices,
Staff/student roles privileges and differences.
5.3 Student data banks, education from other students, communications
5.4 Text lists in each field...alternative to lecture course...credit?
5.5 Compiling good reference lists.
5.6 Obtain course from staff, print notes & refs. & sell at cost price?
5.7 Importance of staff knowledge & personality in determining course.

6.0 Methods of Implementation; 3rd Term, 1972 how to be productive & effective?
6.1 Remainder term 2... How is it best used? Moratorium.
6.2 What,when,how,why. Third term trial period.

6.3 How do we become revolutionary architects? By learning ASA codes?

7.0 Suggested course breakdown;
1. DESIGN
2. Structural Theory & Design (maths, physics, steel, etc.)
3. Building Environment (construction, services, ergonomics)
4. History, Philosophy, Criticism
5. Decision Theory & Methods (computers, logic, design methods)
6. MES(sociology, psychology, management, ie social-psychology)
7. Environmental Sciences (geography(esp. urban,)ecology)
8. Economics, politics
9. "Art" & Photography, Drama, Music, Etc
10. Material Technology(workshop, material performance)
11. Others( incl. non-faculty courses)

These are only some of the topics which must be resolved. XXXXXXXX

**Figure 5** — "Points for Discussion and Resolution Staff/Student Meeting 25 July," 1972. Private collection.

Three years passed between Ashworth's departure and a new appointment, and in that period the relationship between academia and practice, normally articulated by the chair, was significantly recalibrated in the absence of an appointee. One of the factors in the Professorial Board's recommendation of Ashworth's initial appointment had been that his primary interest was teaching, not practice. [^35] When the position of Head of Department and Chair of Architecture was initially advertised, applications came in from architects and professors from around Australia and across the world. [^36] An early enquiry from Walter Gropius, who was interested in maintaining his professional practice, came to nothing. By contrast, when RN Peter Johnson was eventually appointed to the Chair in Architecture and Head of the Undergraduate School, he was encouraged to maintain his practice, offering a firmer bridge between the academy and the profession.

For much of the local architecture profession, Johnson arrived as an impeccable appointment; he was an alumnus of the faculty (an Honours graduate under professors Wilkinson, Hook and Ashworth), an emerging design talent, and an energetic, sociable influencer. [^37] While dean, he continued as a senior partner in the Sydney firm of McConnel, Smith and Johnson, where, by the late 1960s, he had already played a key role in the design of some significant Sydney buildings. [^38] His own family house had won the Wilkinson Award in 1964 and would later figure as a seminal work in historical formulations of the "Sydney School" (see Lassen and Willis, Chapter Five). [^39]

[^34]: Meyer was a member of what was then called the Department of Architecture for over 20 years. He studied under Wilkinson and promoted the election of Lloyd Rees as acting Dean of the Faculty of Architecture in 1962. R Thorne, "Death of Mr Ron Meyer," *The University of Sydney News*, 29 March 1983, 50.

[^35]: Report of the Advisory Committee, 16 June 1948 (University of Sydney Archives); Minutes of the Professorial Board, 16 August 1948 (University of Sydney Archives).

[^36]: Applications for the Chair of Architecture, 1963–1965 (University of Sydney Archives).

[^37]: However, there were reservations among some in the profession. A number of prominent Sydney architects wrote to the Vice-Chancellor to protest Johnson's appointment. At least one asked that the decision be reconsidered and suggested that he and many colleagues were gravely concerned that the position had not been offered instead to Harry Seidler, who had been approached by Professor Denis Winston. Applications for the Chair of Architecture (University of Sydney Archives).

[^38]: J Taylor, "Johnson, Peter," in *The Encyclopedia of Australian Architecture*, ed. P Goad and J Willis (Melbourne: Cambridge University Press, 2012), 370–71; J Taylor, "Obituary: Peter—Richard Norman Johnson," *Architecture Australia* 92, no. 4 (July 2003). Richard Norman "Peter" Johnson remained dean until his retirement from the university in 1986. He later became Chancellor of the University of Technology, Sydney, as well as the Inaugural Chair of the Conference of Heads of Schools of Architecture in Australia.

[^39]: The Wilkinson Award is presented by the Australian Institute of Architects (NSW Chapter), recognising excellence in residential building. Taylor, "Johnson, Peter," 370–71.

a project done with Arch and Fine Arts students with the help of the "Eventstructure Research Group" (an international group centred in Holland).
Syd Uni swimming pool, 1972

**Figure 6** — Under the guidance of the Eventstructure Research Group, Architecture and Fine Arts students collaborate on an inflatable installation at the university swimming pool in 1972. University of Sydney Archives.

Johnson was also heavily engaged in professional advocacy as the Vice-Chairman of the Board of Architects of New South Wales, Vice-President of the New South Wales Chapter of the Royal Australian Institute of Architects, a member of the Faculty of Architecture Advisory Board, and a part-time design tutor. He was a respected and generally well-liked appointment. The licence given to his continued practice and his energetic presence among the profession eased some of the long-standing anxieties about the disengagement of university-based training from architecture's technical and commercial realities.

It was likely expected that, on his appointment, Johnson would reinforce the development of a degree program that obtained its relevance through close attention to the requirements for professional registration. His initial influence was certainly in that direction. In 1969, he oversaw the implementation of a six-year, two-degree course responding to the curriculum review of the early 1960s. It consisted of a three-year Bachelor of Architectural Studies, mandatory work experience, and a two-year Bachelor of Architecture. The emphasis across the degrees was on covering subjects necessary for registration as an architect and for membership of the professional institute, with some specialisation possible in the second degree. [^40] It followed a thoroughly conventional teaching pattern: the design studio, based on projects of gradually increasing complexity, was the recurring core of instruction, with other mandatory subjects in support. In the first year, alongside the studio, students took courses named "Environmental Sciences," "Design History and Theory," and "Materials, Structures and Methods." In each of the final two years, they took

[^40]: Connell et al, *Australia's First*, vol. 2, 282–83.

"Applied Environmental Sciences," "Building Science," and "Applied Management." There were no elective choices, although a thesis was required on a subject approved by the Head of Undergraduate Studies. [^41]

The 1969 curriculum change gestured towards both professional sobriety and academic rigour. With its multiple invocations of the word science (see Hill, Chapter Seven), the revised subject pattern suggested a properly academic constitution via the growing prominence of architectural science since Cowan's arrival as chair in 1953, given an appropriately "applied" bearing. It proposed a moderating accommodation of the longstanding agitation among Australian architecture's institutions for education and registration between the most pragmatic expectations for professional training and those firmly identifying architecture with the liberal and applied arts. As the newly minted dean, Johnson's 1967 Occasional Address foreshadowed the eventual curriculum revision and characterised the crowd of caps and gowns before him as "singularly fortunate" to be graduates in science. [^42] The address also signalled evolving understanding of architecture's epistemological underpinning. He spoke optimistically of emerging fields such as anthropometrics, cybernetics and ergonomics enabling architects to apply scientific method across all of design. [^43] A year on from that address and the mood was very different. Even as the new curriculum came into effect, Johnson found himself having to engage with student concerns for "relevance" expressed in a more strident register. Johnson unsettled the 1968 Architecture Student Revue audience with a downbeat introduction that looked to discern architecture's possible response to troubling times: "when events throughout the world emphasise the failures of human contact, when students particularly, respond with fear and doubt to these events and question the values that allow them to happen." [^44]

Johnson's empathetic tone and progressive disposition seemed to reinforce the break with the Ashworth era.

There were other indications that the character and configuration of the faculty, especially the architectural discipline, were changing. Under Johnson, belying the rigid shaping of the curriculum, a series of transformative appointments were made. The arrival in 1969 of Amos Rapoport, at the time developing a reputation for his forays into architectural anthropology, was indicative of the growing importance of research to the foundations of university-based architectural education and an accompanying questioning of architectural design's epistemology. [^45] 1969 also saw the UC Berkeley-trained environmental artist Marr Grounds join the faculty. [^46]

A commune-dwelling, military uniform-wearing iconoclast, Grounds helped establish the University of Sydney Fine Arts Workshop, the "Tin Sheds," with fine arts lecturer Donald Brook and the architectural historian David Saunders. [^47] The dilapidated corrugated iron sheds adjacent to the architecture faculty were occupied under the pretence of providing training in traditional techniques, but, from the start, they were a crucible for much more radical art practices and ideas. Through that embryonic institution and his environmental design teaching, Grounds began to connect architecture students with an array of contemporary art practices, often at odds with the conservative aesthetic tradition established by Wilkinson and still embodied

[^41]: University of Sydney Yearbook 1972, 219–20.
[^42]: P Johnson, "Occasional Address for Conferring of Degrees Ceremony to Science Graduates—12th April, 1967," Peter Johnson Papers and Pictorial Material, 1945–2001, State Library of New South Wales (SLNSW), Sydney.
[^43]: Johnson, "Occasional Address for Conferring of Degrees Ceremony to Science Graduates."
[^44]: Johnson, "Occasional Address for Conferring of Degrees Ceremony to Science Graduates."
[^45]: Rapoport prepared his seminal House Form and Culture (Englewood Cliffs, NJ: Prentice-Hall, 1969) while at the faculty. One of his earliest postgraduate students was the architect Peter Hamilton, who undertook ground-breaking field work in Aboriginal Australia, living with his family in a remote traditional camp of the Yankuntjatjara people, according to P Memmott and C Keys, "The Emergence of an Architectural Anthropology in Aboriginal Australia: The Work of the Aboriginal Environments Research Centre," Architectural Theory Review 21, no. 2 (1996): 220. In 1969–70, the US Fulbright Scholar Sam Sloan also worked within the faculty on proxemics research. The role of the faculty as early ground for environment behaviour research is taken up by Glen Hill in Chapter Seven.
[^46]: Grounds had tutored at UC Berkeley for 15 years until the elections of Richard Nixon as President and Ronald Reagan as Governor of California encouraged his move to Sydney. "Art Workshop Pioneer to Retire," University of Sydney News, 29 October 1985, 255.
[^47]: On the Tin Sheds' history, see T Kenyon, Under a Hot Tin Roof: Art, Passion, and Politics at the Tin Sheds Art Workshop (Sydney: State Library of New South Wales Press, 1995). Another foundational story for this iconic, rogue institution has it that activities commenced with Lloyd Rees' earlier appropriation of the sheds for life drawing classes with his architecture students (see Chapter Three).

in the teaching of Lloyd Rees. Grounds, for instance, arranged for architecture students to help construct Christo and Jeanne-Claude's 1968–69 *Wrapped Coast* installation at Little Bay [Figure 3]. Johnson was largely supportive of such initiatives; under his deanship, the Tin Sheds were funded and expanded, developing, not only as a site for architecture students to practice sketching, but also as a hotbed of countercultural politics (it was home to anarchist poster collective Earthworks) and a place where conceptual and post-object art was discussed and made. [^48] At the same time, Johnson continued to find a place in the faculty for the artist Lloyd Rees as a Lecturer in History of Sculpture and Painting and part-time instructor of drawing. [^49]

However, in this period, Rees' techniques and sensibility were increasingly challenged or overlooked as student radicalism and pedagogical experimentation began to take hold. While the faculty's architecture programs were structured conventionally, Johnson's eyes were open to change. In 1970, he visited the experimental Environmental Design program in Hobart, where students designed their own learning experience and self-assessed their work, and he returned there in 1972. [^50]

Johnson's tactful reformism wove a path through the jostling demands and ambitions of the local profession, diverse teaching staff, researchers and, particularly, the students. In a 1970 end-of-year article prepared for the *Sydney Morning Herald*, he sympathised with the broader student discord, suggesting that his audience should "have patience with emerging ideas, particularly of the younger generation." [^51] Student reception of such sentiment was presaged a year earlier in the title of the 1969 Architecture Revue; "The Great Wall of Porridge" referred pointedly to Johnson's diplomatic style. [^52]

Five years after his appointment as dean, in May 1972, Johnson gave an Occasional Address that had a touch of prophecy. [^53] His speech emphasised architecture's growing integration of human sciences alongside a recognition of an increased questioning of the environments that "science and technology" had provided. [^54] He described a general air of community unease and suggested that, while his own tendency was towards "reasoned modification of existing systems", the present situation appeared to have reached a crisis point. [^55] The young, as he saw it, were being led to protest and violence through a sense of genuine concern and dismay at the inaction of established social and political organisations. Johnson discussed anti-war and anti-apartheid movements, the growing Green Bans, and "environmental pressure groups." [^56] He closed by urging graduands to question and push for change. Two months later, it was not those graduates pushing for radical change but Johnson's own students. Perhaps his tendency to pluralism further fuelled the desire

[^48]: The Tin Sheds Art Workshop programs and studios would later become formally integrated with the teaching programs of the Faculty of Architecture, Design and Planning. The Tin Sheds, with a focus on arts in particular, eventually allowed architecture students to explore a whole series of new disciplines that could be incorporated into their future practice. Photography, carpentry, computer design, painting, printing and other allied subjects, including performance and street theatre (taught at one time by George Molnar), all became available to study. The Tin Sheds Gallery was constructed within a 1990s refurbishment of the Wilkinson Buildings and still operates. Kenyon, *Under a Hot Tin Roof*, 32.
[^49]: Rees taught in the faculty from 1946 to 1986. Significant Australian architects such as Penelope Seidler and Philip Cox have remembered his lectures and classes fondly: for instance, the hours spent sketching plaster casts of antiquarian objects in the Nicholson Museum. P Donnelly, "Return of the Warrior," *Muse* (March 2018): 13.
[^50]: "Visitors," *I.E.* (December 1972): 41–43. The Environmental Design program founded by Hobart architect Barry McNeil at the recently established College of Advanced Education was one of the most radical experiments in tertiary education of the period. On McNeill, see L Woolley, "McNeill, Barry," in *Encyclopedia of Australian Architecture*, ed. Goad and Willis. At least one University of Sydney architecture student transferred their studies to the Hobart program, drawn by its radical qualities, according to R Fay, "School of Architecture and Design" (University of Tasmania), http://125timeline.utas.edu.au/timeline/1940/school-architecture-design/, accessed 9 October 2018. The criticism the striking Sydney students made of their own program and the changes they demanded strongly echo the principles and procedures of the Hobart Environmental Design program, and it is highly likely that there was regular communication. The student magazine of the Hobart program carried a lengthy article about the Sydney strike, W Hudson, "REVOLUTION," *I.E.* (December 1972): 11–14.

[^51]: P Johnson, "Draft end-of-year article," 1970, Johnson Papers, SLNSW.
[^52]: The 1967 revue was led by Graham Bond, who would go on to wear a dress and fake moustache as the outrageous Australian television character Aunty Jack. Bond graduated with a Bachelor of Architecture degree in 1967 and began tutoring in design at the University of Sydney in the late 1960s. "The Great Wall of Porridge" also involved fellow architecture student Geoffrey Atherden (writer of *Mother and Son*), as well as arts students Peter Weir (director of *Picnic at Hanging Rock* and *The Truman Show*) and Peter Best (composer for *Muriel's Wedding* and *Crocodile Dundee*).
[^53]: P Johnson, "Occasional Address 27 May 1972," Johnson Papers, SLNSW.
[^54]: P Johnson, "Occasional Address 27 May 1972."
[^55]: P Johnson, "Occasional Address 27 May 1972."
[^56]: P Johnson, "Occasional Address 27 May 1972."

**Figure 7** — A "Utopian Fair" at the student-built Autonomous House, 27–28 May 1978. Photograph by Tone Wheeler.

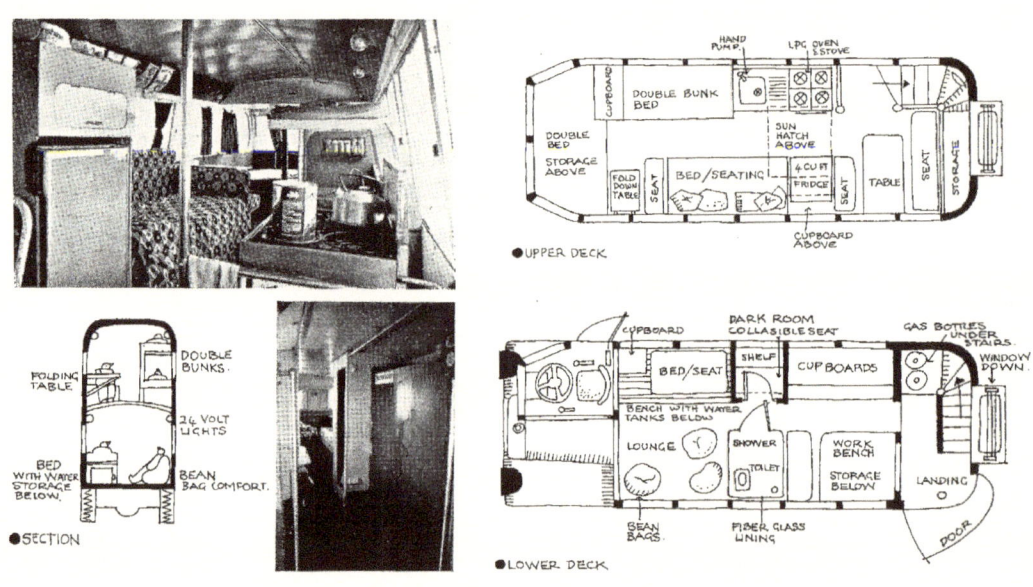

**Figure 8** — The layout and interior arrangement of the Australian Communications Capsule bus. Originally published in *Architecture in Australia* 64, 2 (1975). Architecture Media, Sandra Meihubers, Phil Rose, and Irene and Wally Zagoridis.

for change. [^57] In any case, a significant number of architecture students, with the support of some staff, had decided they would not be assuaged by curriculum tinkering or quiet counsel in the hushed rooms of the professoriate. They demanded fundamental, immediate changes to their education.

## STRIKE

According to an account written by students and published in *Honi Soit*, the catalyst for the strike was 20 July 1972, when frustrations among second-, third-, and fourth-year student groups boiled over [Figure 4]. The frustrations ranged from unhappiness with the lack of relevant courses in environmental design and the impersonality of methods taught to the faculty's rejection of a student proposal for alternative assessment methods. [^58] The fourth-year group was especially provoked by what they experienced as an alienating and pointless coursework exercise, in which they had undertaken research and made recommendations regarding the purpose and requirements of a proposed new architecture building. The students argued that their accommodation in the extremely utilitarian, but very flexible, corrugated asbestos cement-clad "Transient Building" was preferable to the planned extension of the faculty's primary home, the Wilkinson Building. Citing environmental concerns and the satisfactory functionality of their current situation, they argued against the need for new construction. They deemed the new proposal an inappropriate "monument." However, their research and advice seemed to have no effect. [^59] In response, some students formed the NOZZA Co-operative and decided to leave the course, inviting others to join them. A second-year group moved to shut the faculty down and was joined by the other year groups. [^60]

Events unfolded quickly. In the following days, the students met to formulate strike tactics. [^61] It was decided that "the daily running of the Faculty" needed to be stopped in order to force change in a situation the students now found untenable. [^62] They prepared for both strike and forced occupation; although, in the end, the latter was not necessary. On Monday 24 July, students and some staff of the undergraduate school of architecture went on strike. The shutdown lasted for the final two weeks of term—24 July until 6 August—during which all lectures, tutorials and other teaching activities were suspended. [^63] The students established a "Centre of Operations" within the faculty, equipped with their own printing press. [^64] They proceeded to bluntly and directly attack the education they had been receiving:

> We intend to continue [to strike] until its authoritarianism, its inability to accommodate the individual's own aims in using educational resources, its 'product-orientation,' its perpetuation of social inequalities, its pandering to society's privileged elites at the expense of the underprivileged [...] have been [...] replaced by an education geared towards responsibility—responsibility to one's self, to other people and to the earth. [^65]

[^57]: The staffing in architecture, for example, had become increasingly diverse since Johnson's arrival. By 1972, those teaching in the architecture programs included the historian Jennifer Taylor, who was in the midst of building her account of the "Sydney School's" regional modernism; Amos Rapoport had not yet moved to Berkeley, and faculty alumni who had joined the staff (such as Ross King and Tom Heath) were beginning to explore the regrounding of architectural modernism in relation to the burgeoning social sciences. Note that Heath was a founding member of the Environmental Design Research Association, as well as a Director at McConnel, Smith and Johnson. The Wilkinson legacy was carried on by his former student Ron Meyer, as well as the ongoing teaching by Lloyd Rees and newer recruits to the tutoring staff such as sculptor Bert Flugelman and painter Guy Warren. Milo Dunphy, a graduate of the faculty's town planning degree, was tutoring alongside his active environmental campaigning. A young Glenn Murcutt, who had recently established his own practice, taught in the design studios, and there was even the appointment of Liz Fell, a young radical feminist and Sydney Push affiliate, to teach political science to the architecture students.

[^58]: It has also been suggested that participation by students in the production of the 1971 exhibition "The Changing Heart of Your City" was a catalyst for student disquiet. The exhibition was collaboratively staged by the Faculty of Architecture and the *Sydney Morning Herald*. Its theme was "citizen involvement in the development of the city." "You Can Help Plan a Future Sydney," *The Sydney Morning Herald*, 21 August 1971, 2.

[^59]: "Drawing the Line," *The Bulletin*, 5 August 1972, 18.
[^60]: Architecture Students, "Faculty Strikes: Reassessment of Courses, System and Department," *Honi Soit* (7 September 1972): 1.
[^61]: Students, "Faculty Strikes," 1.
[^62]: Students, "Faculty Strikes," 1.
[^63]: Students, "Faculty Strikes," 1.
[^64]: Students, "Faculty Strikes," 1.
[^65]: *Mushroom Students—Kept in the Dark and Fed on Shit...*, anonymous pamphlet c1972 (private collection).

An intense period of meetings and workshops, involving rapidly formed student committees and working groups, examined new approaches to "architectural" education and developed the design for a new course. [^66] Displaying a facility for bureaucracy rivalling that of the university itself, the students' work groups and their appointed chairs deliberated on various topics—subjects, resources, structure, subject weighting, externalities, implementation— and subsequently reported their results to other relevant work groups and an overseeing committee [Figure 5]. [^67]

After an exhausting week of debates and propositions (one set of student notes has "I wan[sic] go sleep" scrawled in the margins), the draft outline of a completely new course was tabled. This demanded, among other things, a "free elective" system, "abolition of 'year' system," student participation in their own assessment, and the establishment of an elected Review Board of students and staff members. The students maintained the strike for a further week, with the aim of effecting full implementation of a course that would provide, as they put it, "in-depth environmental design studies" in 1973.

The action at Sydney was distinctive in its effectiveness, at least in the short term. The striking student group was disillusioned by a course they felt was inadequate to address the "environmental chaos" they saw around them and one that was oriented towards a too-narrow conception of architectural practice. [^68] In response, the students negotiated the development and implementation of a new curriculum, reflecting their demands for its relevance. The pivotal change within the curriculum was a dramatically increased freedom of choice for students in the subjects they undertook and an increase in the range of available options. New regulations for the undergraduate degree provided a framework for this, requiring that students were equipped with:

1. The development of a general understanding and awareness of the built environment and its components;
2. The provision of an introduction to the social, economic and political factors which effect [sic] environmental design decisions;
3. The provision of an introduction to the sciences and technologies which must be considered in the process of designing for environmental change;
4. The provision of an understanding of the process of design itself. [^69]

The rebelling students had effectively outflanked university procedures and managed to convince the faculty to consider a far-reaching reform of the regulations for the undergraduate degree. The Sydney strike was, in many ways, a stunning success. While the students' full proposal was not accepted in the end, substantial changes were made, particularly to the level of self-determination in terms of subject choice and to the variety of available subjects. [^70]

Rather than a prescribed set of subjects in each year, students were to accumulate a certain number of "units" over three years through freely chosen subjects given varying unit values. There was some restriction (for example, a quota of architectural science subjects such as structural design or materials science were required for entry to the Bachelor of Architecture), but the possible options had increased dramatically and included a range of new topics. Fuelled also by the growth of the planning department and its interdisciplinary grounding, there were now 62 different subjects from which to choose. [^71] Some were a familiar presence such as Art, Design, Principles of Structural Design, and Construction Documentation. Others give a clear indication of the newly expanded scope of study: Urban Ecology, Contemporary Environmental Design

[^66]: Agenda for General Meeting of Staff and Students, 28 Friday July 1972 (private collection).
[^67]: Proposed Subjects for Work Groups 1972 (private collection).
[^68]: A Sydney Correspondent, "Quibbling Over By-Laws," unattributed newspaper clipping c1972 (private collection).
[^69]: "Report of the University of Sydney for the Year ended 31st December, 1972," in *University of Sydney Calendar 1974*, vol. 2 (University of Sydney), 14.
[^70]: Changes to University Senate Resolutions took effect on 8 August 1973. See *University of Sydney Handbook*, vol. 1 (1974), 246–52; "Faculty of Architecture Revision of Degrees Report," *University of Sydney Handbook*, vol. 2, 14.
[^71]: Connell et al, *Australia's First*, 283.

Figure 9 — Marr Grounds and Paul Pholeros' "Top End" art installation at Rocky Point Out Station. Marr Grounds and Sandra Meihubers.

and Theories, Introduction to Man-Environment Studies, Ethology Ecology in Design, and Political Science applied to Design. It was not everything the striking students wished for, but it had an atmosphere of possibility [Figure 6].

## Legacy

The Sydney strike was significant and not just for the educational experimentation and countercultural concerns it introduced to the school. Its impact was a marker of serious broader questioning of the architect's professional identity, and the episode points to what are still open questions about the effects of the 1960s' social movements and counterculture on the practices and self-understanding of the architecture profession and the architecture school as a key site for its reproduction.

The students' actions had dramatic and immediate effects, but they also brought about more lasting developments; the program structure set in place after this episode remained essentially the same throughout the next two decades, even if specific subjects would come and go. One of the most obvious early consequences was the new program's capacity as a substrate for shared pedagogical experimentation by staff and students. This was further fuelled by a newfound sense of fluidity and mobility, in which local exploration was often directly in dialogue with concepts and practices from the United States, the UK and beyond. With the aid of some sympathetic staff, students were able to petition for new subjects (leading to figures such as Patricia Apps teaching public economics and Sydney Push affiliate Liz Fell teaching political science to first-year architecture students) and to pursue self-directed thesis projects. They also took the opportunity to turn the design studio towards engaging with pressing social and environmental issues. Some of the best-known projects emerging from the fertile post-strike period revolved around the 1973 Aquarius Festival. More than 5000 people, mostly students from the major university campuses in Sydney, Brisbane, Canberra and Melbourne, attended the festival, which has become an enduring expression of the 1970s Australian counterculture, replete with tales of sexual and social experimentation, drugs, expanded consciousness, and a wild array of performances. [^72] The architect-planner Colin "Col" James, a recent addition to the faculty's teaching staff and a strong supporter of the student strike, was critical to the festival's formation. He made the pivotal suggestion that the Australian Union of Students, the festival's organising body, should "recycle a town." [^73] James took charge of the overall planning for the festival's infrastructure, in which architecture students played a key role. [^74] Gary Fidler reminisces on the students' energetic and optimistic focus on ecological and participatory design:

[^72]: For an introduction to the Aquarius Festival and its legacy see R Garbutt, J Dutton and J Kijas, eds, "Counterculture," *M/C Journal* special issue 17, no. 6 (2014).
[^73]: Col James quoted in V Bible, *Aquarius Rising: Terania Creek and the Australian Forest Protest Movement* (Masters diss., University of New England, 2010), 19. On the economic situation of rural NSW and the influx of "new settlers," see P Murphy, "Sea Change: Re-Inventing Rural and Regional Australia," *Transformations* 2 (March 2002).
[^74]: M Smith and D Crossley, eds, *The Way Out: Radical Alternatives in Australia* (Melbourne: Landsdowne Press, 1975).

> We came up on a bus, probably about a dozen students, with people like Glenn Murcutt and Richard Leplastrier who are really well-regarded architects now. We came up and designed toilets with alternative technologies, natural saunas utilising steam tents, hot rocks, and creeks with geodesic domes and all sorts of things like that. Also, social experiments—like setting up the food co-ops where it was up to you to decide what you were going to pay for the fruit and vegetables. [^75]

The festival experience was an important spur to the 1974-1978 Autonomous House Project, one of the more ambitious (and notorious) projects to emerge from the new program [Figure 7]. The house, a bricolage of alternative technologies on a derelict site behind the architecture faculty's Wilkinson Building, was part of a wave of similar experiments around the world. [^76] Designed and constructed by architecture students using recycled and donated materials, it employed passive solar strategies, including a Trombe wall built from beer bottles, and ambitiously aimed to generate its own power, harvest and heat its own water, produce its own food supply, and recycle all of its waste (although biogas production was thwarted by the local council's refusal to allow pigs on campus). [^77] Experiences at the Aquarius Festival and with the Autonomous House Project led to over a decade of faculty involvement in research, advocacy and technical support for the intentional communities that sprung up post-festival. As part of these efforts, staff, including James and Graham Holland, collaborated with students on the development of the innovative self-build technical manual *Low Cost Country Home Building*. [^78] Desires expressed during the strike period for the possibility of an education that fostered new modes of professional intervention were finding avenues for realisation.

Beyond changing the circumstances of their own education, the strike had opened up possibilities for remaking architectural practice and culture. Students became involved in an array of pedagogical experimentation, community advocacy and engagement, participatory design initiatives, and design-build projects. During the late 1970s and early 1980s, Morrice Shaw led students in collaboration with schoolchildren and community groups to produce, through participatory design-build processes, a series of playgrounds and parks in inner Sydney. In 1978, for example, 60 first-year architecture students worked for eight weeks to help design and build a sandpit, tree platforms, a bunker, retaining walls, bamboo maze, extendable fence, and a multi-level stage at the North Sydney Community Centre. [^79] A measure of the success of these ventures was the 1981 RAIA NSW Outstanding Environmental Design Award, received for the collaborative redesign of a municipal park in Balmain. [^80]

Shaw's efforts were part of what became a strong strand of socially engaged design education within the faculty. James was the most prominent figure in this, involving students in collaborative design projects with local Indigenous organisations such as the Aboriginal Housing Company. [^81] Energetic and inspirational, James often prompted and facilitated similar endeavours from his students. One instance saw Tone Wheeler, a participant in the Autonomous House project, oversee the development and realisation of James' notion, dating to the early 1980s,

[^75]: J Kijas, *Caravans & Communes: Stories of Settling in the Tweed 1970s & 1980s* (Murwillumbah, NSW: Tweed Shire Council, 2011), 106.
[^76]: L Stickells, "Journeys with the Autonomous House," *Fabrications* 27, no. 3 (2017): 352–75.
[^77]: Stickells, "Journeys with the Autonomous House," 3. The Autonomous House building site incorporated Michael White's construction and operation of an Indonesian *warung*, or food stall, as his thesis project. Soon after, in what was supposed to be a break from his studies, White travelled to Bali where he reinvented himself as Made Wijaya, eventually developing a highly successful landscape design practice and publishing a series of books on the island's temple architecture. J James, "Made Wijaya, Landscape Architect, Author and Stranger in Paradise," *Sydney Morning Herald*, 8 September 2016.

[^78]: Technical Assistance Group, *Low Cost Country Home Building: a Handbook on the Essentials of Low Cost Construction for the Guidance of Australian Rural Homebuilders* (Sydney: Department of Architecture, University of Sydney, 1982).
[^79]: During the same period, Shaw was completing his well-known "Wave" House on Scotland Island.
[^80]: "Council Park Allocation Creates Employment," the *Sydney Morning Herald*, 18 August, 1980 14; "Shaw, Morrie," in *Encyclopedia of Australian Architecture*, ed. Goad and Willis, 625.
[^81]: *University of Sydney Annual Report 1992* (University of Sydney Archives).

that disused inner-city warehouses should become cooperative housing for university students. Eventually completed in 1991, STUCCO involved students in designing the conversion of an old factory and warehouse into apartments and communal facilities for low-cost student accommodation. [^82] While never the dominant focus of the faculty's architecture programs, this kind of activity and the reputation of the faculty as a supportive niche for socially and environmentally responsible design continued into the 21st century. [^83]

The strike's energy also rippled beyond the curriculum; students sought to experiment with environmental processes and design practices as part of a much larger countercultural imperative in Australia. James again figured strongly, encouraging student involvement with the then-ascendant Green Bans movement and collaborating with former students in a pro-bono design advice and technical aid collective named ARCHANON. [^84] There were other offshoots: in late 1973, architecture students Phil Rose, Paul Pholeros (later to found Healthabitat), and Wal Zagoridis, as well as school teacher Irene Zagoridis, began work on The Australian Communications Capsule, also known as The Media Bus Project [Figure 8]. [^85] Having completed their first three years of study, the group retrofitted a Leyland Titan bus as a mobile living and working space, complete with photographic darkroom and bean bag zone. In 1974, they circuited Australia conducting interactive workshops on environmental design themes.

Pholeros later recalled the significance of the student strike in provoking the group's "mood of exploration" and inspiring them to utilise their architectural training in wider community settings. [^86] Pholeros offers an emblematic example of the strike's catalytic effect. Soon after the Media Bus adventure, he went on to a similarly peripatetic collaboration with the lecturer Marr Grounds; together they flew across northern Australia to work with a number of Indigenous communities on collaborative environmental sculptures and exhibitions [Figure 9]. [^87] By the mid-1980s, he was providing courses as part of the faculty's continuing education program and launching Healthabitat. [^88] Healthabitat was a not-for-profit partnership focused on improving Indigenous Australia's housing, health and environmental health. Pholeros, who died in 2016, eventually became an adjunct professor in the faculty and was admitted to the Order of Australia in 2007 for his work in Indigenous communities.

The strike, the radical architectural pedagogies installed in its wake, and the broader architectural initiatives with which they connected, aimed at challenging the status quo. The activities described above formed just part of a galaxy of experimentation filled with interventions in political and environmental activism, conceptual art practices, inflatable architectures, global communication networks, self-regulatory and cooperative learning, design-build projects, and community outreach programs. The students and staff involved interrogated and critiqued the traditions at work in the faculty and its modes of academic and institutional dissemination. They attempted to transgress disciplinary limits and to destabilise architecture's relationship to social, political, economic and technological conventions. In so doing, they quickly generated forms

[^82]: *University of Sydney Annual Report 1991* (University of Sydney Archives). The first of its kind in Australia, STUCCO still operates via its original principles of democratic self-management.
[^83]: For example, during the mid-2000s, Anna Rubbo took up a particular interest in design within cross-cultural and community development issues. Global Studio grew out of Rubbo's work with the United Nations Millennium Project Task Force on Improving the Lives of Slum Dwellers and involved partnerships with Columbia University and the University of Rome La Sapienza.
[^84]: ARCHANON derived from ARCHitecture for the ANONymous client. "ARCHANON II," *Architecture in Australia* 63, no. 4 (1974): 79–83; D Mayes and J Stack, "Architecture, Professional Crisis, Survival," *Tharunka* (4 June 1975): 17.
[^85]: The project featured in the 1975 student-edited issue of *Architecture in Australia*. T Wheeler, "Soft Architecture Learning and Working," *Architecture in Australia* 64, no. 2 (1975): 50–51.

[^86]: Pholeros quoted in J Harris, "On the Buses: Mobile Architecture in Australia and the UK 1973–75," *Architectural Histories* 4, no. 1 (2016): 9.
[^87]: M Grounds and P Pholeros, *Sculpture at the Top Ends* (Adelaide, South Australia: Experimental Art Foundation, 1976). The pair later collaborated on another, similar project: M Grounds and P Pholeros, *Oxide Street: An Environmental Artwork on the Dingo Fence in Central Australia* (St Peters, South Australia: Experimental Art Foundation, 1981).
[^88]: A not-for-profit organisation Pholeros founded with Dr Paul Torzillo and Stephan Rainow, Healthabitat has been awarded many prizes, including the 2011 World Habitat award from the United Nations' Habitat and Building Social Housing Foundation. Pholeros, as an architect, was awarded the inaugural International Union of Architects (UIA) Vassilis Sgoutas Prize in 2008.

**Figure 10** — McConnel, Smith and Johnson's addition to the Wilkinson Building under construction (on right of image). The student-built Autonomous House lies to its south. 1975. University of Sydney School of Architecture, Design and Planning.

of institutional critique and an emerging disciplinary self-reflexivity. In fact, it was not long before misgivings emerged, and the longer arc to the strike's radical claims and actions began to grow uncertain.

The strike had delivered material gains, but the aspirations to redirect the faculty's culture and have the architecture program reflect a new social order were always idealistic. In a notably unguarded address to the Australian Institute of Engineers in June 1972, Peter Johnson drew attention to his ongoing discussions with students about their opposition to the new faculty extension, the design of which was being undertaken by Johnson's own practice. He described their questioning as "sincere" but "fumbling and inconclusive." [^89] He ended his speech by declaring: "The building, will I hope, be built." [^90] Johnson's remarks presaged the later limits to the acceptance of student demands and pointed towards the enduring asymmetry of staff-student relationships. It wasn't long before the persistence of that power balance became clearer. Four months after the strike, in November 1972, a filing cabinet was stolen from the faculty and the contained records burnt. The police were called, and students were questioned, but the incident remained unresolved. An anonymous account explained the motive for the break-in as disgust at a secret, prejudicial system of student profiling undertaken by staff. Records were, apparently, being kept on the psychological complexion, design aptitude, and professional disposition of individual students. [^91] The anonymous author questioned whether the students had truly gained from the strike action. A little later, in 1974 and 1975, two student-edited issues of the professional journal *Architecture in Australia* severely criticised and satirised conventional educational and professional practice models.

Despite the flexibility of its new program, the University of Sydney still came under attack. Mark Stiles, one of the strike leaders, wrote in the 1974 issue that an opportunity for self-directed education had been missed. Stiles argued that students' subject choices were still too constrained and disconnected from the rest of the university; that there was too much teaching by dilettante architects; and, returning once more to the theme of social relevance, he proclaimed that, in the strike action, "what was being demanded (and wasn't recognised) was an honest and committed view of design as a socially responsible act, including the possibility that the best design might be no design at all." [^92] The frustration of the student

[^89]: P Johnson, "Address to Institute of Engineers' Lunch," 8 June 1972, Johnson Papers, SLNSW.
[^90]: Johnson, "Address to Institute of Engineers' Lunch."
[^91]: "Confrontation," unattributed magazine clipping (c1973), Barry McNeill Papers, Tasmanian Archives, Hobart.
[^92]: M Stiles, "Contribution from Sydney University," *Architecture in Australia* 63, no. 4 (February 1974): 63. Stiles was almost certainly referring here to an article elsewhere in the issue, in which he and fellow student Dave Muir described their distressing experience of a studio focused on the design of a high-security prison; "Fear and Loathing in Long Bay: A Savage Journey into the Heart of the Ultimate Slammer," *Architecture in Australia* 63, no. 4 (February 1974): 87.

body, their anxiety about the course direction and their employment opportunities continued also to be expressed through the newspaper of the University of Sydney Architecture Society, *The Good Oil Drum.* [^93] Of course, disillusioned, some just walked away from their education and the profession. But examining what those who decried the profession and its institutions tried to do from within at a particular point in time, within a specific context, points us towards perennial uncertainties and problems faced in the ongoing construction of a discipline and profession. [^94] In particular, it reveals how notions of educational, professional and societal "relevance" are formed and re-formed.

Disillusionment was not the only sentiment being expressed in the faculty. The reaction of Cowan, Chair of Architectural Science, was emblematic of the bemusement and disappointment, if not outright hostility, some felt regarding the striking students and their activity. Largely dismissive of what he considered their privileged concerns, Cowan questioned whether the most aggrieved students should not simply be studying something other than architecture. [^95] Certainly, the effects of the intervention were ambiguous by the mid-1970s. Apart from the undergraduate architecture program, the faculty's other courses continued to operate largely unperturbed. Students were inducted and students graduated; the Department of Town and Country Planning introduced a Graduate School of Planning in 1974, while university budgetary constraints and poor economic conditions meant a freeze on establishing full-time faculty positions and turned many students' minds towards simply gaining employment. [^96] Alongside such developments, traditional Beaux Arts drawing and rendering exercises were pursued into the 1990s, and critique of the school as a mechanism for the production of a cultural elite was persistent. [^97]

So, what to make of the strike at the University of Sydney and its outcomes? How to gauge its influence and legacy or to judge its failure or success? The campus upheavals of the long 1960s, and their appearance in schools of architecture, seriously challenged understandings of the university's role and place in society. They also foregrounded recurrent questions about the architect's specialist knowledge, the position of architectural training in the university, and the profession's agency. The striking Sydney students held the school's curricula and teaching methods as being incapable of addressing architecture's relationship to contemporary social and political maladies and demanded that their vision of a new social order be reflected in the very basis of their studies. In this, the students were challenging those things that had seemed radical and innovative in architectural education at the end of the First World War, including the ascension of design studio teaching and the role of history and art practices, and again at the end of the Second World War, with the new scientific footing, but which had since ossified.

The striking students were concerned about their future social impact as expert professionals, keen to introduce a renewed social and moral conscience to the practice of architecture, and viewed the relevance of their education in terms quite distinct from most of their teachers. They demanded the redesign of the undergraduate architecture curriculum and the possibility of new educational experiences in line with their quest for a progressive, anti-elitist, environmentally sensitive professional identity. As much as it was shaped by currents of student radicalism and the protest movements of the period, the belligerence of the striking architecture students was also impelled by deep-rooted

[^93]: *The Good Oil Drum*, 1975–1979 (Sydney: University of Sydney Architecture Society) (University of Sydney Archives).
[^94]: The point was sometimes made during this period that students would garner more agency and relevance for the discipline they sought to remake through gaining their degrees and professional registration. See, for example, P Blake, "Cityscape: Yale on Ice," *New Yorker*, 11 August 1969, 54–55; Vincent Scully quoted in Stern and Stamp, *Pedagogy and Place*, 300–2.
[^95]: J Cowan, *A Contradiction in Terms: the Autobiography of Henry J Cowan, Foundation Professor of Architectural Science, University of Sydney* (Sydney: Hermitage Press, 1993), 214.
[^96]: Connell et al, *Australia's First*, vol. 2, 283.

[^97]: For a caustic analysis of the architectural profession and a specific account of tensions in the educational program at the University of Sydney by a former researcher at the university, see G Stevens, *The Favored Circle: The Social Foundations of Architectural Distinction* (Cambridge: MIT Press, 1998).

disciplinary agitation regarding the orientation of architectural education and the trajectory of internal transformations of the faculty according to Wilkinson's founding program. Many of the experiments undertaken had a short lifespan and were abandoned or dissolved within months or years or terminated due to financial and/or political constraints. Others became assimilated into a generic mainstream education.

Taking a longer view, the episode added to the kaleidoscopic quality of the programs developed at Sydney over the 20th century—which ranged across countercultural art practices, modernist design, environmental sustainability, architectural science, urbanism, social justice initiatives, community participation, and environmental psychology—and their jostling disciplines, ideologies and characters.

However, the strike also exposed the limitations to the prospects for professional reform from within. A tense dynamic remained between the students' desire for expert knowledge and status, an understanding of professional knowledge as political force, disciplinary autonomy, and concerns about the social responsibility of architects and the role of university-based education as a vehicle for radical change. If anything symbolised the ambiguous legacy of the strike and its complex outcomes, it was that the faculty forged on with the construction of the new facilities that had been so contentious in the lead-up to the strike [Figure 10]. In 1976, the students began to move into McConnel, Smith and Johnson's new brutalist extension to the Wilkinson Building, a limit to the effects of the students' activism conspicuously materialised in off-form concrete. [^98] ≡

[^98]: T Howells has caustically suggested: "Later named in honour of the founding professor of Architecture, ... the Wilkinson Building is an edifice singularly devoid of any Wilkinsonian character and so-named, fortunately, well after [Wilkinson] had been laid to rest." *University of Sydney Architecture* (Sydney: Watermark Press, 2007), 103.

# The Expanded Field

**Introduction —** We might say things "loosened up" in the 1970s and have since never been the same. Certainly, the relevance of the faculty's educational programs to the world beyond the university was significantly rethought. One of the most prominent transformations was that the traditional aesthetic values and practices that Wilkinson had hoped to install—the "fine taste" and "good sense" through which the faculty's graduates would lead society beyond its errors in building and planning—were giving way to an embrace of other values: accessibility, eclecticism, and an upturning of established educational and organisational hierarchies (expert and client, teacher and student). The Sydney University Art Workshop, more commonly known as the Tin Sheds, played a critical role in the shift. Lloyd Rees began occupying the ramshackle buildings on City Road, Darlington, during the late 1960s in order to teach basic and life drawing to architecture students. By the late 1970s, via haphazard development, the sheds were a hothouse for radical art production and activism and were being used to extend art education to groups who would not normally have access [^1]. The founders of the art workshop included the environmental artist Marr Grounds, architectural historian David Saunders, and the art critic and theorist Donald Brook. The sheds became a key Australian site in the 1970s growth of post-object and conceptual art. It also hosted anarchist and feminist printmaking collectives. Influential artists connected to the sheds included the Earthworks Poster Collective, Frances Phoenix, Joan Grounds, Toni Robertson, Mike Parr, Alex Danko and Tim Burns. Architecture students drawn to its experimental activities included Imants Tillers, who would go on to become a significant artist and critic; and Alec Tzannes, who contributed to the Harold Szeeman-curated *I want to leave a well done child here* (Bonython Gallery, 1971) before becoming one of Australia's most respected architects. The architecture faculty provided financial and other support from the start. By the 1990s, with the construction of the Tin Sheds Gallery within the Wilkinson Building, it had organisationally and physically absorbed the art workshop.

The following images offer a glimpse of the way the energy of the Tin Sheds period affected the educational atmosphere of the faculty: its outputs range from *Circa 70*, a short-lived faculty journal including articles from Clement Greenberg, Donald Brook and Terry Smith and architecture students' engagement in experimental art practices, to the changing ambitions of student design projects and their exhibition in the Tin Sheds Gallery.

— Lee Stickells

[^1]: The key publication on the Tin Sheds' history is Therese Kenyon, *Under a Hot Tin Roof: Art, Passion, and Politics at the Tin Sheds Art Workshop* (Sydney: State Library of New South Wales Press, 1995).

**Figure 1** — Cover of *Circa 70: A Journal of the Department of Architecture and the Architectural Research Foundation, University of Sydney* (1971). Reproduced courtesy of the University of Sydney School of Architecture, Design and Planning.

**Figure 2** — Students in a silk screen workshop at Sydney University Art Workshop, 1972. University of Sydney Archives.

**Figure 3** — Life drawing class at Sydney University Art Workshop, 1973. University of Sydney Archives.

**Figure 4** — Experimental project involving students from fine arts and architecture taking the option "Spatial Dynamics," which was held in the clubroom at the Seymour Centre, 1979. University of Sydney Archives.

**Figure 5** — Sketches of keynote speakers for the information pack for the Australasian Architecture Students Association Sydney Convention, 16-23 May 1970. Courtesy of RMIT Design Archives.

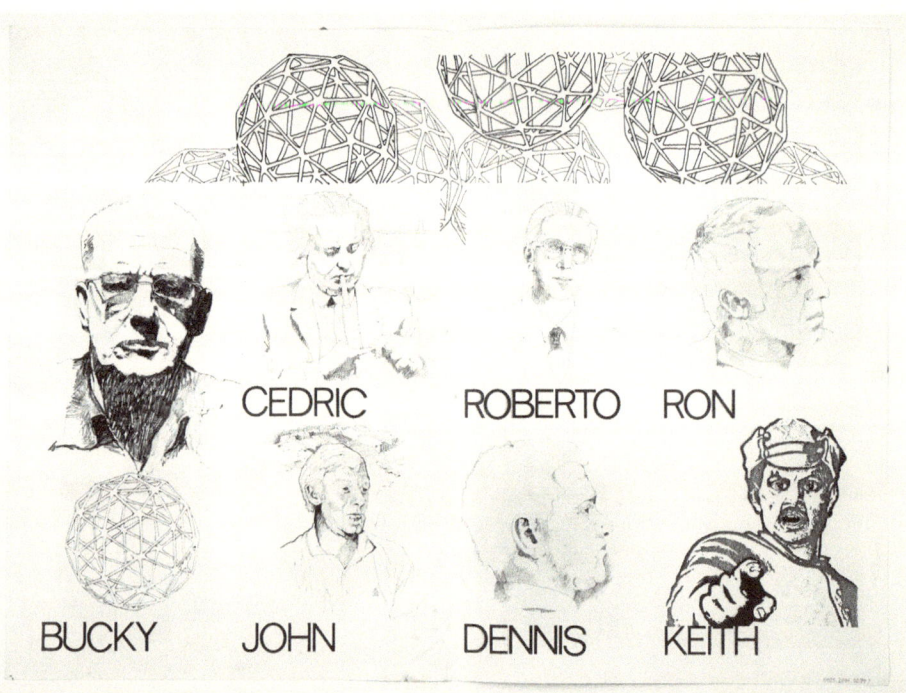

**Figure 6** — *Superarcheroo* cartoon from the information pack for the Australasian Architecture Students Association Sydney Convention, 16-23 May 1970. Courtesy of RMIT Design Archives.

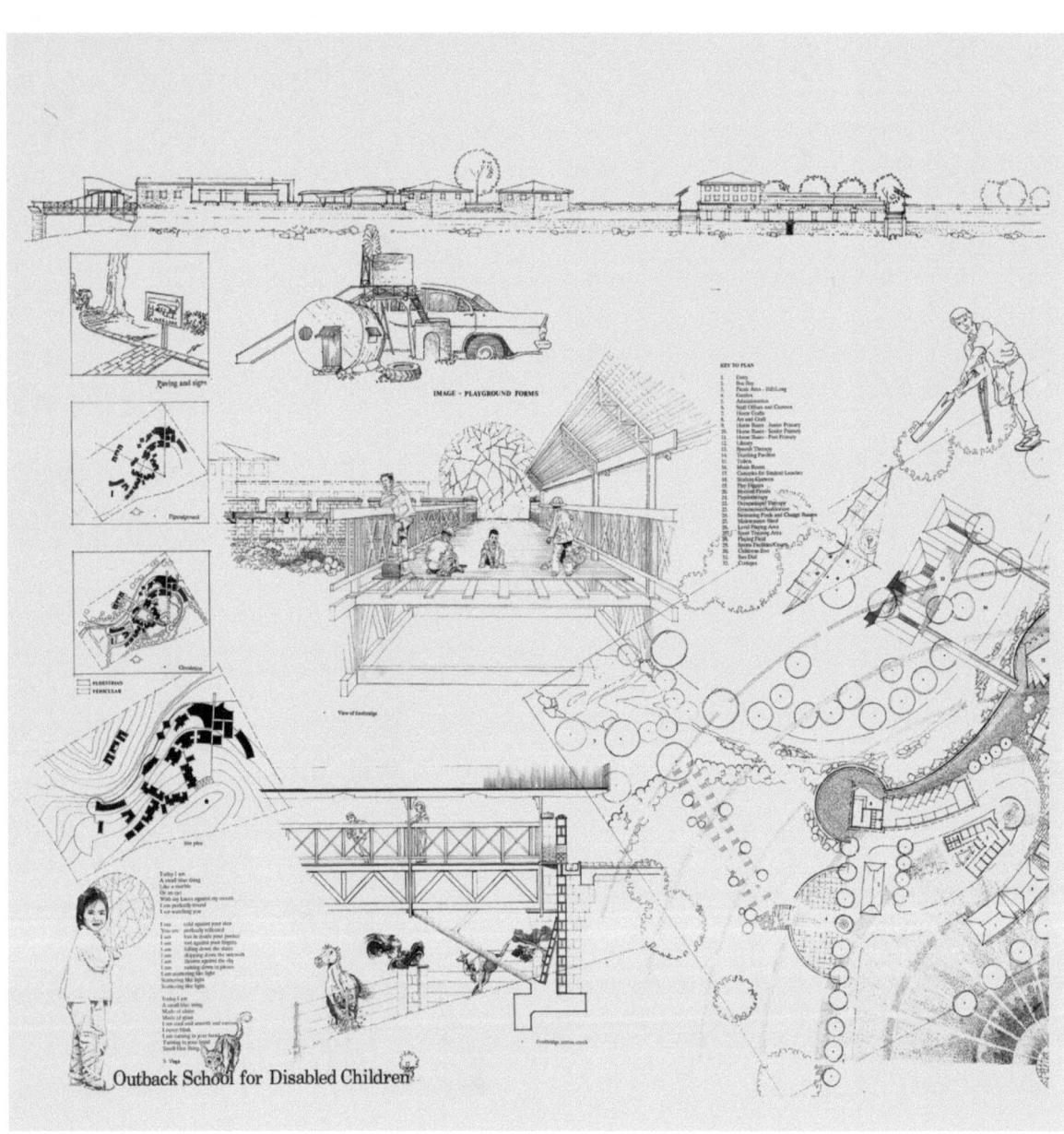

**Figure 7** — John Le Breton, *Outback School for Disabled Children*, Panel 1, sixth-year student project presentation drawings, c.1990.
McConnel Drawings Collection, University of Sydney Library, Rare Books and Special Collections.

**Figure 9** —
Mark Arbuz and Stephen Stokes,
*Alternative Technology Fair*, 1976.
Screenprint, 38.2 x 55.8 cm.
National Gallery of Australia, Canberra.

**Figure 10** (opposite page)—
Mark Arbuz and Stephen Stokes,
*Utopian Technology Fair, Autonomous House*, 1978.
Screenprint, 49 x 72 cm.
National Gallery of Australia, Canberra.

**Figure 11** — Sculpture in the Advanced Art Semester Unit Course exhibiting at the Tin Sheds Gallery, c.1990. University of Sydney Archives.

Internationally, three new architectural research fields were emerging in which the faculty would come to play an important role: man-environment studies, design computing, and architectural phenomenology.

– Glen Hill, "The Seventies Science Wars"

**Figure 1** — Professor John Gero cheerfully showing off the first SUN Workstations in Australia in 1983. In 1984, the design computing unit acquired the first 128K Apple Macintosh on campus, which tour parties would come to view. University of Sydney Archives.

# Chapter 7: The Seventies Science Wars: Cognitive Science, Computer Science and Counter Science
— Glen Hill

*The scene: February 1971, a small lecture theatre.* Newly arrived students in the University of Sydney's architecture program take their seats for their first lecture. Liz Fell, a young "radical feminist" seconded from the Faculty of Arts to teach an undergraduate architecture subject titled "Political Science Applied to Design," stands confidently in front of her first architectural class for the year. The students—timid, fresh from high school—are unsure what to expect from the architectural education ahead of them. Fell looks around the room, glares at all the young males in the class and declares, "*You* are the problem!"

The scene is loosely interpreted from a 2014 interview given by Paul Pholeros, a student at the University of Sydney in the 1970s. [^1] In the interview, he recalls the profoundly positive impact Fell, together with the many other diverse and powerful voices he encountered in his architectural education in the 1970s, had on his extraordinary career as a social activist-architect. [^2]

The 1970s were the beginning of a remarkable period of experimentation in architectural education and scholarship at the University of Sydney's Faculty of Architecture and indeed at many architecture faculties around the Western world. Influenced by developments at architectural schools such as the Architectural Association in Britain and Harvard, Yale, Columbia, and the University of California in the United States and accelerated by the 1972 architecture student strike discussed by Lee Stickells in Chapter Seven, the University of Sydney's Dean of the Faculty of Architecture, Professor Peter Johnson, oversaw a wholesale review of the curriculum that introduced a melting pot of diverse people and their ideas about teaching and research. [^3] Subjects from disciplines as disparate as sociology, psychology, anthropology, ethology, politics, philosophy, and religious studies intermingled with conventional architectural offerings, while radical new ways of approaching architectural design were explored in both theory and practice.

Perhaps paradoxically, given the general mood of hippie non-conformity at the time, the new pedagogical offerings and the scholarly research increasingly occurring in the faculty still seemed to require epistemological legitimisation. In line with a shift that had long been underway in higher education, that legitimisation was sought in science or, in some cases, in the rhetoric of science. Drawing upon scientific content, using the scientific method, or simply invoking the word science, became increasingly popular in the faculty's academic scholarship in the 1970s and 1980s. Recall that even Fell's activist teachings were delivered under the authorising title of "Political *Science* Applied to Design."

## Science and the Academy

The rise of science and its displacement of the humanities in the Western university system is said to begin in the 19th century, when universities in North America started to emulate the German model of dividing their

[^1]: E Charlesworth, *Humanitarian Architecture: 15 Stories of Architects Working After Disaster* (London: Routledge, 2014), 56.
[^2]: Charlesworth, *Humanitarian Architecture*, 53–66. Paul Pholeros (1953–2016) received an Order of Australia in 2007 for services to architecture, Indigenous housing, and health.
[^3]: An account of selected historical case studies of experiments in architectural pedagogy has been assembled as part of the Radical Pedagogies Project led by Beatrice Colomina: "Radical Pedagogies," http://radical-pedagogies.com, accessed 17 May 2018. Of the University of Sydney Faculty of Architecture academics, Marr Grounds had trained at UC Berkeley and Colin James had studied at Harvard. Clare Cooper Marcus, the prominent UC Berkeley academic known for her strong social agenda, visited the faculty in 1970.

institutions into specialised disciplines with an emphasis on expertise and the creation of new know-ledge. [^4] Political scientist Patrick J Deneen suggests, however, that the shift began much earlier, claiming that "[t]he crisis of the humanities in fact began in the early modern period with the argument that a new science was needed to replace the 'old science' of the liberal arts, a new science that no longer sought merely to *understand* the world and its creatures, but to *transform* them." [^5] Much closer to our period of interest in the middle of the 20th century, North American universities further diminished the authority of the humanities when they began to place "renewed emphasis upon scientific training and technological innovation—spurred especially by massive government investment in the "useful arts and sciences." [^6]

Following the lead of the US and Canada, an increasing emphasis on science and technological training became evident in Australian universities in the wake of the Second World War. [^7] The rise of the authority of science led to the desire to give a scientific gloss to both existing and new university disciplines. This is readily evidenced in the scurry to invent academic disciplinary titles containing the word "science." Australian university offerings came to include disciplines such as natural science, human science, social science, political science, behavioural science, medical science, health science, business science, life science, environ-mental science, veterinary science, marine science, design science, cognitive science and, more recently, computer science and data science. The University of Sydney's Faculty of Architecture was one of the earliest to incorporate a Department of Architectural Science and a Chair of Architectural Science, as discussed in Daniel Ryan's chapter in this volume.

At the same time that Fell and other "radicals" were participating in the drama of staff and student activism over Indigenous, social and environmental issues, the University of Sydney's Faculty of Architecture was experiencing equally radical shifts in its academic trajectories as an outcome (or response) to the rise of science in academia. [^8] Internationally, three new architectural research fields were emerging in which the faculty would come to play an important role: man-environment studies, design computing, and architectural phenomenology. The first two brought specific scientific content and scientific methods into a fresh relationship with architecture and design; the last was an intense reaction against attempts to apply the rationality of scientific method to design and architecture. While often at odds with each other, all three added to the richness of the intellectual ferment of the faculty throughout the last decades of the 20th century.

## Man-Environment Studies

One of the earliest texts setting out the scope of the new architectural field of man-environment studies was Amos Rapoport's *Human Aspects of Urban Form: Towards a Man-Environment Approach to Urban Form and Design.* [^9] Discussing the provenance of his book, Rapoport, who had taken up an academic position at the University of Sydney's Faculty of Architecture between 1969 and 1972, acknowledged that the "[a]ctual writing began and the early, and hence crucial, drafts were completed while I was at the University of Sydney." [^10]

[^4]: L Menand, P Reitter and C Wellmon, eds, *The Rise of the Research University: A Sourcebook* (Chicago: University of Chicago Press, 2017).
[^5]: PJ Deneen, "Science and the Decline of the Liberal Arts," *The New Atlantis: A Journal of Technology and Society* 26 (Fall 2009/Winter 2010): 60–68.
[^6]: Deneen, "Science and the Decline of the Liberal Arts," 60–68.
[^7]: G Stevens, *The Favored Circle: The Social Foundations of Architectural Distinction* (Cambridge, MA: MIT Press, 1998), 3. Garry Stevens gives a more British-centric explanation of the emergence of architectural and design science at the University of Sydney's Faculty of Architecture, suggesting that it was "a product of the enthusiasm for bringing science into architecture that swept the British Commonwealth in the 1950s." See also A Dutta, ed., *A Second Modernism: MIT, Architecture, and the "Techno-Social" Moment* (Cambridge, MA: MIT Press, 2013); J Ockman, ed., *Architecture School: Three Centuries of Educating Architects in North America* (Cambridge, MA: MIT Press, 2012).
[^8]: Political activist and journalist Wendy Bacon taught in the faculty with Liz Fell. Architect Colin James worked on "green bans" with the Builders Labourers Federation and assisted the Aboriginal Housing Cooperative.
[^9]: A Rapoport, *Human Aspects of Urban Form: Towards a Man-Environment Approach to Urban Form and Design* (Oxford: Pergamon Press, 1977).
[^10]: Rapoport, *Human Aspects of Urban Form*, viii. Amos Rapoport is an architect and one of the founders of man-environment studies. He moved from Melbourne to the University of Sydney in the year of publication of his influential book: A Rapoport, *House Form and Culture* (Englewood Cliffs, NJ: Prentice-Hall, 1969).

Man-environment studies' goal, simply put but not simply achieved, was to understand the relationship between people and their environment. Rapoport encapsulated this in three key questions:

1. What bio-social, psychological and cultural characteristics of human beings (as members of species, of various groupings, or as individuals) influence, and in design should influence, which characteristics of the built environment?
2. What effects do which aspects of which environments have on which groups of people, under what sets of conditions, and why?
3. What are the mechanisms of these two-way interactions between people and environments? [^11]

Man-environment studies emerged out of, and alongside, similar research occurring in a wide range of disciplines beyond architecture, particularly in psychology. The specialist research area of architectural psychology, or, as it is now more popularly known, environmental psychology, was first discussed in German psychologist Willy Hellpach's 1935 book *Geopsyche*. [^12] The area grew gradually during the 1950s and 1960s, eventually gaining a significant academic presence with the 1970 publication of Harold Proshansky's *Environmental Psychology*. [^13] Its academic resilience was confirmed a decade later with the founding of a journal of the same name.

As well as psychology, man-environment studies drew upon many established disciplines, including anthropology, sociology, and human geography. Nevertheless, early man-environment studies researchers recognised the need for a unique, architecturally focused disciplinary area because, as Rapoport notes, man-environment studies:

> [w]hile basing its knowledge of people on the findings and approaches of a number of social and behavioural sciences, it differs from them by its stress on the physical environment which, by and large, these disciplines have neglected. [^14]

Since the emergence of the discipline, man-environment studies has been transformed, both in nature and name. Perhaps in part because gendered language was becoming a sensitive issue in the 1970s, man-environment studies evolved into "people-environment studies" and is now commonly referred to, among other appellations, as "environment behaviour studies." [^15]

The deployment of the authority of science, both in terms of its content and method, was central to environment behaviour studies. Rapoport believed that it was vital that there should be a scientific basis to understanding the relationship between people and their built environment, even recently suggesting that, as well as the scientific areas it has employed, the field would also have benefited from other science-based disciplines such as "neuroscience, cognitive neuroscience, cognitive science, genetics, evolutionary science, evolutionary psychology, evolutionary ecology, sociobiology, integrative ecology, systems ecology, ethology, evolutionary economics, behavioural economics, and network theory." [^16]

Indeed, it was the emphasis on science and the systematic accumulation of knowledge that differentiated Rapoport's vision for environment behaviour studies from traditional approaches to architectural design, as well as the views of many of his fellow environment behaviour researchers. (And it was this emphasis that made the field even more discordant with its academic cousin, architectural phenomenology.) Reflecting upon

---

[^11]: Rapoport, "Environment-Behavior Studies: Past, Present, and Future," *Journal of Architectural and Planning Research* 25, no. 4 (Winter 2008): 277–78.
[^12]: W Hellpach, *Geopsyche* (Leipzig: Verlag Wilhelm Engelmann, 1935).
[^13]: H Proshansky, *Environmental Psychology: Man and His Physical Setting* (New York: Holt, Rinehart and Winston, 1970).
[^14]: Rapoport, *Human Aspects of Urban Form*, 1.
[^15]: EBS (Environment Behaviour Studies) is also the acronym for Environment, Behaviour and Society. See GT Moore, *Environment Behaviour and Society: A Brief Look at the Field and Some Current EBS Research at the University of Sydney*, http://netedu.xauat.edu.cn/sykc/hjx/content/ckzl/1/3.pdf, accessed 17 May 2018.
[^16]: Rapoport, "Environment-Behavior Studies," 278.

his dissatisfaction with the path that some of the environment behaviour disciplinary sub-groups were taking in the early years, Rapoport describes his desire as having a strong scientific ground:

> One group, always a very small minority, which included myself, was interested in founding a scientific discipline of environment-behaviour relations (EBR). They were interested in *understanding* the world through basic research aimed at understanding this particular domain. Not necessarily interested in design itself, they believed that it could not be improved without knowledge and, above all, without an explanatory theory of EBR ... [^17]

Rapoport considered that other disciplinary groups in the environment-behaviour studies domain were too quick in attempting to use the findings of environment-behaviour studies for *"changing* or improving the world" without first doing the necessary preparatory work of creating a consistent and coherent body of knowledge and a theory capable of being applied to design problems. [^18] Without a sound scientific grounding, Rapoport argued "… attempts to improve the built environment, what is usually called 'design,' were likely to fail, since no outcomes could be reliably predicted." [^19] Understanding architectural design as a process of scientifically grounded rational thinking led to Rapoport's legendary refusal to teach in the design studio, which he felt was flawed because of its lack of scientific rigour. [^20]

Even from its earliest beginnings in the late 1960s, environment behaviour studies mutated and diverged into a variety of professional and academic groupings. Early groups included population and environmental psychology, which was associated with the journal *Population and Environment*, and environmental psychology, a new division created by the International Association of Applied Psychology (IAAP). The Environmental Design Research Association (EDRA), which focused on the social aspects of the environ-ment, traced its roots to the social activism of the late 1960s. [^21] A later grouping, the International Association for the Study of People in their Physical Surroundings (IAPS), was founded in 1981. The Man-Environment Relations Association (MERA) emerged in Japan, while the Environment Behaviour Research Association (EBRA) was established in Dalian, China. Because Rapoport perceived this collection of disciplinary groupings as unable to link up and sustain a consistent and coherent body of knowledge and methodology, he referred to them as "islands of knowledge in a sea of ignorance." [^22]

After Rapoport's departure from the University of Sydney's Faculty of Architecture in 1972, academics in the faculty continued to develop their own "island" of environment behaviour research. Perhaps because it was generally scientific in its orientation, Rapoport would likely have approved of its research direction. Ross Thorne was a key player in the development of this research. Thorne had been at the faculty since 1961, well before Rapoport's arrival in 1969. Already well recognised as the architect of a number of remarkable early Sydney School houses, discussed in Catherine Lassen and Julie Willis' chapter in this volume, as an academic, Thorne nurtured early environment behaviour research at the faculty. By 1980, he had established the People and the Man Made Environment group, based in the Ian Buchan Fell Housing Research Centre at the

[^17]: Rapoport, "Environment-Behavior Studies," 277.
[^18]: Rapoport, "Environment-Behavior Studies," 277.
[^19]: Rapoport, "Environment-Behavior Studies," 277.
[^20]: T Heath, *Learning Architecture, Teaching Architecture: A Guide for the Perplexed* (Toowong, Queensland: Denarius Design Books, 2010), vii–x.
[^21]: "The Environmental Design Research Association (EDRA) is an international, interdisciplinary organization founded in 1968 by design professionals, social scientists, students, educators, and facility managers. EDRA came into being during a period of social awareness and social unrest. Consequently, our agenda, the social aspects of the environment, was clearly a product of the times. The 1960s were a period of new horizons and new visions." Environmental Design Research Association, "About EDRA," https://edra.site-ym.com, accessed 17 May 2018. Prominent architectural practitioner and theorist Tom Heath, who was a principal of McConnell, Smith and Johnson from 1964–79 and taught theory at the University of Sydney Faculty of Architecture during that time, was a founding member of EDRA.
[^22]: Rapoport, "Environment-Behavior Studies," 280.

Faculty of Architecture. [^23] Working with other Australian and New Zealand universities, the group organised conferences in the area of environment behaviour. After a productive conference in Auckland, New Zealand, in June 1983, Australasian researchers established the People and the Physical Environment Research (PaPER) group in July of that year. By 1990, the regular academic newsletters from this group had expanded and transformed into the *The Person-Environment and Cultural Heritage Journal of Australia and New Zealand*. Thorne also continued an active engagement with environmental psychologists, establishing an Architectural Psychology Research Unit in 1991.

The PaPER group included many other academic contributors from the University of Sydney's Faculty of Architecture. Trained as a psychologist, Thorne's long-time academic colleague, Terry Purcell, was a good fit with the emerging architectural environment behaviour research discipline and became a significant contributor to environment behaviour research at the faculty. The cognitive science dimension of Purcell's research, which included the cognitive processes involved in the formation of mental representations of the environment and the cognitive processes involved in design problem solving, particularly the role of sketching and drawing, also had research crossovers with the faculty's other major architectural research field, design science. Anthropologist Paul Memmott, who was an honorary research associate at the Faculty of Architecture from 1987 to 1989, extended environment behaviour research into the domain of Australian Aboriginal architecture in his research at the University of Queensland. Richard Lamb, a scientist trained in ecology and botany, joined the faculty in 1988 and brought a green perspective to the faculty's environment behaviour research. Marking the temporary ascendancy of the discipline within the faculty, Gary Moore, an already well-established Canadian environment behaviour researcher who had co-founded the Environmental Design Research Association (EDRA), joined the faculty as dean in 1997. As part of his desire to strengthen environment behaviour research within the faculty, Moore, along with Hilaire Graham, Wendy Sarkissian and Peter Droege, organised a major conference on the people and physical environment research at the University of Sydney in 1998.

Rapoport recently lamented what he perceived as the limited impact the environment behaviour field has had on the design of the built environment. [^24] According to Rapoport's diagnosis, this was due to the lack of a sound scientific basis to enable the discipline to make any predictive contribution to design. However, others involved in the discipline, including some in the Faculty of Architecture at the University of Sydney, pointed to different reasons for the weak traction environment behaviour studies has had in architectural design. These reasons also related to science, but, rather than suggesting that finding solid scientific ground offered a solution, they saw the very search for such ground as the problem.

## Design Science

In 1966, just as the new field of man-environment studies was emerging, John Gero, a recent graduate of the University of Sydney's Master of Building Sciences program (another of the recently created academic disciplinary titles containing the word science), joined the academic staff at the Faculty of Architecture. In time, he was to become a giant presence in the faculty and in his field. [^25]

Although arriving at the faculty with a building engineering background, Gero became increasingly enamoured with the potential of the new-fangled, clunky, expensive, digital computing machine [Figure 1]. Looking back over the long arc of Gero's research, it is possible to identify a pattern in which his research sits on

[^23]: Ian Buchan Fell, who died in 1961, left the income from his estate to the university for the promotion and encouragement of education and research on housing.

[^24]: Rapoport, "Environment-Behavior Studies," 276–81.
[^25]: John Gero is now Research Professor in Computer Science and Architecture at the University of North Carolina, Charlotte, and a Research Professor at the Krasnow Institute for Advanced Study and at the Department of Computational Social Science, George Mason University.

the cutting edge of the engineering and design potential offered by every new generation of computer. An historical review of Gero's remarkable scholarly output of over 50 books and 700 book chapters, articles and papers reveals how his research developed, beginning with the early use of primitive computers to assist with basic engineering calculations and progressing toward frontline research into the use of artificial intelligence in design.

In 1968, two years after joining the faculty, Gero organised the Computer Applications Research Section of the Department of Architectural Science, bringing together staff and student researchers with a common interest in the emerging potential of the use of the computer for building design. [^26] In 1969, in one of the first papers written after the formation of the group, Gero described the range of architectural domains that he believed would be impacted by the computer: management; computer-aided design; design of technical systems; economic studies; and documentation. [^27]

Reflecting the diversity in the research domains he had identified, during the early 1970s, design computing research at the Faculty of Architecture tackled a range of computer applications across broad areas of engineering and building design, including innovative modes of structural analysis; [^28] determining site feasibility; [^29] sun shading and overshadowing; [^30] preparing specifications; [^31] and the design of complex structures such as cable networks. [^32]

By 1975, Gero was even able to venture some early thoughts about the ethical implications of computers in architectural design. [^33] In his perceptive discussion, he looks towards a future in which interactive computing would be sufficiently developed to allow the value system of the design context to be interrogated, rather than just accepting the ethics embedded in the "well-defined" problem that the computer was capable of handling at that time. It was a prescient observation in light of the contemporary debate over problematic values "hidden" in the algorithms of contemporary artificial intelligence platforms.

Although Gero's initial research fell under the rubric of "computer-aided" design, even this early work signalled an interest in the use of computers that went well beyond merely using them as an aid to building design, prefiguring later intensive research into ways to automate the design process. From the middle of the 1970s, Gero's research became increasingly focused on the use of computers for optimisation. In a 1975 paper, he points out that, in the architectural domain, optimisation had been evolving for a decade, with mixed success in areas such as site development, building services, materials selection, and space planning. [^34] Architecturally, the capacity for the computer to determine optimum space relationships and generate "ideal" floor plans, placed the research squarely on a path towards the automation of key aspects of architectural design. [^35] The following year, Gero presented research describing how dynamic programming might handle the integer non-linear programming required to develop an optimisation algorithm for dimensioning architectural plans. [^36] During the second half of the 1970s, the Faculty of Architecture's design computing unit explored the use of optimisation on a large range of architectural design applications.

[^26]: J Gero, "The Work of the Computer Applications Research Section of the Department of Architectural Science, Sydney University," *Architectural Science Review* (hereafter *ASR*) 15, no. 3 (1972): 58–63.
[^27]: J Gero, "Computers in Architectural Science," *ASR* 13, no. 1 (1970): 11–16.
[^28]: J Gero, "Pneumatic Structures Constrained by Networks," in *Proceedings of 1st International Colloquium on Pneumatic Structures*, ed. D Feder (Stuttgart: IASS and Stuttgart University, 1967), 134–138; J Gero, "Prestressed Masonry," *Building Forum* 1, no. 1 (1971): 15–19; J Gero, "A Prestressed Masonry Reinforced Concrete Space Structure," in *Designing, Engineering and Constructing with Masonry Products*, ed. B Johnson (Houston: Gulf, 1971), 210–15.
[^29]: J Gero, "Computer-Aided Interactive Site Feasibility Studies for Architects and Designers," in *ONLINE 72* (Uxbridge: Brunel University, 1972), 857–77.
[^30]: J Gero, "Sunshading, Shadows and Effects on Traffic," in *Planning and Design of Tall Buildings* (ASCE, DS, 1972), 43–47.
[^31]: J Gero, "Specification by Computer," *ASR* 19, no. 1 (1976): 10–13.
[^32]: J Gero, "The Behaviour of Cable Network Structures," in *2nd International Conference on Space Structures* (Surrey: University of Surrey, 1975), 368–78.

[^33]: J Gero, "Ethics in Computer-Aided Design: A Polemic," *ACM SIGDA Newsletter* 5, no. 4 (1975): 9–14.
[^34]: J Gero, "Architectural Optimization: A Review," *Engineering Optimization* 1, no. 3 (1975): 189–99.
[^35]: Gero, "Architectural Optimization," 189–99.
[^36]: J Gero, "Synthesis and Optimization of Small Rectangular Floor Plans," *Environment and Planning B* 4 (1977): 81–88.

**Figure 2** — While Snodgrass is widely recognised for his scholarly research, the high quality of his architectural design work is less well known. Shown here is a perspective drawing of a 1975 house project for the New Zealand photographer Brian Brake. Peter Muller, *Adrian Snodgrass* (San Francisco: Blurb, 2016), 7. Courtesy Peter Muller.

By the early 1980s, Gero was writing on the potential of knowledge engineering, expert systems, and artificial intelligence in design. [^37] In the medical field, knowledge engineering had famously been used at Stanford University to develop the first expert system in the 1970s. MYCIN, as it was called, was capable of artificially replicating the medical knowledge required to recognise infections and recommend dosages of appropriate antibiotics based on a patient's body weight. A similar potential to capture the expertise of architectural designers and replicate their capacity for decision making in architectural expert systems was an exciting prospect that occupied a great deal of the computer applications research at the university's architecture faculty during the 1980s.

In 1982, an inspired graduate from the University of Melbourne, Richard Coyne, joined the design computing unit to undertake a PhD under the supervision of Gero. While completing his undergraduate degree in landscape architecture, Coyne had developed a fascination with computer graphics programing that he sought to extend into artificial intelligence. [^38] Coyne quickly became a vital member of the design computing unit. As well as publishing his own book on expert systems, Coyne led the design computing unit's team of authors for one of the most significant books on knowledge-based design, *Knowledge Based Design Systems*. [^39] While he continued to build an impressive research and publishing portfolio, his later work was not always in conformity with the epistemological position of the design computing unit.

In the late 1980s, Gero began collaborating with an extraordinary researcher from Carnegie Mellon University, Mary Lou Maher, around the future of artificial intelligence. Their first joint paper in 1987 identified the contemporary limitations of computer aids for architectural design, which at that time centred around drawing programs and detailed evaluation programs. [^40]

They envisaged that the immediate future of design computing research would be the continuation of the development of knowledge-based systems, particularly for design integration and detail design. However, these systems were restricted to predetermined scenarios and therefore incapable of novel designing. The long-term goal was to create a generation of artificial intelligence capable of "creative" design; Gero and Maher's restrained academic language could hardly conceal their excitement.

In 1990, Maher moved to Sydney and joined the architecture faculty's design computing unit, giving further clout to the artificial intelligence research being carried out at the University of Sydney. In 1993, the esteem of the unit was acknowledged when it gained the status of an Australian Research Council-funded Key Centre. Gero and Maher became co-directors of the Key Centre for Design Computing. As well as furthering the computing unit's research, Maher went on to establish the first Bachelor of Design Computing program at the faculty.

The design computing unit's study of cognitive behaviour and human reasoning, particularly its use of research from psychology, overlapped directly with the contemporaneous cognitive science research being undertaken in the man-environment field. This shared interest in the cognitive processes of design led to a collaboration between researchers from the Faculty of Architecture's Environment Behaviour and Design Computing units. As an outcome of this collaboration, Gero and Purcell, the psychologist working in the faculty's environment behaviour unit, were invited to

[^37]: J Gero, "Object Modelling Through Knowledge Engineering," in *Utilization of Artificial Intelligence and Pattern Recognition in Manufacturing Engineering* (Tokyo: CIRP, 1984), 19–25.
[^38]: Richard Coyne commenced his PhD at the University of Sydney in February 1982 and completed the degree in 1986. He is now Professor of Design Computing at the University of Edinburgh.
[^39]: R Coyne, *Logic Models of Design* (London: University College, 1988); R Coyne, et al., *Knowledge-Based Design Systems* (Reading, MA: Addison-Wesley, 1990).
[^40]: J Gero and ML Maher, "Future Roles of Knowledge-Based Design Systems in The Design Process," in *CAADFutures* 87 (Amsterdam: Elsevier, 1987), 81–90.

be joint guest editors of a special edition of the prestigious design and planning journal, *Environment and Planning B*, dedicated to new research into the cognitive processes involved in design. [^41]

While the design process modelling used in optimisation and knowledge-based systems required design knowledge to be made explicit, the design processes themselves were derived either from introspection or "proposed formalisable processes." [^42] An alternative way of modelling design processes was to base the models on the cognitive behaviour of real human designers. During the 1960s and 1970s, various design research centres around the world had been conducting cognitive experiments with protocol analysis techniques aimed at elucidating the design processes used by designers. [^43] Their methods included studying designers in the act of designing; interviewing designers about their designing; getting designers to "think-aloud" while they were designing; combining "thinking-aloud" with the analysis of CAD drawings produced concurrently by that designer; studying the categorisation process and its role in concept formation; and applying human reasoning and problem-solving research from psychology to design process models.

The alliance between researchers in design computing and architectural psychology highlights the ambition of the faculty's design computing project to one day be able to model the reasoning of human designers and thereby achieve the holy grail of automating creative design. This was a vision that relied on a particular epistemological position: scientific realism. However, not all in the faculty, or even within design computing, shared this epistemological position, and some became openly sceptical about its achievability.

# Architectural Phenomenology

Living in Australia after the Second World War was, for many, a claustrophobic experience. In the late 1950s, many young professional Australians dreamed of escaping to England, and quite a few did. [^44] In the 1960s, many "free-thinking" and "free loving" Australians dreamed of joining the "hippie trail" in search of ashrams in India and, again, a few did. [^45] Very much ahead of the curve, in the final years of the 1940s, Adrian Snodgrass abandoned his architectural undergraduate degree at the Sydney Technical College and departed the parochial confines of Australia to begin a long sojourn in Asia. Throughout the 1950s and early 1960s, Snodgrass travelled to India, Ceylon, Tibet, Hong Kong, China, Bhutan, the Philippines and Japan. In his extended stays in India and Ceylon, Snodgrass became a serious student of Sanskrit. He kept in touch with the cutting edge of Sydney architecture [Figure 2] through intermittent return trips to Sydney to work in the office of his friend and remarkable architect Peter Muller, discussed in Lassen and Willis' chapter in this volume. In 1967, he undertook a short stint in the more conventional world of architecture, working as an associate with the Hong Kong-based interior design firm Pacific House. From 1968, he spent five years in Kyoto, Japan, studying Sanskrit, Chinese and Japanese Buddhist texts. This was followed by another period in a commercial architectural practice in Hong Kong. [^46] In 1975, he relocated to Indonesia to make documentary films with the photographer Brian Brake, after which he finally returned to Australia and began an equally unconventional architectural and academic career path.

---

[^41]: J Gero and T Purcell, "Cognitive Modelling in Design: Editorial," *Environment and Planning B* 20 (1993): 253–56.
[^42]: Gero and T Purcell, "Cognitive Modelling in Design," 253.
[^43]: Research centres included the School of Architecture at Carnegie Mellon University, the Design Computing Program at the Georgia Institute of Technology College of Architecture, and the Department of Computer Science at the Helsinki University of Technology.

[^44]: R Crawford Bridge and D Dunstan, eds, *Australians in Britain: The Twentieth Century Experience* (Clayton, Victoria: Monash University ePress, 2009).
[^45]: S Gemie and B Ireland, *The Hippie Trail: A History* (Manchester: Manchester University Press, 2017).
[^46]: During 1974 in Hong Kong, Snodgrass was executive associate with commercial interior designer Dale Keller & Associates and worked in the architectural firm, Palmer and Turner.

In 1976, Snodgrass began teaching at the University of Sydney in an unusual shared arrangement between the Department of Religious Studies and the Faculty of Architecture. With the support of the dean of the architecture faculty, Peter Johnson, and without having completed an undergraduate degree, Snodgrass enrolled in a postgraduate research degree in 1978. In 1981, he was awarded a Master of Science in Architecture (ironic, given the damning critiques of the use of science in architecture that he would shortly mount). His masters thesis, "The Symbolism of the Stupa," was published as a book in 1985 and is now internationally recognised as a seminal work in the field. In 1981, Snodgrass accepted a joint appointment as Japan Foundation Lecturer in Religious Studies and Architecture and began work on his doctoral dissertation, which he completed in 1985. The dissertation, *Stellar and Temporal Symbolism in Traditional Architecture*, used Chinese, Indic, pre-Columbian, African, Christian and Islamic materials to analyse the ways in which temporal concepts and cycles of time are incorporated in buildings. This work was later published as *Architecture, Time and Eternity*. In 1988, Snodgrass published a third major work on Asian architecture, *The Matrix and Diamond World Mandalas in Shingon Buddhism*.

At the same time that Snodgrass was researching and writing on the cosmology of Asian architecture, an epistemological upheaval was occurring in English-speaking universities across the world: the advent of postmodernism. Perhaps because the continental philosophical tradition that grounded the emergence of postmodernism had many affinities with the eastern epistemological positions with which Snodgrass had been working, or perhaps because postmodernism challenged the rationalist, scientific scholarship being pursued at the faculty, Snodgrass was attracted to its revolutionary thinking. [^47]

Postmodernist thought, the basis of which had been fermenting in the German and French philosophical movements of phenomenology, hermeneutics, existentialism, structuralism, post-structuralism and deconstruction, did not make a significant impression on the English-speaking world until translations of key works began to appear in the 1960s. [^48] When they did arrive, the writings of Gilles Deleuze, Jacques Derrida, Michel Foucault and Martin Heidegger were an explosive challenge to the Anglo-American analytical philosophical tradition. In opposition to the analytical tradition's realist assumption that truths pre-existed and could be found through methodical, disciplined enquiry, postmodernism suggested that truths were socially constructed.

In Western architectural discourse, discussion of postmodernism became prominent from the mid-1970s, particularly in the idiosyncratic form popularised by critic and architect Charles Jencks. [^49] In architectural practice, postmodernism manifested formally in at least two major streams: an historicist stream that often made ironic use of historical architectural styles; and a deconstructivist stream, likened formally to a Russian Constructivist "train wreck," intended as an experiential disruption to the habitual grounds of architecture.

Snodgrass began to draw upon post-modern thought in his writing and teaching, particularly the existential phenomenological thinking of Heidegger. He also introduced this lens to the coordination of a series of radical architectural design studios, which experi-mented with poststructuralist approaches to design. These studios did not, however, set out to produce "postmodern-looking" buildings. [^50]

[^47]: One of the foundations of philosophical postmodernism was the work of Martin Heidegger. For a discussion of the relation between Heidegger's thought and Eastern philosophy, see CY Cheng, "Confucius, Heidegger and the Philosophy of the I Ching: A Comparative Inquiry into the Truth of Human Being," *Philosophy East and West* 37, no. 1 (1987): 51–70.

[^48]: Heidegger extended the older hermeneutic tradition of interpreting religious texts, arguing that all human actions are acts of interpretation and therefore hermeneutical.

[^49]: See, for example, C Jencks, *The Language of Postmodern Architecture* (London: Academy Editions, 1977).

[^50]: Charlesworth, *Humanitarian Architecture*, 53–66. This is not to suggest that other design studios in the faculty did not embrace the formal language of historicist or deconstructivist postmodernism. Indeed, at the end of his time as a student, Paul Pholeros, the prominent graduate referred to at the outset of this chapter, lamented the infiltration of postmodern formalism and what he saw as a corresponding reduction of emphasis on social and environmental issues in architecture.

Instead, they encouraged students to make what may have seemed from the outside to be bizarre and fantastical interpretive leaps in their designing. In doing so, the studios sought to challenge the assumption that design could be reduced to rational, logical, systematic processes of the sort assumed by design science and man-environment studies.

Serendipitously, a number of the design studios were co-taught with a prominent member of the faculty's design computing unit, Coyne, initiating an unlikely alliance that was to bloom into a productive research association responsible for numerous ground-breaking publications. [^51] As Coyne notes:

> Snodgrass introduced me to philosophy and architectural theory. Engagement with the practices of the design studio and my increasing awareness of the limits of computation led me to embark on a series of critiques of digital cultures. [^52]

Coyne's 1995 book, *Designing Information Technology in the Postmodern Age: From Method to Metaphor*, was an outcome of this increasing awareness, pitting phenomenology, hermeneutics, and the thinking of Heidegger against many of the assumptions grounding computer-aided design. [^53] As these were assumptions that most of the design computing world held and that Coyne himself had used only a few years earlier in the influential book *Knowledge-Based Design Systems*, the resonance with Ludwig Wittgenstein's famed rejection of his own early positivist philosophy comes to mind. [^54]

The problem Snodgrass and Coyne saw with both man-environment studies and design science stemmed from the unquestioned assumption that a "scientific," rationalist, realist way of seeing should be operative in the man-environment studies and design science domains. [^55] Snodgrass and Coyne instead understood design thinking as categorically different to scientific thinking. In a series of remarkable papers that were later published as *Interpretation in Architecture: Design as a Way of Thinking*, they argued that design is a hermeneutical process. Following Heidegger, this implies that design involves pre-understandings and future projections that are tacit and can therefore never be fully articulated. If true, this would undercut the psychological investigations of man-environment studies, which aimed to articulate the grounds of the decision making of designers. It would also undercut design science, as the inarticulable nature of pre-understandings in the design process, and projections operative in the process, would render these pre-understandings unamenable to being digitised and programmed. Rather than rational accounts of step-wise logic, Snodgrass and Coyne proposed that design instead proceeded by way of metaphorical play. The picture thus painted of design was one involving unexpected and a-rational leaps, rather than systematisable or formulisable increments of logic. [^56]

[^51]: Many of these texts are gathered together in a later book: A Snodgrass and R Coyne, *Interpretation in Architecture: Design as a Way of Thinking* (London: Routledge, 2006).
[^52]: R Coyne, "Bio: Reflections on Technology, Media & Culture," https://richardcoyne.com/richard-coyne/, accessed 17 May 2018.
[^53]: R Coyne, *Designing Information Technology in the Postmodern Age: From Method to Metaphor* (Cambridge, MA: MIT Press, 1995).
[^54]: Coyne, et al., *Knowledge-Based Design Systems*. Wittgenstein's seminal 1921 text, *Tractatus Logico-Philosophicus*, was lauded by logical positivists. Wittgenstein subsequently undermined the thesis he had put forward in the *Tractatus*, describing it as dogmatic. Snodgrass and Coyne were well aware of Wittgenstein's dramatic "turn" and enjoyed discussing it with students. See "Ludwig Wittgenstein" in *The Stanford Encyclopedia of Philosophy*, https://plato.stanford.edu/entries/wittgenstein/#TranCritTrac, accessed 17 May 2018.
[^55]: A Snodgrass and R Coyne, "Models, Metaphors and the Hermeneutics of Designing," *Design Issues* 9, no. 1 (Autumn 1992): 56–74.
[^56]: While the critique mounted by phenomenological and hermeneutical thinking may have challenged the use of a scientific epistemology in both man-environment studies and design science, this does not diminish the contribution each made to understanding human decision making and to the artificial intelligence (AI) revolution that is now transforming all aspects of contemporary human life, not least the way architectural design itself is practised. What remains undecided is whether or not it will ever be possible to automate the creative moment at the heart of design or whether the human contribution of design decision making (involving interpretation and metaphorical leaps) will simply be relocated into ever narrower "political" moments in the formulation of AI algorithms or the selection of AI data points.

## Conclusion

The three new academic trajectories that emerged in the University of Sydney's Faculty of Architecture in the latter part of the 20th century all bore fruit. Many of the scholars involved became internationally recognised in their fields, and the research they produced added significantly to the scholarship of their disciplines. However, tensions between the disciplines within the faculty during the period described in this chapter gave rise to a perception of internal dysfunction. Architectural sociologist Garry Stephens, who both studied and taught at the faculty during this period, goes as far as to say that the relations among the disciplines was akin to "fratricidal warfare." [^57]

Given the productivity of many within the faculty during this period, it might therefore be tempting to describe the academic environment during these decades as productive in spite of the friction between the disciplines. This may, however, be a misreading. Rather, it might instead be suggested that the academic environment during these decades was made even more productive *because* of this friction. All of the researchers believed passionately in their different research perspectives. This led them to also disagree passionately. Competing views, criticisms and the need to mount cogent arguments and defences kept these scholars on their academic toes. While fences may have been erected between their disciplines, there were also gaps in the fences that allowed scholars to interact productively with the territory of the others: Gero with man-environment studies, Purcell with design science, and Coyne with hermeneutic phenomenology were all examples of this.

The productive ferment within the University of Sydney's Faculty of Architecture during the latter part of the 20th century was a microcosm of the creative turbulence occurring within universities throughout the world. Postmodernism in its various forms was challenging the dominant epistemology of science. The debates that resulted were often lively, occasionally rancorous, and sometimes highly productive. Even now, the competing positions that emerged during this period remain unsettled and continue to provide grounds for scholarly argument in many disciplinary areas, including architecture. ≡

[^57]: Stevens, *The Favored Circle*, 4.

In the exciting environment of a rapidly developing city and the pressure to resolve demanding challenges, there was a tendency, consciously or otherwise, to regard "theory" as irrelevant.

– Duanfang Lu and Peter Webber, "A Theory Moment"

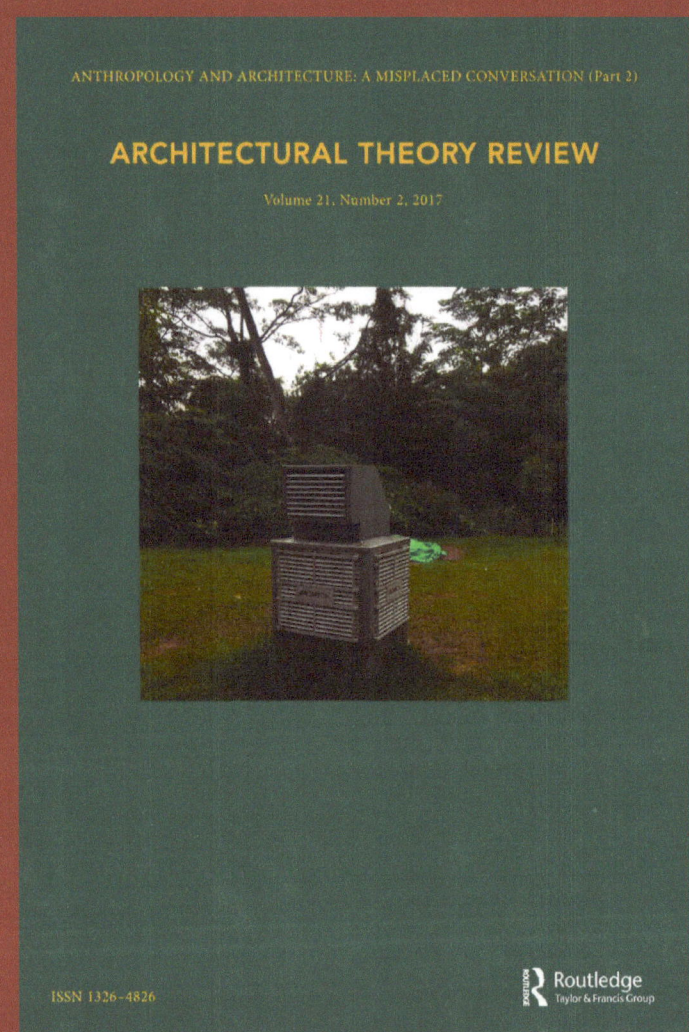

**Figure 1** — Cover of *Architectural Theory Review* 17, no. 2 (2017).

# Chapter 8: A Theory Moment
— Duanfang Lu and Peter Webber

*Architectural Theory Review* (*ATR*) was launched as a house journal of the Department of Architecture at the University of Sydney in April 1996. By adopting situated, multi-dimensional frames of reference, *ATR* was distinctive among the architectural theory journals at the time. In the decades since its inception, sweeping changes have taken place in the disciplinary culture of architecture and its interlocutors. Following the radical avant-garde practices of the 1960s and 1970s, and the autonomous theoretical pursuits of the 1980s and 1990s, the 21st century has witnessed the rise of the post-critical and historiography as new paradigms for architecture's reaction to the widely perceived self-indulgence of mainstream architectural theory in the late 20th century. The conclusion of the influential theory journal *Assemblage and Architecture New York* in 2000, itself an uptake of the project of *Oppositions* and progenitors of, respectively, *Grey Room* and *Log*, marked the turning point. Across a decade of disciplinary transition, *ATR* has thrived. Starting out as a regional journal with most of its contributors and audience from Australia, the journal has gradually acquired an international audience, with contributions from around the world. Recognising its potential, Taylor and Francis acquired *ATR* and has published the journal in print and online formats since August 2007, the three issues each year "generating, exchanging and reflecting on architectural theory" [Figure 1]. [^1]

Following the approach adopted by C Greig Crysler in his 2003 book *Writing Spaces*, this chapter will track the development of *ATR* as an instance of "situated social practices grounded in specific institutions and the actions of particular agents." [^2] The chapter will first reconstruct a trajectory across the "theory moment" of the faculty in the late 20th century, which led to the conception of *ATR*. Positioning *ATR* as a journal consolidating Sydney's regional importance to theoretical debate, it will then offer an account of how *ATR* has developed over the past two decades to allow a broader range of issues related to the development of the discipline and built environments to be interrogated in the context of post-critical architecture. The chapter will close with a reflective discussion of *ATR* as a vehicle for understanding how the faculty has related to, absorbed, positioned itself with respect to, and engaged with developments in architectural theory since the 1980s.

## A Confronting Context

From the end of the Second World War to the 1970s and 1980s, the architectural profession in Sydney had considerably expanded; many outstanding buildings were designed, with graduates of the University of Sydney often at the forefront. Numerous elegant dwellings were created, many in a bushland context and utilising a palette of natural and traditional materials: timber, brick, quarry tile, corrugated iron. As Catherine Lassen and Julie Willis have discussed earlier in this book, Ken Woolley, Richard Leplastrier, Bruce Rickard and Tony Moore are some of the better-known architects whose work was later described as architecture of the "Sydney School." [^3] Similarly, many

[^1]: "Aims and Scope," *Architectural Theory Review* (hereafter *ATR*) 22, no. 1 (2018): front matter.

[^2]: CG Crysler, *Writing Spaces: Discourse of Architecture, Urbanism, and the Built Environment, 1960–2000* (New York: Routledge, 2003), 5.

[^3]: This movement was first posited and discussed in J Taylor, *Australian Architecture Since 1960* (Sydney: Law Book Company, 1986).

large works of architecture in the city were designed by University of Sydney graduates: the elegant stadia and exhibition buildings by Philip Cox; the innovative State Office Block and urbane Hyatt Hotel opposite the Opera House in Sydney Cove, both by Woolley; significant new public buildings such as those at Parliament House and the Art Gallery of New South Wales by Andrew Andersons; and the extraordinary contribution to the completion of the Opera House and the design of its forecourt by Peter Hall. At the urban level, unremarkable streets and car park areas were transformed into attractive public spaces, notably Sydney Square and Martin Place, with Sydney graduates Woolley and George Clark the respective leaders of these projects. Such buildings and urban spaces were, without doubt, some of the most successful examples of their type anywhere in the world, and their architects had in common a commitment to prioritise the social needs of users, the efficient function of buildings and spaces, a resolution of environmental challenges, a creative response to context, and an achievement of elegant and urbane outcomes.

In the exciting environment of a rapidly developing city and the pressure to resolve demanding challenges, there was a tendency, consciously or otherwise, to regard "theory" as irrelevant. For those who did scour international journals, the propensity of those architectural critics and historians who would adopt the mantle of "theorists" to indulge in language tending to the arcane and inaccessible hardly encouraged local engagement in international debate. Architects who had studied at the University of Sydney have vivid memories of senior lecturer George Molnar, the expatriate Hungarian architect and talented if irascible teacher who was far better known as a cartoonist. His sardonic drawings were featured in the centre page of the *Sydney Morning Herald* for several decades [Figure 2]. [^4] Many of the outstanding practitioners of the era had matured under his influence. While hardly nurturing what we would now call a conventional theoretical discourse, he certainly strongly encouraged critical review of architectural projects. If students were tempted to propose construction techniques that were illogical, building forms that were irrational, or façade patterns that were irrelevant, they risked exposure in front of their classmates to sarcasm which, despite its humorous overlay, was often both incisive and embarrassing

Figure 2 — Cartoon by G Molnar in *Insubstantial Pageant* (Sydney: Angus and Robertson, 1959).

For a few brief years during the 1960s, debate about the nature of architecture had flourished among younger architects under the auspices of an informal discussion group called The Architectural Society, largely led by recent graduates and activists such as Tom Heath, who would later be appointed to a research chair at what was then the Queensland Institute of Technology. Heath advocated a somewhat extreme rationalist view of the nature of the design process, and internal disagreement over his stance was one of the factors that contributed to The Architectural Society fading into obscurity.

[^4]: G Molnar, *Insubstantial Pageant* (Sydney: Angus and Robertson, 1959).

The culture of the Faculty of Architecture of the day had moved beyond endorsement of modernism, but it did not embrace any of the various postmodernist movements that successively pervaded many of the architectural schools in the United States and Europe, whether as design or intellectual styles. Rather these were shunned for their introspectiveness, mocked for their exclusivity. In the world of local practice, a mischievous group in the office of the NSW Government Architect concocted the term "New Materialists" (distinct from the term's later appearance in the lexicon of philosophy) to describe certain tendencies among practitioners. One of the first books, published in 1967, to review the Jørn Utzon design for the Opera House, and the fatal flaws in his concept for the concert hall, included a chapter titled "Function is not a 'Dirty Word'." [^5]

## Towards "The Moment"

Not unsurprisingly in this context, even by the beginning of the 1980s, the curricula for neither the first Bachelor of Science nor the second Bachelor of Architecture degree at the University of Sydney included formal, core courses devoted to the theory of design or architecture. There were, however, distinguished staff making invaluable contributions in related areas. Jennifer Taylor and Trevor Howells were already celebrated for their outstanding research and publications in the history of architecture. A remarkable group of full and part-time staff had a deep commitment to exploring social and political issues, often as the genesis of design initiatives. None were more creative than Colin "Col" James and Paul Pholeros, with their deep empathy and understanding of Indigenous issues; Anna Rubbo and her commitment to social housing and global cultural issues; and Adrian Snodgrass, with his profound knowledge and writings on Asia's cultures. The bulk of design studio teaching was undertaken by part-time design tutors from varied backgrounds, inevitably exposing students to a rich vein of informal debate about design ideas. Dean Peter Johnson, liberal and benign, was tolerant and supportive. He was a firm believer in the potential of cultural diversity and social engagement. He fostered a diverse range of academic enterprises and encouraged the development of sometimes competing views about theory and practice.

Before joining the faculty, Peter Webber, joint-author of this chapter, had extensive experience in the design of buildings for the public sector: from schools, hospitals and universities to police stations and jails. His philosophical and political position had been strongly influenced by the then highly unconventional teachings of Percival Goodman, to which he had been exposed during a postgraduate year at Columbia University in 1961. Together with his psychologist brother, Paul, who espoused social equity and reform of the culture of consumption rampant in post-war United States, Goodman lamented in their co-authored, landmark book, *Communitas* (1960), that "we spend our money for follies, that our leisure does not revive us, that our conditions of work are unmanly, and our beautiful American classlessness is degenerating into a static bureaucracy; our mass arts are beneath contempt." [^6] The purpose of design, they argued, must begin and end with satisfying the needs of all in the community, not the whims of architectural fantasists. A contrary and increasingly powerful influence within the faculty at the University of Sydney came from the Department of Architectural Science, which was generating substantial funding from outside sources and publishing a plethora of research papers in scientific journals. Led by the research of John Gero in computer-aided design technology, discussed elsewhere in this book by Glen Hill, an ultra-rationalist approach to the design process was promulgated and was permeating the minds of many students. The time had surely come for questioning irrational and extremist viewpoints. Exposure

[^5]: M Baume, *The Sydney Opera House Affair* (Melbourne: Nelson, 1967).

[^6]: P Goodman and P Goodman, *Communitas: Ways of Living and Means of Life* (New York: Random House, 1960), 5.

to balanced debate about the nature of the discipline to which they would devote their careers was long overdue. The vision of both an academic course devoted to theory and an academic journal devoted to its investigation was forming on a distant horizon, but there was much to be done before the flash of a theory moment.

## The Theory Course

In academia, the introduction of new courses is never easy or immediate. For the Faculty of Architecture, the process began with lengthy discussions in the newly formed Board of the Department of Architecture, comprising all members of the academic staff. A discussion paper was presented by Webber in 1985 as the basis for determining the form and structure of the course. [^7] After reviewing courses then offered in architectural schools in Britain and North America, the paper noted that there was little commonality among them and that generally their emphasis was "towards design method or process, sometimes towards an historical overview of theoretical approaches, occasionally towards principles of architecture and architectural concepts which have a 'timeless validity'." [^8] The University of California, Berkeley, at that time offered six diverse courses in the area of "Design, Theory and Method." It was recommended that, in the first degree program, then devoted to design in its broadest sense, a new course should "develop an understanding of the nature of theories, recent developments in the concept of theory, explore the nature of aesthetics and analyse the design process itself." [^9] In the second, "the concentration should be firstly upon the nature of architecture itself, architectural principles, and the integration of areas of knowledge which are supportive of the design process." [^10] The proposed reading list in the new course was to include,

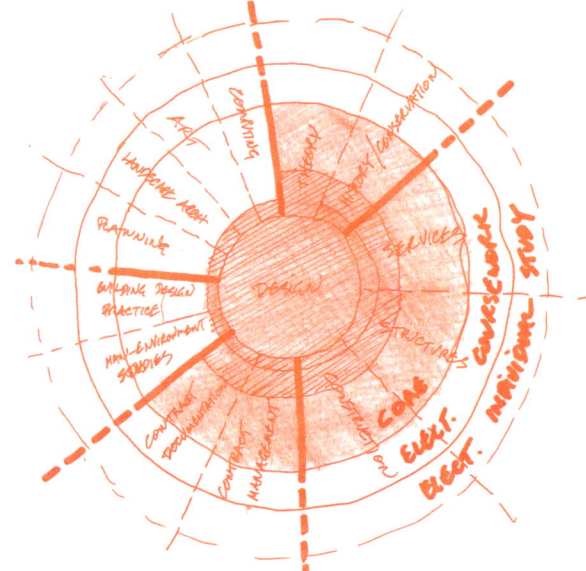

**Figure 3** — Course Diagram in P Webber, "Theory of Architecture Courses in the B. Arch Degree: Discussion Paper," unpublished paper, 1985.

not only traditional practitioner-theorists from Vitruvius and Andrea Palladio to Eugène Viollet-Le-Duc and John Ruskin, but also, critically, contemporary theorists, including Sigfried Gidieon, Nikolaus Pevsner, Wolfgang Braunfels, Donald Preziosi and Roger Scruton. The last was seen to be moulding his words with "the vigorous discipline of the trained philosopher."

The teaching of both architectural history and architectural theory was to be closely related but separately delivered, a proposition at first not endorsed by all and one which continues to be debated. Joan Ockman eloquently put the question: "Who put the slash in history/theory? It was a consequential stroke, although its origin is hard to pinpoint. It seems to have appeared in the late 1960s or early 1970s, when architecture schools began to accord theory the same value as history." [^11] In Sydney, a diagram accompanying Webber's paper illustrated the relationship between these courses and emphasised how all courses ultimately would inform the activity of design, which was at the very heart of the program [Figure 3]. After much debate, substantial restructuring of the entire undergraduate

[^7]: P Webber, "Theory of Architecture Courses in the B. Arch Degree: Discussion Paper," unpublished paper, 1985.
[^8]: Webber, "Theory of Architecture Courses."
[^9]: Webber, "Theory of Architecture Courses."
[^10]: Webber, "Theory of Architecture Courses."

[^11]: J Ockman, "Slashed," *e-flux architecture*, https://www.e-flux.com/architecture/history-theory/159236/slashed/, accessed 22 May 2018.

program, and exhaustive development of detail, the second term in 1988 saw the very first "Theory of Architecture" course delivered. It was comprised of a series of lectures addressing the timeless attributes of architecture, structure and form, materials and ornament, architecture-environment-place and typology, and placed substantial emphasis on moral and social concerns. Predictably, little credit was given to the ephemeral "-isms" that pervaded both popular and rarefied journals of architectural criticism. Importantly, the formal sessions were interspersed with small group seminars chaired by younger graduates and doctoral students to encourage enquiry and creative written contributions. Inspired by Ruskin's *Seven Lamps of Architecture*, seven critical questions were posed to participants, with the hope that, by the conclusion of the course, each student would have contemplated what might be their own responses:

- Is the integration of structure and architectural form an imperative for all good architecture?
- Should the nature of materials be expressed in the character of a work of architecture?
- Does it matter if the architectural expression of the building does not respond to environmental conditions?
- In the international environment of today, is there any longer value in buildings being related each to a particular place?
- Does the satisfaction of social/cultural needs and aspirations of the users determine architectural form?
- Is the expression of a unifying theme or related set of themes a prerequisite for every satisfying work of architecture?
- Can architecture have meaning?

The positive impact of the new "Theory of Architecture" course was soon to be apparent, albeit impossible to quantify. Debate in the seminars was lively and well informed. Students began to produce erudite papers, drawing on interrelated ideas discussed in other courses, particularly in architectural history.

# The Journal

By the 1990s, academic publishing in architectural history and criticism focused, in Australia, on *Transition*, which was founded in 1979 and had been published by RMIT University since the early 1980s; and *Fabrications*, the journal of the Society of Architectural Historians, Australia and New Zealand, founded in 1987 and initially edited out of UNSW. Whereas the former had been curious about developments in theory, it grew to focus on the experimental design culture anchored to RMIT, while *Fabrications* took seriously its mission to offer a record of new historical research on the region's architecture. The journal of the Royal Australian Institute of Architects, *Architecture in Australia*, had for decades been publishing only occasional critical reviews of new buildings. A frequent contributor, the Sydney graduate Tom Heath published an annual "Discourse" issue during his tenure as editor in the second half of the 1980s. [^12] At that time, the University of Melbourne's architecture school was perceived as the proprietor of theoretical debate in Australian academia. Its graduates had been embedded in postmodern theoretical debate and were creating postmodern buildings in a wide range of registers.

Recognising that there was, at this time, no journal, either academic or professional, devoted to architectural theory in particular, the Board of the Department of Architecture at the University of Sydney discussed the options for format and philosophy and unanimously resolved to launch a journal of its own. Since the Department of Architectural Science, on the initiative of the first chair, Jack Cowan, had been responsible for the journal *Architectural Science Review* for many years, it was determined to complement this with the title *Architectural Theory Review*. The first edition was quietly launched in April 1996 by founding editors Anna Rubbo and Adrian Snodgrass.

[^12]: A Leach, "*Transition* to 'Discourse': Architectural Theory in Postmodern Australia," in *Mediated Messages: Periodicals, Exhibitions and the Shaping of Postmodern Architecture*, ed. V Patteeuw and LC Szacka (London: Bloomsbury, 2018), 135–50.

A large advisory editorial board was established, comprising representatives of all other architectural schools in Australia, together with supportive colleagues from universities in Auckland, Edinburgh, Papua New Guinea, Vienna and elsewhere. The ambition of the board and the founding editors was for *ATR* to be inclusive and responsive to the concerns of its readers and a broader public but also, critically, readable and accessible to all.

From the very beginning, the journal reflected a commitment to a multi-vocal and multi-regional approach to architectural theory. As Rubbo and Snodgrass put it in the inaugural editorial, *ATR* stresses "diversity, regionalism and a plurality of voices as a counter to threats of uniformity in the face of globalization and the information explosion." [^13] Considering that "[architectural] theory means different things to different people," they invited members of the editorial board to respond to the following question in 1000 words: "What do you think are the most important questions facing architectural theory as an idea and practice, and what are the issues it could/should be concerned with?" [^14] The act of asking for an unconventional short response instead of a full-length academic article turned out to be an effective strategy to push scholars to unlearn the conceptual frameworks they have been trained to accept and to participate in dialogue with an open mind. Nine short responses were published in *ATR*'s second issue, with additional responses published in the issues that followed, offering readers a diverse range of fresh and embodied perspectives on architectural theory. Most of the responses adopted a humanistic perspective and stressed the social and cultural meanings of the built environment. Rory Spence, for example, considered it important for both architectural practice and theory to explore "the ways in which architecture can reconnect with the things that make us most human" and to discover "how it can achieve greater human resonance." [^15]

Similarly, and expressing a deep dissatisfaction with mainstream North American architectural theory, Webber conceptualised architecture "as a service to community and as a reflection of its values," calling for specific emphasis on "community renewal and civic engagement" as the bedrock of architectural theory. [^16] Others, such as Laurie Hegvold, Stanislaus Fung and Susana Torre, focused on the importance of the cross-cultural dimension in architectural theory. [^17] Hegvold's essay, in particular, highlighted Australia as a regional centre, where architectural schools nurtured, not only architects who worked in Australia, but also many architects who would work in Southeast Asia. As such, he argued that the discourse in design pedagogy must ensure that teaching in the programs "encourage suitable design solutions which express regional values relevant to their cultural context, be it Australian or Asian." [^18] These open-ended debates, together with a section of "Student Essays" and articles on gender, non-Western, and Indigenous built environments, are reflective of the journal's multi-vocal approach during its early development.

Much like the idea of the "Sydney School," which had been developed by Australian architects, historians and critics as a regional reaction against international modernism, *ATR*'s approach to architectural theory can be considered a deliberate reaction against the metropolitan theory culture of North America, which, to some extent, was also reflected in some European platforms such as *AA Files*, *Archplus* and *Quaderns*. This culture fostered two dominant approaches to critical theory in architecture. The first followed the neo-Marxist criticism of society and culture developed by the Frankfurt School: the critic was tasked with destroying those ineffectual myths that had given architects false hopes for social transformation through design. [^19]

[^13]: A Rubbo and A Snodgrass, "Editorial," *ATR* 1, no. 1 (1996): 1.
[^14]: A Rubbo and A Snodgrass, "Editorial," *ATR* 1, no. 2 (1996): i.
[^15]: R Spence, "Architectural Theory," *ATR* 1, no. 2 (1996): 1.
[^16]: P Webber, "Critical Concerns of Architectural Theory," *ATR* 1, no. 2 (1996): 11–13.
[^17]: L Hegvold, "Cultural Crossings – Quo Vadis," *ATR* 1, no. 2 (1996): 7–9; S. Fung, "Architectural Theory as Cross-Cultural Study," *ATR* 1, no. 2 (1996): 5–7; S. Torre, "Theories, Not Theory," *ATR* 1, no. 2 (1996): 15–17.
[^18]: Hegvold, "Cultural Crossings," 9.
[^19]: M Tafuri, *Architecture and Utopia: Design and Capitalist Development* (Cambridge, MA: MIT Press, 1976), 181–82.

The second, mainly developed among East Coast academics and professionals in the United States, followed a mode of critical analysis established in the text-based humanities disciplines since the 1960s, which posits the text as an autonomous and confined system of meaning and hence architecture as text. In an editorial in the 30th issue of *Assemblage*, K Michael Hays reflected on this approach to which the journal had committed: "[If] the theory of the 'Assemblage' generation has taught us anything, it is that what used to be called the sociohistorical context of architectural production... as well as the objects produced are both themselves texts (call them constructions if you don't like texts), in the sense that we cannot approach them separately and directly, as distinct unrelated things in themselves, but only through their prior differentiation and transmutation." [^20] Underpinning this approach is an assembly of sociological, psychological, philosophical or linguistic texts by French structuralist and poststructuralist authors such as Jean Baudrillard, Jacques Lacan, Roland Barthes, Michel Foucault, Jacques Derrida and Gilles Deleuze. Unlike Manfredo Tafuri, who insisted on the autonomy of architectural history from design practice, protagonists of this second path sought to develop an operative theory of the critical architect, as in Peter Eisenman's "critical practice." [^21] However, with architecture being employed as a text for autonomous play, its connection with the social was left unaddressed, and the disruption of this theory moment turned out to be a reproduction of a self-referential, socially abstracted architecture. [^22]

Coincidentally, in the same year in which Hays wrote the aforementioned editorial for *Assemblage*, ATR published a student essay entitled "Meaning in Architecture ... Is the Traditional Semantic Method Adequate?" [^23] Based on a reading of works by Tadao Ando, the Buddhist Water Temple in Hyogo, Japan, and Peter Eisenman's House II, Jodie Niven's essay argued: "One communication model is clearly inadequate in trying to find 'meaning in architecture,' but is this necessary or even possible? Surely, as the messages are different, the models used to understand them should be. Saussure's semantic theories are not invalid in understanding architecture, but neither are they universal." [^24] Despite its brevity, Niven's essay echoes, not only the institutional culture and new pedagogical objectives of the faculty in these years, but also the multidimensional approach that the journal had adopted as its complement. The project of *ATR* is well articulated in a 1999 editorial, which says it is not intended to "act as a mouthpiece for the promulgation of any particular outlook, but to provide a forum for the expression of divergent interpretations"; the journal "exists to mirror these divergences." [^25] The enduring presence of the "Student Essays" section until 1999 indicates how teaching and publishing interacted around the journal in its early years, just as discussion on "theorising architectural education," which would gain traction in the early 2000s, further indicated *ATR*'s commitment to exploring new pedagogical developments in architecture.

## (Re)Situated Theories

Beyond the neo-Marxist approach, with its stress on the structural, and the poststructuralist approach, with its stress on the syntactical, the temporal approach has been a particularly crucial dimension for *ATR*. A strong sense of situatedness has been a common thread connecting the editorials over the past two decades, although this has been uttered differently at different times and employed to different ends. In their inaugural editorial, Rubbo and Snodgrass stated that *ATR* was interested in "theoretical responses to the challenges that face architecture in

[^20]: KM Hays, "On Turning Thirty," *Assemblage* 30 (1996), 8.
[^21]: C Rowe, "Introduction," in *Five Architects* (New York: Oxford University Press, 1975), 15–17.
[^22]: Crysler, *Writing Spaces*, 79.
[^23]: J Niven, "Meaning in Architecture ... Is the Traditional Semantic Method Adequate?" *ATR* 1, no. 1 (1996): 130–34. Niven was a third-year BSc (Architecture) student at Sydney when the essay was written in 1995.

[^24]: Niven, "Meaning in Architecture," 134.
[^25]: A Rubbo and A Snodgrass, "Editorial," *ATR* 4, no. 2 (1999): 1.

this age of rapid and radical change." [^26] Their initial strategy was to remain open to divergent interpretations of architecture and its problems, to encourage debate and welcome disagreements. [^27] This sense of openness helped shaped the development of architectural history and theory within the faculty. Starting with predominantly academic members adopting humanistic and phenomenological approaches, this increasingly well-defined element grew to accommodate scholars with sometimes markedly different approaches to the history and theory of architecture. With these newcomers becoming engaged in the project of *ATR* as editors and authors, ever new perspectives were brought to bear on the journal and its project.

Gevork Hartoonian, for example, brought to the journal a new reading of critical practice as an active author and a guest editor of a number of issues in the early 2000s. Having received his doctoral training from the University of Pennsylvania and having taught at Columbia University and the Pratt Institute before joining the faculty at the University of Sydney, Hartoonian offered a counterpoint to the history and theory culture that Sydney had cultivated up to the end of the century. Instead of being sceptical about the project of critical architecture, he sought to reclaim it from the debris of post-critical architectural technocracy. Following Kenneth Frampton, he also explored the ontology of tectonics as a way to fight against postmodern nihilism. In his editorial for a special issue published in 2002, Hartoonian resituated critical practice in the aftermath of September 11 in New York, bringing the importance of the presence of the "other" to the fore: "Critical practice involves … negotiating with the other within that space of in-betweenness that belongs to anybody, to anybody who has come to terms with the project of modernity as the 'destiny' prompted by the cosmopolitan-humanism flourishing since the dawn of modernity." [^28] Recalling Françoise Choay's observation that our "competence to build," that is, the homology between the body, landscape and technology, is on the verge of disappearance, his special issue summoned a stellar line-up of scholars and professionals attached to Columbia's Graduate School of Architecture, Preservation and Property to address the problem of critical practice in a new historical condition. [^29] Apart from scholarly articles, the issue included interviews with Frampton, Mary MacLeod, Bernard Tschumi and Mark Wigley, each offering an updated, reflective view of their own work.

Trained at Tsinghua University and the University of California, Berkeley, Duanfang Lu, co-author of this article, joined the Faculty of Architecture in 2004, thereby helping to strengthen the study of non-Western modern architecture. The mainstream histories of modern architecture had long focused on its development in Europe and the Americas, with academic inquiry on the built environment in other societies often concentrating on traditional forms and overlooking their modern architecture. Lu's book, *Remaking Chinese Urban Form*, provided a new perspective on the development of the work unit called danwei, the walled compound that integrated working and living, as an urban form under Maoist socialism, while her edited book *Third World Modernism* opened up new perspectives on modern architecture in developing countries in the 1950s and 1960s. [^30] In 2008, her special issue "Unthinking Spectacle" addressed the tension between the universal theoretical claims of "spectacle" and the specificities of cultural, historical and geographic locales. While the writers in this issue all somehow used spectacle as an analytical tool, they analysed the complexity and multiplicity of regional or local practices in radically different ways, focusing variously on the visual practices in Victorian Britain, the conservation of Carcassonne in southern France, retail spaces in Dubai, the resurrection of the Kul-Sharif Mosque in post-socialist Tatarstan, refugee detention centres in Australia, street graffiti

[^26]: Rubbo and Snodgrass, "Editorial" (*ATR* 1, no. 1), 1.
[^27]: Rubbo and Snodgrass, "Editorial" (*ATR* 4, no. 2), 1.
[^28]: G Hartoonian, "Editorial," *ATR* 7, no. 1 (2002): 1.

[^29]: Hartoonian, "Editorial," 1.
[^30]: D Lu, *Remaking Chinese Urban Form: Modernity, Scarcity and Space, 1949–2005* (London: Routledge, 2006); D Lu, ed., *Third World Modernism: Architecture, Development and Identity* (London: Routledge, 2010).

in Melbourne, and traditional Chinese material culture. The situatedness and diversity illustrated through one special issue here serve as perfect testimony to the *ATR*'s approach to theory as situated practice.

The 2011 editorial, "Untimely Prospects," not only celebrated the journal's 15-year history, but also conceptualised its transition to a new editorial team, comprised of Naomi Stead, Lee Stickells and Michael Tawa, and a new approach to the theory's questions. They addressed situatedness by explicating the temporal sense of "review" in the title of the journal, thus tackling two enduring problems in the field of architectural theory:

> **First, a lack of emphasis on the history and historicity of theory— the specific temporal contingencies and circumstances in which theories emerge, are disseminated, are put to work, and in which they also age, become irrelevant, pass out of timeliness. Second, there was ... a lack of current address to ideas that are now themselves out of time: the un-contemporary, the dated and outdated, the blunt rather than the cutting edge.** [^31]

Seeing theory as "world-forming" and review as "[undoing] a seeing," they reformulated the journal's key task as allowing for "critical, digressive and even subversive readings of what architectural theory has been, can be and will be." [^32] By doing so they situated the work of review "within a distinctive temporality of presence which presents the futural potential of what has passed." [^33] Based on a new conceptualisation of temporality and a greater insistence on exploring defined themes, special issues began to concentrate on "reviewing the implications and legacies of a particular object." [^34] A recent series of issues has explored how built environments reveal, accentuate or challenge various structures of power: "The Right to the City," edited by Lee Stickells in 2011; "On the Margin," edited by Michael Tawa and Linda Marie Walker in 2013; "Spatial Violence," edited by Andrew Herscher and Anooradha Iyer Siddiqi in 2014; "Corruption," edited by Adam Jasper in 2015; and "Resist, Reclaim, Speculate," edited by Isabelle Doucet and Hélène Frichot in 2018. [^35] This approach remained in place as the new editors of 2011 were replaced by Sean Anderson, Jennifer Ferng and Adam Jasper in 2014 and, beyond, to the current editorial direction of Andrew Leach.

Despite the different approaches adopted in each issue, what remains consistent is the core conviction of "architecture's position as an exercise of power." [^36] In neo-Marxist critical theory, architecture is treated purely as an epiphenomenon determined by the economic base, hence foreclosing any significant initiative on the part of architecture. In contrast, following the "space-is-political" move of the social sciences and humanities in the past three decades, this body of publications in *ATR* asserts that architectural space is not a harmless material substratum or an innocent backdrop for the free play of human agency but rather can play an active role in shaping the social. [^37] The discussions in its pages have consistently opened up a new set of issues about "architecture's agency—the social efficacy of architecture as built form, the position of the architect as designer/citizen, the power of its educational and professional structures," to quote Lee Stickells' editorial from "The Right to the City." [^38] Notably, in questioning the capacity and effects of architectural interventions in this and other issues listed above, an interdisciplinary endeavour that overlaps with recent developments in the social sciences and humanities, including human geography, cultural studies, anthropology, gender studies and postcolonial studies, has gained significant traction, and the boundaries between the

[^31]: N Stead, L Stickells and M Tawa, "Untimely Prospects," *ATR* 16, no. 2 (2011): 77–83.
[^32]: Stead, Stickells and Tawa, "Untimely Prospects," 80.
[^33]: Stead, Stickells and Tawa, "Untimely Prospects," 81.
[^34]: L Stickells, "Right to the City: Rethinking Architecture's Social Significance," *ATR* 16, no. 3 (2011): 213–27.
[^35]: *ATR* 16, no. 3 (2011); *ATR* 18, no. 1 (2013); *ATR* 19, no. 3 (2014); *ATR* 20, no. 2 (2015); *ATR* 22, no. 1 (2018).
[^36]: Stickells, "Right to the City," 213.
[^37]: H Lefebvre, *The Production of Space* (Oxford: Blackwell, 1991), 28; D Hebdige, "Subjects in Space," *New Formations* 11 (1990), vi–vii.
[^38]: Stickells, "Right to the City," 214.

discipline of architecture and other disciplines have been productively blurred. This is evident in a series of more recent issues dealing with such topics as "Terra Firma" and "Animal, Mineral, Vegetable," both edited by Ferng in 2015, and "Architecture and Anthropology," a double issue edited by Jasper in 2016-17. [^39]

## Becoming Minor: The Role of Theory at the University of Sydney

In their books *Kafka: Towards a Minor Literature* (1975) and *A Thousand Plateaus* (1980), Gilles Deleuze and Félix Guattari envisaged the process of becoming-minor as one that widens the gap between oneself and the norm. [^40] Understood in a qualitative rather than a quantitative sense, for them the minor is what deviates from the bearer of the dominant social code. The significance of the minor lies in the political potential of its divergence from the norm. This conceptualisation of becoming-minor is useful to illustrate the role of theory at the University of Sydney. When the Faculty of Architecture degrees began to include courses in architectural theory in the 1980s, they served an audience attentive to metropolitan architectural theory. However, this period did not last long. The faculty's commitments to cultural diversity and social engagement inevitably led to a scepticism about the usefulness of the various "-isms" of the metropolitan centres. The inception of *ATR* could be considered an attempt to deal with both the inadequacy of theory's vocabulary and the uncertainty associated with the tools needed to cope with radical shifts brought by the rapid processes of globalisation and digitalisation. It is worth noting that the school's positioning of itself as a regional leader of architectural education and research has shaped both this uncertainty and the ambition to which it has given rise since the 1980s and 1990s. The strategy of being open to divergences in architectural theory, a strategy adopted by both the faculty and its journal, should be viewed in this context.

Under this strategy, those scholars and doctoral students in architectural history and theory within what is now the University of Sydney School of Architecture, Design and Planning have gradually come to comprise one of its largest research groups. The scholars and students work at the intersection between architectural, urban, social, intellectual and cultural debate. This growth has been tracked in the fortunes of *ATR*, which has, in many respects, outgrown the setting from which it originally appeared. In the past two decades, the journal has served as a fertile ground that enacts multiple minors that are divergent from mainstream architectural theory. Its impacts range from new speculative investigations in architectural theory beyond the dominant discourses on critical theory in architecture, to acts of resituating critical theory in a post-critical mentality to assess legacies and plan agendas, to more recent explorations in new territories such as the making of architects, spatial violence, and corruption. With special issue editors and papers now drawn from across the world, it has put forward a wide range of competing positions geographically, institutionally and historically, reflecting parallel debates in the social sciences and humanities. With a combination of critical, interpretive and speculative scholarship, the journal has provided a global audience with a significant forum for probing new directions for research, education and practice, and has served as a vital site of international exchange. ≡

[^39]: *ATR* 20, no. 1 (2015); *ATR* 20, no. 3 (2015); *ATR* 21, no. 1–2 (2016–17).

[^40]: G Deleuze and F Guattari, *Kafka: Towards a Minor Literature*, trans. D Polan (Minneapolis: University of Minnesota Press, 1986); G Deleuze and F Guattari, *A Thousand Plateaus*, trans. B Massumi (London: Continuum, 1980).

# Postscripts

The Great Hall, University of Sydney, set for examinations, 1900, photographer unknown. University of Sydney Archives.

# What Universities Are For: An Address on the Occasion of the 29 September 2017 Graduation Ceremony, Great Hall, University of Sydney
— Andrew Leach

**Author's Note**
*The text that follows faithfully records the address noted in the title, without the modifications I was tempted to make to ameliorate the aspirational tone the occasion required. As an argument, it is inevitably incomplete, and its themes certainly demand elaboration: something I will attempt at some later date. It captures, however, a moment of discussion and reflection in the lead-up to the centenary that has ultimately given rise to this book and to the public programming of 2018, and it reflects a commitment to the idea that the past is an enduring source of provocations for our social (and hence institutional) conscience.*

Professor Masters, Professor Ewing, Professor Redmond, esteemed colleagues in the Sydney School of Education and Social Work and the Sydney School of Architecture, Design and Planning, please allow me to begin by adding my congratulations to you, the newest graduates of this university, and to those of your family and friends who have joined you here on this fine occasion. [^1]

Some of you have today received degrees in the field of architecture, which is my discipline as well. In my school, we are preparing, next year, to celebrate the centenary of the appointment of Australia's first Chair of Architecture in the person of Professor Leslie Wilkinson, whose buildings form a substantial backdrop to your time on this campus—whether you know it or not. He arrived in 1918 and became the inaugural dean of the newly founded Faculty of Architecture in 1920. This appointment was a milestone in the history of architecture in Australia that we are rightly celebrating. It was a milestone, too, in the history of professional and technical education. It cemented this field's place in the university after decades of local debate in the University Senate and in meetings of the New South Wales Institute of Architects over the proper formation of the architect as an educated professional. It built on the earlier success of engineering and laid, for us, a foundation on which town planning would soon build, and architectural science and design thereafter.

Universities are not static. They are responsible for defending knowledge and for testing it. This inevitably brings change in the institution's character, composition and outlook, all of which can be read through its architecture.

[^1]: These first lines are directed to Tony Masters, chair of the university's Academic Board; Robyn Ewing, AM, Head of the School of Education and Social Work, Faculty of Arts and Social Sciences; and John Redmond, Dean and Head of the Sydney School of Architecture, Design and Planning.

Wilkinson's appointment in 1918 notwithstanding, the University of Sydney first added courses in architectural design and architectural history to its catalogue of offerings in 1882, 135 years ago. Students taking these courses would either be students of this institution heading towards a Certificate in Engineering or students of the Sydney Technical College who were after something beyond the purely technical training they were receiving on Harris Street. The courses in architecture were first taught by Cyril Blacket, whose father, Edmund Blacket, conceived of the building in which we sit and who would enjoy a distinguished career in technical education. He was followed by John Sulman, later Sir John Sulman, who, in his later years, helped to realise the plan for the national capital first conceived by Marion Mahoney Griffin and Walter Burley Griffin, but who taught architectural history and design here for a quarter of a century and then town planning for some years beyond that.

Sometimes buildings express values that pass into history while serving as anchors for tradition. Sometimes they work as markers of time and of the changes to which institutions are subject. In 1882, the university let architecture in through the doors and in the same year allowed women to enrol in the same courses that men had been taking since the 1850s. An undistinguished building was commissioned to mark this monumental change: the Women's Common Room. It was demolished in 1917 to make way for Manning House—a reflection that something that had once seemed peculiar to this university had become absorbed—but it is important to mark those moments of change, to reflect on how they were formalised by our institutions, and to think about what we, today, have gained from them. I say this, in part, to mark a coincidence I find to be meaningful but also because it seems to me, as it perhaps should, that architecture has a role in mediating those changes, not least because of how that field itself evolved through being taught as a university subject.

When Wilkinson gave his inaugural address, it began inauspiciously, reflecting the values of his day, by dismissing the building culture of the original Australians. But he suggested a way out of his own poor judgment by noting that Sydney had set the right course in welcoming architecture into the university, wherein his students and colleagues, and us in their wake, could test all we know of our field.

You have proof, here and now, of your education and your achievement. If the gowns feel a little heavy on your shoulders, good. You have done more than tick boxes. More than clear hurdles. More than keep us faculty happy or swap fees for grades. You have followed through on a process in which we are all, evidently, deeply invested. This process has, one way or another, changed you, and in ways that you may not yet have registered. Just as teaching you changes us. Or should. The teachers among you know this already; it is why we can speak of our vocation beyond our profession.

Some advice in passing: keep reading. No one is setting texts for you anymore, and staying on top of your professional literature, whatever your field, is only part of the answer. Read books. Books that take you further into the worlds that interest you and books that introduce you to new worlds, that force you to encounter new ways of seeing the worlds you think you know well. Read carefully, just as you have been taught to do. Whether you will step into an office, a classroom, or some other setting, be contagious in your disregard for complacency.

One book that has stuck with me is the first novel of British author Jon McGregor, published in 2002. Called *If Nobody Speaks of Remarkable Things*, it recalled the events on a nondescript street from several points of view, but I have found the line, given to a father speaking to his daughter, hard to shake: "If nobody speaks of remarkable things," he says, "how can they be called remarkable?" If we have a job to do now, it is to speak of remarkable things, to equip the children, teenagers or adults in our classrooms to see the world beyond looking out of habit. To bring into the office unfamiliar ideas and new ways of looking at the world. To offer moments of resistance to a world that can seemingly be absorbed in passing. Let me make this point with an example, prefaced by an acknowledgment that I might have made earlier.

As Professor Masters noted at the outset of these proceedings, this building, and we inside it, are sitting on Gadigal country, where people have lived for thousands, tens of thousands, of years. Congratulations are particularly due to those graduates today whose forebears were here before Tasman and Cook first charted these shores. It will take a long time yet to rectify the damaging impact of colonisation, but the educated mind is a powerful and enduring tool in the struggle for cultural change.

Talking with my colleague Michael Mossman a few weeks ago, he recalled something to me that he had heard Shane Houston, until recently one of this university's Deputy Vice-Chancellors, say in this room. Forgive me if you heard this first hand, but it bears repeating, even if imperfectly. The lengths of timber above you come from specific places in the area in and around modern Sydney, as do the slabs of stone with which we are surrounded. [^2] For those with the right knowledge, which I don't have, this building describes the topography of country. Seen in this way, it transforms from an interior into a map.

This is the kind of thing of which architecture's complexities and contradictions are made, as many of our graduates now very well understand, but this seems a particularly powerful manoeuvre: to read something like this impressive interior, with its allusions to and participation in the university's traditions, and to turn it into something quite different in which different cultural, political and social forces have agency. But think of this: every structure on this campus through which the university has defined itself as a university can be made to enact this transformation of meaning. Each one is at once an expression of the ambitions and cultural claims that my own daughter's forebears brought to New South Wales in the 18th and 19th centuries and that the university pursued into the 20th, but they also offer a living key to the landscape and culture displaced by those ideals.

Now you know what I know, and, on that observation, I will conclude. Congratulations again to you all.

---

[^2]: Houston's comments, made on the occasion of a panel convened on 4 November 2016 for the annual Dr Charles Perkins AO, Memorial Oration and Prize, likewise in the Great Hall, were as follows: "It's an important thing we do to acknowledge Country and traditional owners, and it's important to see in everything around us that part that reflects Aboriginal and Torres Strait Islander peoples and our culture and the 62,000 years that we have been on this land. This marble floor was quarried from Gandangara country to the south west of Sydney. Those sandstone walls [were] quarried from Wangal and Gadigal country down near Pyrmont. And those magnificent timber beams up there were taken from Bundjalung country on the north coast of New South Wales. So we're never too far from the memory and the life of Aboriginal and Torres Strait Islander people wherever we are." The Memorial Oration commemorates Dr Perkins (1936–2000), the first Aboriginal man to be awarded a university degree in Australia, likewise conferred in Sydney's Great Hall.

# Prospects
— Martin Tomitsch

The chapters in this book chart key episodes in the history of the University of Sydney School of Architecture, Design and Planning, addressing the establishment and evolution of its component disciplines. As they illustrate, the school's history over the past century offers many instructive episodes that emphasise enduring concerns and responsibilities—perceived and assumed—that will likely remain imperative for the school's next 100 years. The university's ongoing entanglement with a changing world ensures that, alongside the broader production and dissemination of knowledge, the role of a school such as ours in professional education—its relation to its students and to their future employers—is being continually recast. Milestones like the centenary of Wilkinson's appointment offer an important opportunity to reflect on the implications of the past in the present and in an open future. This postscript takes up that opportunity, offering three contemplative snapshots through three different lenses. The first offers a structural overview of the school in 2018 while invoking some of the aspects of its history that in one way or another remain in play in the present. The second reflects on major global challenges that the school can help address through its research and education across architecture, design and planning. The third snapshot offers a speculative view of emerging fields and opportunities for the built environment and design disciplines.

## The Sydney School in 2018

The School of Architecture, Design and Planning is well known as the home of Australia's first Chair in Architecture. Over time, through a number of other firsts, it has expanded to include a distinct range of disciplines concerned with the built environment and design. In 2018, as the centenary of the appointment of Leslie Wilkinson as the inaugural Chair in Architecture is celebrated, the school is also home to three further disciplinary areas: architectural science, design, and urban planning (not to mention architectural history and architectural theory within architecture).

While the school started with a single full professor of architecture upon Wilkinson's appointment in 1918, it currently includes 11 professors, whose various appointments reflect the school's contemporary diversity and disciplinary alignments. Seven of the appointments are full-time continuing professors (three women and four men); one is a continuing conjoint professor with the School of Civil Engineering; one a fractional fixed-term Professor of Indigenous Creative Practice (in architecture); and two are fractional fixed-term professors (in architectural science and urban planning). These professorial appointments contribute to the total count of 75 members of faculty (43 continuing and 32 fixed-term) and are supported by 26 professional staff and over 200 casual teaching staff members to educate over 2000 students across the school's programs. The Sydney School of Architecture, Design and Planning is now, at heart, a multidisciplinary institution approaching research and education in the built environment and design disciplines through the intertwined intellectual traditions and research paradigms of the humanities, social sciences, physical sciences, and design.

The school offers a range of undergraduate and postgraduate coursework degrees across architecture, design and planning. The Bachelor of Design in Architecture, together with the Master of Architecture, which was awarded as a research degree for many decades, evolved from the original Bachelor of Architecture and the two-degree program of the BSc and BArch, as did the recently introduced, vertically integrated BDes in Architecture (Honours) combined with the MArch. The architecture programs also include the Bachelor of Architecture and Environments (BAE), which enrolled its first cohort of students in 2015 with the aims of offering a broader education across aspects of the built environment by complementing core training in architecture with knowledge from architectural science, urban planning and design, and of reflecting the growing intersectionality of careers in the built environment. It is, for now, a unique degree in that its structure and diverse content blurs traditional disciplinary boundaries. The school's third undergraduate degree is the Bachelor of Design Computing, which focuses on designing the interactions between people and technology and is taught by design academics. So, too, are the Master of Interaction Design and Electronic Arts, which replaced the Master of Digital Media and the Master of Design Computing in 2009, and a new Master of Design, which will be offered for the first time in 2019 with specialisations in Design Innovation and Strategic Design. The school further offers a number of specialised postgraduate programs, including the Master of Urban Design, the Master of Urbanism, the Master of Architectural Science, the Master of Urban and Regional Planning, and the Master of Heritage Conservation.

Faculty teach students enrolled in these various degrees while conducting research within one or more of five groups arranged around the school's current research foci: Architectural Design, Architectural Theory and History, Architectural Science, the Design Lab, and Urbanism. All the school's academic faculty, as well as over 100 current higher-degree research candidates, are affiliated with at least one of these groups.

The school's location, like the disciplines it encompasses, has also changed from time to time; the changing accommodation of its activities tracking the school's evolution and expansion. Its first incarnation was an entity in the University Quadrangle before a move to the other side of City Road, which was led by the Department of Architectural Science's initial occupation of an old terrace house in 1956. This was followed a few years later by the architecture discipline's relocation into what became the Wilkinson Building, located on City Road, across from Victoria Park. [^1] The Wilkinson Building was originally designed by Eric Nicholls and Arthur Baldwinson, with major additions through the 1970s and 1980s (designed by McConnel, Smith and Johnson, the practice of the then-Dean Peter Johnson), and later complemented by interventions by Bates Smart in the 1990s.

**Figure 1** — The Wilkinson Building, home to the School of Architecture, Design and Planning.

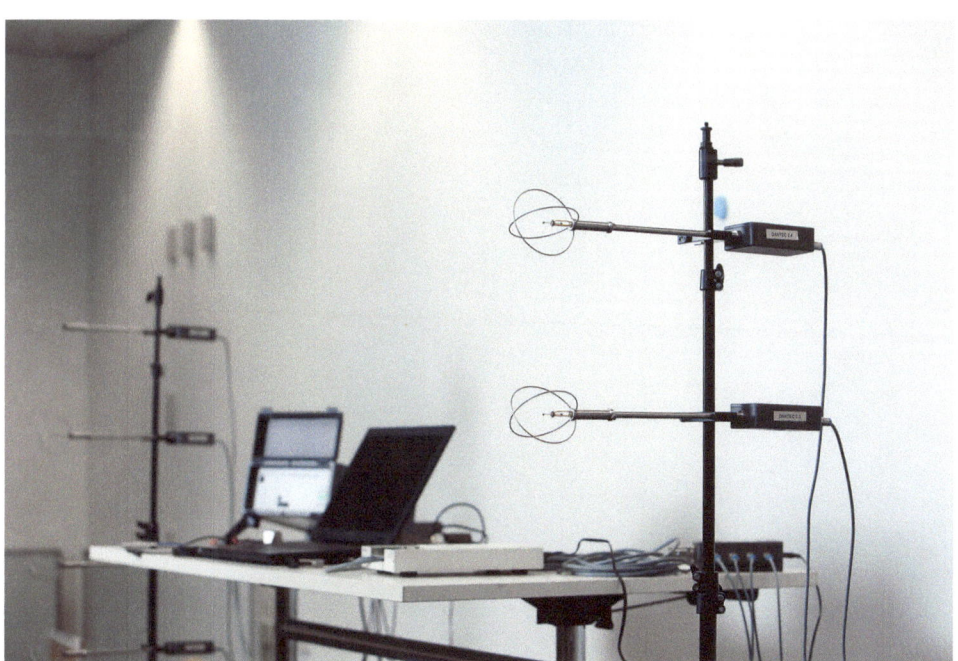

**Figure 2** — The school houses several specialised labs to support research across architectural science and design such as the indoor environmental quality (IEQ) lab pictured in this image, which uses advanced sensors for conducting scientific experiments about the impacts of indoor climate parameters on the comfort, health and productivity of the occupant.

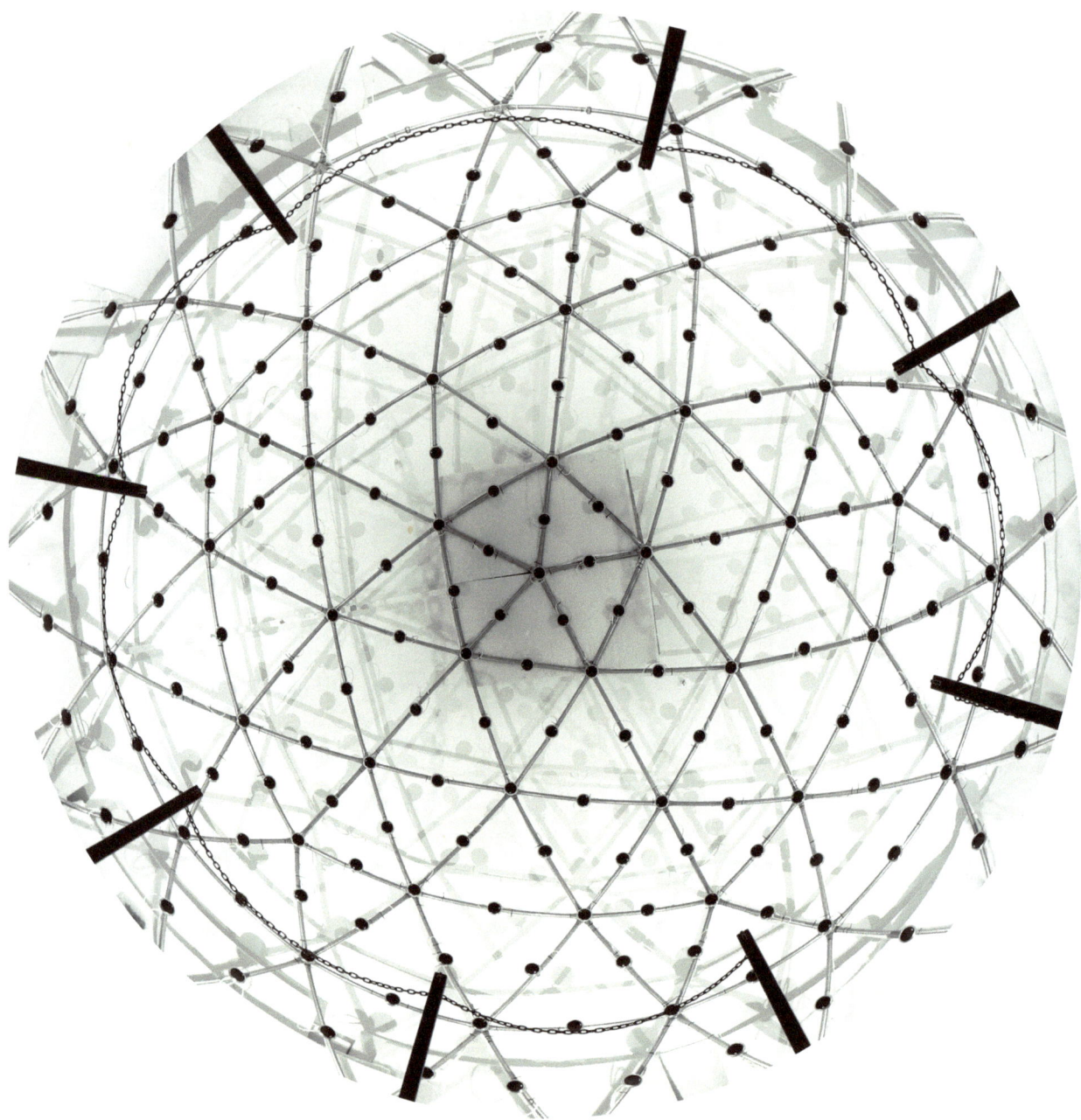

**Figure 3** — High-density hemispherical array of loudspeakers in the school's acoustics lab.

In recent years, the interior of the building has likewise undergone a number of renovations and reconfigurations. Two "homebase" studios designed by Bennett Trimble were added in 2015 and 2016 to provide students with an environment in which to work on their projects outside scheduled class time. Since 2014, the school has also housed one of the most advanced indoor environmental quality (IEQ) labs in the world, established to support scientific experiments dealing with indoor climate, indoor air quality, daylighting, electric lighting, and acoustics, along with their impacts on the comfort, health and productivity of the occupant. Other established facilities include a dedicated lighting lab, an audio and acoustics lab, and a robotics lab, which is integrated into the school's Digital Modelling and Fabrication Lab. All in all, the Wilkinson Building functions both to accommodate a diverse range of students, faculty, public programming, and research activities and to invite, as a prototype, experimentation and appropriation. One might say that the faculty and students have successfully managed to make the building work despite facing ongoing challenges such as sustained growth in the number of students and staff. Indeed, the school's unpretentious building fabric is sometimes viewed as an asset, accommodating architectural interventions that help it to keep pace with institutional transformations and to maintain an experimental atmosphere congruent with the design disciplines to which it is home.

Just as the physical fabric of the school keeps changing, so too does its organisational structure. When Wilkinson argued for the establishment of a Faculty of Architecture in 1920, it was one among 10 faculties in the university (six of which, like the Faculty of Architecture, were founded in that moment). Over time, the university grew to a total of 16 faculties of different sizes and capacities. In 2016, the university outlined a new operating model to reduce this number. The proposed model initially included scenarios that saw what was then the Faculty of Architecture, Design and Planning being merged with either the Faculty of Arts and Social Sciences or the Faculty of Engineering and Information Technologies. The stark incongruities in both of those scenarios served to amplify the internal coherence of the school's unique range of disciplines. In a faculty retreat, held at the university's Sancta Sophia College in August 2015, we had already collectively argued to remain an independent entity consisting of a diverse yet coherent suite of disciplines. The university acceded to the case put by Dean John Redmond for us to remain an autonomous structural element in the institution's organisational chart. At the conclusion of our first century, we are one of three university schools (alongside the School of Law and the Sydney Conservatorium of Music) that sit beside five university faculties.

As the chapters in this book illustrate, a question that has persisted across generations and disciplines is that of relevance: the relevance of our educational programs and research to the world beyond the university. Each building block that contributed to creating the school in its current configuration has been carefully assessed for its value to the attendant discipline, to the future of the school's graduates, and to the wider community. For both architecture and town planning, this was a founding question: how could a university education establish and maintain rigorous professional standards? In this respect, establishing new courses and qualifications and leading new processes of professional registration went hand-in-hand.

It is possible that this preoccupation with the relevance of a university education led academics to embark on visionary, yet deeply grounded, endeavours in teaching and research. The establishment of architectural science as a distinct discipline, and of the Bachelor of Design Computing as a new undergraduate program focusing on how design changes the way we use technology, were both ahead of their time. These endeavours were constructed around research initiatives and implemented through collaborative efforts driven by key academic figures. The assimilation of disciplines that emerged from within the framework of architecture over the past 100 years, not only made us unique as a school, but also contributed to our recent success in global rankings. [^2]

That these efforts have been aided by generous donations from beyond the university demonstrates the high value with which they are regarded. Such donations range from the Lendlease Chair in Urban Design (dating to 1989) to gifts from Penelope Seidler and Garry and Susan Rothwell, enhancing the university's capacity in architectural history and architectural design, respectively, in 2018. The establishment of the Henry Halloran Trust to celebrate the legacy of an important early-20th-century advocate for town planning has allowed the school to expand its social contribution and to foster public outreach through projects such as the Festival of Urbanism.

As our school enters its next century, the question of relevance will remain as essential as ever to everything we do, especially in light of rapid urbanisation and the unprecedented global challenges facing humanity.

## Changing Times

A century ago, one in every 10 people lived in urbanised areas. Today, over half of the planet's population lives in cities, with the urban population predicted to increase by a factor of 1.5 by 2045. [^3] It has rightly been suggested that we have entered the century of the city. [^4] The disciplines of architecture, design and planning will be critical in contributing to the sustainable development of our planet, from capturing knowledge from our past to informing the future with both visions and policy.

In particular, the responsibility of design as a discipline has seen radical transformations over the past 100 years, along with industrial, technological and market shifts. [^5] When design first found its disciplinary feet through the modernist innovations of the Arts and Crafts movement and the Bauhaus, designers began working with artisans and engineers to find more pragmatic, elegant and cost-effective solutions to industrial procedures. As markets and fabrication processes evolved, the role of design shifted to delivering a strategic advantage by having products with better appearance, better human factors or usability, and better market performance. In the late 1990s and early 2000s, the role of design changed again, with companies seeking designers to work with not only engineers but also their business departments to develop better ideas and better integration. [^6] As the global and lived environment becomes more complex, the role of design is changing yet again. Design and its methods are now seen as a "pathway for solving complex, nonlinear problems, which

**Figure 4** — Setting up an experiment in the Lighting Lab.

**Figure 5** — Robotic 3D printing and computational design offer new opportunities for architectural design and advanced manufacturing with the potential to reduce the environmental impact in the construction industry through the use of sustainable materials and more economic processes.

cannot be solved with technological or scientific methods alone." [^7] It provides a framework and a way of thinking to deal with uncertainty, complexity and failure. [^8]

According to the World Economic Forum, we are at the brink of a new industrial revolution. [^9] Each of the previous industrial revolutions, which brought advances in mechanical production, mass production, and automated production, has had significant impacts on the practices and roles of architects, artists, craftspeople and artisans, engineers, social reformers, and entrepreneurs. At the same time, companies and organisations have turned to design to fully utilise the opportunities arising from technological progress, leading most recently to an industrial revolution of "cyber-physical systems." [^10] These changes have catapulted economic growth and enabled new styles of living and working; design in all its forms has been integral to this experience. As we are entering this new phase of industrial change, our economies and our ways of living will shift yet again. Technological progress is changing how we construct buildings, how and where we live, the work we do, and how we drive our cars (or, how our cars drive us). It will herald increased automation at an unprecedented rate, penetrating all aspects of our environment and lived experience, from the fabrication and construction of buildings to the movement of people and goods.

As these shifts unfold, the role of architecture, design and planning must move beyond identifying methods, tools and frameworks for improving the built environment towards a systematic understanding of the long-term impact that our disciplines will create over the next 100 years. The built environment and design disciplines are entangled with technological change. Their role is not to develop new technology but to inform how new technology can be integrated into our lives and, that way, drive societal and environmental change. Reflecting on Winston Churchill's famous remark, "We shape our buildings, and afterwards our buildings shape us," [^11] as architects, designers and planners, we must understand how the tools, materials and processes that we use to shape our lived environment will shape the future of our planet and humanity across generations and centuries.

## A Speculative View on the Road Ahead

Humanity's future is predicted to be urban. [^12] The built environment and design disciplines will therefore play a significant role in leading the agenda for the century ahead. Yet this cannot be done by one discipline alone. The challenges we are facing, from ageing populations to climate change to refugees and decolonisation, will require us to collaborate across fields of knowledge, institutions, regions and generations more than ever before. [^13]

As demonstrated in the preceding chapters and further argued through this postscript, the school's disciplines contribute to shaping people's lives and how they experience the built environment. The way people live in cities has been linked to their health as well as the health of the environment. [^14] The future agenda for research and education in architecture, design and planning, therefore, must also consider a focus on planetary health to ensure humanity's health and well-being and the sustainable development of our planet. [^15] This involves building on a decades-long and ongoing engagement with rural regions and Indigenous communities and the knowledge embedded within their practices, as well as the exploration of emerging design and fabrication processes. [^16] While technological evolution has allowed us to generally live healthier lives, it is increasingly also found to have negatively impacted our environment. The motorisation of cities has led to air pollution, posing one of the greatest health risks of our time. [^17] Modern urban planning initiatives driven by technological innovation in the late 19th century have given rise to the construction of motorways, promoting sedentary lifestyles while reducing habitats for people and wildlife. [^18]

Reflecting on these trends and threats to our health and the health of our environment, global movements are beginning to recognise that, in order to survive as a species, we must preserve the integrity of the Earth's biophysical systems. Technological progress is increasingly making it possible to integrate knowledge from science and biology with architecture and design to create processes, products and environments that are more sustainable and, in many cases, also offer better performance and better experiences. We are only at the beginning of understanding the opportunities afforded through these new systems and cross-disciplinary perspectives. For a future agenda that places an equal emphasis on human health and the health of our environment to be successful, the contribution of all of our school's founding disciplines, from the humanities to the social sciences to the physical sciences to design, are equally critical building components. We must continue to deeply engage with our past, to study the world as it is, and to imagine the world that could be through the creation and interrogation of the "designed" world.

[^1]: HJ Cowan, *A Contradiction in Terms: The Autobiography of Henry J Cowan, Foundation Professor of Architectural Science, University of Sydney* (Sydney: University of Sydney and Hermitage Press, 1993), 97–99; G Molnar, "The Prof," in *Leslie Wilkinson: A Practical Idealist*, ed. S Falkiner (Woollahra, NSW: Valadon, 1982), 89.
[^2]: "University Rankings: Architecture/Built Environment," QS University Rankings, www.topuniversities.com/university-rankings/university-subject-rankings/2018/architecture, accessed 31 May 2018. The 2018 QS World University Ranking lists the University of Sydney as 16th in the world and first in Australia for architecture and the built environment.
[^3]: "Urban Development," World Bank, www.worldbank.org/en/topic/urbandevelopment, accessed 25 May 2018.
[^4]: NR Peirce and CW Johnson, *Century of the City: No Time to Lose* (New York: The Rockefeller Foundation, 2008), 6.
[^5]: CL Owen, "Design Education in the Information Age," *Design Issues* 7, no. 2 (1991), 25.
[^6]: Owen, "Design Education in the Information Age," 26–27.
[^7]: M Tomitsch, C Wrigley, M Borthwick, et al., *Design. Think. Make. Break. Repeat. A Handbook of Methods* (Amsterdam: BIS Publishers, 2018), 10.
[^8]: Tomitsch, Wrigley, Borthwick, et al., *Design. Think. Make. Break. Repeat*, 10–11.
[^9]: K Schwab, "The Fourth Industrial Revolution: What it Means, How to Respond," World Economic Forum, www.weforum.org/agenda/2016/01/the-fourth-industrial-revolution-what-it-means-and-how-to-respond, accessed 25 May 2018.
[^10]: Schwab, "The Fourth Industrial Revolution."
[^11]: R James, *Winston S. Churchill: His Complete Speeches 1897-1963* (New York: Chelsea House Publishers, 1974), 6869.
[^12]: A Capon, "The View from the City," *Healthy City Design*, special issue, World Health Design (July 2011), 6.
[^13]: "Global Issues Overview," United Nations, www.un.org/en/sections/issues-depth/global-issues-overview, accessed 25 May 2018.
[^14]: Capon, "The View from the City," 6.
[^15]: S Whitmee, A Haines, C Beyrer, et al., "Safeguarding Human Health in the Anthropocene Epoch: Report of The Rockefeller Foundation-Lancet Commission on Planetary Health," *Lancet* 386, no. 10007 (2015), 1973–2028.
[^16]: C Nichols, "Discovering Design: Enhancing the Capability to Design at the Cultural Interface between first Australian and Western Design Paradigms" (PhD diss., University of Sydney, 2014), 312.
[^17]: P Head, "Healthy Cities in an Ecological Age," *Healthy City Design*, 11.
[^18]: M Johnson, "Life-Changing Regeneration," *Healthy City Design*, 16.

After practising architecture for 15 years in the office of Peter Hall and Peter Webber, **Glen Hill** returned to the University of Sydney to carry out doctoral research under the supervision of Adrian Snodgrass. His research, which extends into areas of architectural theory, design thinking, ecological sustainability and human rights, has drawn considerably from poststructuralist Continental philosophy. He has taught architectural history, theory, and design at the University of Sydney School of Architecture, Design and Planning for over 20 years.

**Paul Jones** is an Associate Professor and Program Director of the Master of Urban and Regional Planning degree in the Sydney School of Architecture, Design and Planning. Since 2012, he has been teaching the postgraduate unit PLAN9068 History and Theory of Planning and Design. His research interests are in Asia-Pacific urbanisation, specifically informal urbanism and the structure, form and governance of informal settlements, and is an adviser to UNESCAP and UN-Habitat on implementation of the New Urban Agenda and SDG 11.

**Catherine Lassen** is an architect and Senior Lecturer in Architecture at the University of Sydney. Her research and teaching interests investigate modern Australian architectural history, also exploring connections to contemporary practice. Through a focus on architectural drawings, she has written books and curated exhibitions on Glenn Murcutt and Hugh Buhrich. Her architectural work has been awarded and published in Australia and internationally; furniture designs she completed for site-specific art works by Yoko Ono formed part of a major MCA retrospective.

**Andrew Leach** joined the University of Sydney in 2016 as Professor of Architecture and Research Director for Architectural Theory and History. His recent books include *The Baroque in Architectural Culture 1880–1980* (edited with Maarten Delbeke and John Macarthur), *On Discomfort* (2017, edited with David Ellison), *Rome* (2017), and *Gold Coast* (2018). He is a former ARC Future Fellow and Australian Postdoctoral Fellow. In 2018 he held a Wallace Fellowship at the Harvard Center for Italian Renaissance Studies Villa I Tatti. Leach is currently editor-in-chief of *Architectural Theory Review*, the Sydney School's journal.

**Duanfang Lu** is Professor of Architecture and Urbanism in the School of Architecture, Design and Planning at the University of Sydney. Her publications include *Remaking Chinese Urban Form* (2006, 2011) and *Third World Modernism* (2010). Her anthology *The Routledge Companion to Contemporary Architectural History* will be published in 2019. She has been an Australian Research Council Future Fellow (2012–16), served on the Board of Directors of the Society of Architectural Historians (2012–15), and is currently President of the Society of Architectural and Urban Historians – Asia.

**Peter Phibbs** is Professor of Urban Planning and Policy and while an undergraduate was a summer intern at the Federal Department of Urban and Regional Development.

**Daniel J Ryan** is a lecturer at the Sydney School of Architecture, Design and Planning. He received his PhD and a Master of Design Science from the University of Sydney and studied architecture at University College Dublin. An historian of architecture and building science, focusing on Australasia and the Pacific, he is also the director of the Sustainable Design stream of the Master of Architectural Science. He is interested in the exchange of ideas about climatic design and settlement, especially between tropical medicine, science and architecture. His work has appeared in *Architectural Theory Review*, *Fabrications* and *Éditions du Centre Pompidou*.

**Lee Stickells** is Associate Professor in Architecture and Associate Dean for Research Education in the University of Sydney's School of Architecture, Design and Planning. His research is characterised by an interest in the potential for architecture to shape other ways of living, particularly its projection as a means to reconsider the terms of social life – of how we live together. Lee is currently an editorial committee member of the journal *Architectural Theory Review* and a SAHANZ Editorial Board member.

**Martin Tomitsch** is Associate Professor and Chair of Design and Director of the Design Lab at the University of Sydney School of Architecture, Design and Planning. His research focuses on the role of design for shaping the interactions between people and technology. He is co-founder of the Austrian Network for Information and Communication Technologies for Development (ICT4D.at) and the Media Architecture Institute (www.mediaarchitecture.org) and holds adjunct positions at the Vienna University of Technology and the Beijing Central Academy of Fine Arts.

**Peter Webber** is Emeritus Professor of Architecture at the University of Sydney and a town planner, urban designer and architect. His career has included the roles of Government Architect of New South Wales, NSW State Planning Commissioner, Professor of Architecture at Sydney University, Board Member of the National Trust as well as appointed member of many statutory and advisory panels. Among his many publications are three books: *The Design of Sydney: Three Decades of Change in the City Centre* (1988); *EH Rembert: The Life and Work of the Sydney Architect* (1982); and *Peter Hall Architect: The Phantom of the Opera House* (2012).

**Simon Weir** is an Academic Fellow in Architecture at the University of Sydney. His research on Salvador Dalí's surrealist theories of art and classical theories of architecture have been published in the RIBA's *Journal of Architecture*, the journal of the Interior Design/Interior Architecture Educator's Association (IDEA), and Routledge's *Interior Architecture Theory Reader*. His technical research, focused on the construction of stone architecture, can be found in *RobArch*, and the *Nexus Network Journal of Architecture and Mathematics*.

**Julie Willis** is Professor of Architecture and Dean of the Faculty of Architecture, Building and Planning at the University of Melbourne. She is an expert in Australian architectural history of the late 19th and 20th centuries. Her current research examines the transmission and translation of architectural knowledge through professional networks in architecture. Major works include the *Encyclopedia of Australian Architecture* (2012, edited with Philip Goad) and, with Kate Darian-Smith, the edited collection *Designing Schools: Space, Place and Pedagogy* (2017).

**Sydney School:**
Formative Moments in
Architecture, Design
and Planning at the
University of Sydney

First published in 2018
by Uro Publications,
Melbourne, Australia
uropublications.com

Editors: Andrew Leach and Lee Stickells

Essays by
Glen Hill, Paul Jones, Catherine Lassen and Julie Willis,
Andrew Leach, Duanfang Lu and Peter Webber, Daniel J Ryan,
Lee Stickells, Martin Tomitsch, and Simon Weir,
with a lecture by Gough Whitlam.

Publication design: Michael Bojkowski
Printing: Lightning Source

© Uro Publications 2018

All rights reserved. No part of this publication may be reproduced
or transmitted in any form or by any means, electronic or mechanical,
including photocopy, recording or any other information or storage system,
without prior permission in writing from the publisher.
Any copy of this book issued by the publisher is sold subject to the condition
that it shall not by way of trade or otherwise be lent, resold, hired out or
otherwise circulated without the publisher's prior consent
in any form or binding or cover other than that in which it is published and
without a similar condition including these words being imposed
on a subsequent purchaser.

Every effort has been made to trace accurate ownership
of copyrighted text and visual materials used in this book.
Errors or omissions will be corrected in subsequent editions,
provided notification is sent to the publisher.

ISBN: 978-0-9943966-5-5

Distributed in Australia by Books at Manic
and internationally by Idea Books.

 A catalogue record for this book is available from the National Library of Australia

www.ingramcontent.com/pod-product-compliance
Lightning Source LLC
Chambersburg PA
CBHW041441010526
44118CB00003B/139